CONVEYANCING 2004

CONVEYANCING 2004

Kenneth G C Reid WS

Professor of Property Law in the University of Edinburgh

and

George L Gretton WS

Lord President Reid Professor of Law in the University of Edinburgh

with a contribution by Alan Barr of the University of Edinburgh

Avizandum Publishing Ltd
Edinburgh
2005

Published by
Avizandum Publishing Ltd
58 Candlemaker Row
Edinburgh EH1 2QE

First published 2005

ISBN 1-904968-01-5

British Library Cataloguing in Publication Data
A catalogue record for this book is available from the British Library.

Typeset by Waverley Typesetters, Galashiels
Printed and bound by Bell & Bain Ltd, Glasgow

CONTENTS

Table of statutes   xi

Table of orders, rules and regulations   xv

Table of cases   xvii

PART I: CASES

  Missives   3
  Options   5
  Statutory notices   5
  Servitudes and rights of way   5
  Real burdens   9
  Common property   10
  Property enquiry certificates   11
  Execution of deeds   12
  Competition of title   13
  Completion of title   14
  Right-to-buy legislation   15
  Leases   16
  Heritable securities and floating charges   21
  Solicitors, estate agents, surveyors and architects   22
  Boundary disputes/prescription   26
  Miscellaneous   28

PART II: STATUTORY DEVELOPMENTS

  Nature Conservation (Scotland) Act 2004 (asp 6)   31
  National Health Service Reform (Scotland) Act 2004 (asp 7)   31
  Antisocial Behaviour etc (Scotland) Act 2004 (asp 8)   31
  Tenements (Scotland) Act 2004 (asp 11)   31
  Finance Act 2004 (c 12)   32
  Civil Partnership Act 2004 (c 33)   32
  Land Reform (Scotland) Act 2003   33

Agricultural Holdings (Scotland) Act 2003   36
Building (Scotland) Act 2003   37
Abolition of Feudal Tenure etc (Scotland) Act 2000   37
Title Conditions (Scotland) Act 2003   38
Fees in the Property Registers   38
New application form for Register of Sasines   38
Amendment of Land Registration (Scotland) Rules 1980   39
Conservation bodies   39
Rural housing bodies   39
Fees in the Lands Tribunal   40

PART III: OTHER MATERIAL

Charities and Trustee Investment (Scotland) Bill   43
Longer-term fixed-rate mortgages   43
Regulation of the mortgage market   44
CML Lenders' Handbook for Scotland: new home warranties   44
Contacting lenders   45
Endowment mortgages   45
Standard securities in favour of Woolwich plc   46
Online PECs   47
Coal mining reports: money up front   47
Delay in conclusion of missives   47
Registers of Scotland   48
    Hello to the Register of Community Interests in Land   48
    Goodbye to the Register of Entails   49
    Freedom of information   49
    Registration of company securities   49
    Volume of business   49
Register of Scottish Baronies   50
Reform of land registration   50
Reform of bankruptcy and diligence   51
Reform of housing law   51
Reform of registration of company securities   52
House price service   52
Letters of obligation and SDLT   52
Purchases or sales by non-solicitors   53
Books   53
Articles   54

PART IV: COMMENTARY

Missives of sale   59
    Self-satisfaction   59
    D-I-Y missives   60
Cohabitation blues   63
    Two recent cases   63
    Co-purchase agreements   66
Real burdens   71
    Security services   71
    Factoring services   73
    Feudal abolition   77
    Enforcement by contract   78
Passing of property and the question of trust clauses   78
    Burnett's Tr v Grainger: the House of Lords decides   78
    Trust clauses: to use or not to use?   79
Servitudes   85
    Parking—again   85
    Prescriptive acquisition: possession as of right   89
Antisocial Behaviour etc (Scotland) Act 2004   91
    Part 7: penalising landlords for antisocial tenants   91
    Part 8: compulsory registration of private landlords   92
Preservation Notices   95
    Old notices   95
    New notices   95
    Notices of preservation   97
    Notices of converted servitude   102
Offside goals, possession and bad faith   103
Leases   104
    Irritancy and acceptance of rent   104
    Is a successor landlord bound?   104
    The unreasonably unconsenting landlord   107
    Rescinding a lease for material breach   108
Descriptions, boundaries and prescription   109
    Descriptions: conflicting elements   109
    Prescription: foundation writs   111
    Prescription: walking on water   112
Stamp duty land tax   112
    Introduction   112
    Partnership transactions   113
    Other changes   115

Ex facie absolute dispositions   117
Tenements (Scotland) Act 2004   121
    Introduction   121
    A default law   122
    Meaning of 'tenement'   122
    Ownership   123
    Limits and boundaries   124
    Pertinents   125
    Tenement Management Scheme   127
    Scheme property   129
    Scheme decisions   130
    Subject-matter of decisions   131
    Challenging scheme decisions in court   132
    Maintenance: making the decision   133
    Maintenance: apportionment of liability   136
    Maintenance: acting alone   138
    Maintenance: access   140
    Flat sold in mid-repair   140
    Insurance   143
    Common interest   144
    Demolition and abandonment   144
    Missing items: aerials and gas pipes   145
    Sale of new flats: some drafting implications   146
    Purchase of flats: some implications for practice   149

PART V: TABLES

Cumulative Table of Appeals 2004   153
Table of Cases Digested in Earlier Volumes but Reported in 2004   155

PREFACE

This is the sixth annual survey of new developments in the law of conveyancing. As in previous years, it is divided into five parts. There is, first, a brief description of all cases reported or otherwise drawn to our attention since *Conveyancing 2003*. The next two parts summarise, respectively, statutory developments during 2004 and other material of interest to conveyancers. The fourth part is a detailed commentary on selected issues arising from the first three parts. Finally, in part V, there are two tables. The first, a cumulative table of appeals, is designed to facilitate moving from one annual volume to the next. The second is a table of cases digested in earlier volumes but reported, either for the first time or in an additional series, in 2004. This is for convenience of future reference.

We do not seek to cover agricultural holdings, crofting, public sector tenancies (except the right-to-buy legislation), compulsory purchase or planning law. Otherwise our coverage is intended to be complete.

We are grateful to our colleague Alan Barr for providing the text on stamp duty land tax, and for help and support in other ways.

Kenneth G C Reid
George L Gretton
7 March 2005

TABLE OF STATUTES

1868 Land Registers (Scotland) Act
    s 6 38
    Titles to Land Consolidation (Scotland)
    Act
    s 25 84
    s 26B 15, 38
    s 142 38
1890 Partnership Act
    s 20(1) 11
1913 Ancient Monuments Consolidation
    and Amendment Act 9
1921 Trusts (Scotland) Act 43
1933 False Oaths (Scotland) Act 102
1959 Building (Scotland) Act 37
1961 Trustee Investment Act 43
    Trusts (Scotland) Act
    s 2 82
1964 Succession (Scotland) Act 32
    s 2 15
1970 Conveyancing and Feudal Reform
    (Scotland) Act
    s 9(3) 117
    s 24 21
    s 25 22
    sch 4 note 1 47
1973 Prescription and Limitation (Scotland)
    Act
    s 1 111
    s 3(3) 8
    s 11(1) 23
    (3) 22, 23
    (4) 23
    sch 1 para 1(ab) 138
1974 Land Tenure Reform (Scotland) Act . 94
1979 Ancient Monuments and
    Archaeological Areas Act 9
    Land Registration (Scotland) Act
    s 6(1)(a) 111
    (5) 49
1980 Law Reform (Miscellaneous Provisions)
    (Scotland) Act
    s 6 . . . . 15, 38
1981 Matrimonial Homes (Family
    Protection) (Scotland) Act 32
    s 18 63
    Wildlife and Countryside Act
    part II (ss 28–52) 31
1984 Roads (Scotland) Act
    s 91(2) 5

1984 Roads (cont)
    s 140(6), (7) 5
    s 141(2) 5
1985 Bankruptcy (Scotland) Act
    s 33(1)(b) 14, 80
    Companies Act
    s 410 49
    Law Reform (Miscellaneous
    Provisions) (Scotland) Act 19
1986 Insolvency Act
    s 145 84
1987 Housing (Scotland) Act
    s 64(1) 16
1988 Court of Session Act
    s 47(2) 27
    Housing (Scotland) Act
    s 32(1) 16
1992 Protection of Badgers Act 31
1995 Requirements of Writing (Scotland)
    Act
    s 1 . . . . 4, 13, 14
    (2)(a)(i) 7
    (b) 12
    (3) 4, 13
    (4) 4, 13
    (7) 12
    s 6(3)(a) 102, 142
    s 14(5) 13
    sch 2 102
1998 Scotland Act
    s 29(2)(d) 123
    s 104 . . . . 128, 146, 148
2000 Abolition of Feudal Tenure etc
    (Scotland) Act
    s 1 37
    s 5 37
    s 18 . . . . 77, 95
    s 18C 31
    s 43 96
    s 44 96
    s 45 37
    s 46(1) 37
    s 52 49
    s 63 . . . . 13, 50
    (2) 50
    s 68 37
    s 75 78
    s 76(1) 13
    sch 12 para 58 13

2001 Housing (Scotland) Act
    sch 1 para 1(1) 15
2002 Freedom of Information (Scotland) Act
    s 1(1) 49
    part 2 (ss 25–41) 49
    sch 1 para 12 49
2003 Agricultural Holdings (Scotland) Act
    part 2 (ss 24–38) 36, 48
    s 25 36
    s 26 36
    Building (Scotland) Act 37
    s 7 37
    s 31 37
    Finance Act
    s 44A 116, 117
    s 77(2A) 117
        (3)(b) 117
    sch 3 para 3A 116
        para 4 116
    sch 4 para 8A(1) 116
    sch 15 part 1 (paras 1–4) 113
        part 3 (paras 9–14) 113
        para 9 113
        para 10 114
            (1) 113
        para 14(1) 114
            (6), (7) 115
        para 17 115
        paras 18–24 115
    sch 17A 116
    para 13 116
    Land Reform (Scotland) Act
    part 1 (ss 1–32) 33
    part 2 (ss 33–67) 33, 34–35, 48
    s 33 35
    s 37(6)(c) 33
    s 52 33
    s 56(3)(a), (b) 33
    s 57 33
    s 63 33
        (1) 34
    s 64 34
    part 3 (ss 68–97) 33, 35–36
    s 73 36
    s 75 36
    s 89 35
        (1) 36
    s 90 35
    Title Conditions (Scotland) Act
    ss 1–6 75
    s 2 87
    s 3(1), (2) 72
        (6) 75
        (7) 72
    s 4 97
        (2)(c)(ii) 138
        (4) 138
    s 5(1)(a) 72
    s 8(2)(c) 138
    s 10 141
        (2) 143

2003 Title Conditions (cont)
    s 11(5) 138
    s 12 97
    s 18 138
    s 23 40
    s 25 147
    s 26(2) 128
    ss 28–31 128
    s 28 . . . . 73, 128
        (1)(b) 132
    s 29 . . . . 128, 135
    s 30 . . . . 128, 132
    s 31 128
    s 31A 128, 132
    s 34 40
    s 37 40
    s 38 39
    s 43 39
    s 46 31
    s 49(2) 98
    s 50 . . . . 98, 99
        (1) 100, 102
        (2)(e) 100
        (3) 102
        (4) 101
        (5) 102
        (6) 98
    s 52 . . . . 97, 102
    s 53 . . . . 97, 102, 138
        (2)(d) 138
    s 56 . . . . 77, 97, 102
        (2) 77
    s 58 102
    s 63 . . . . 77, 132
        (9) 77
    s 64 73
    part 6 (ss 71–74) 38
    s 71 128
    s 73 40
    s 76 86
        (2) 85, 87
    s 79 . . . . 87, 102
    s 80 102
    (1) 102, 103
    (5)(f) 98
    s 90 40
    s 91 40
    s 115(2) 101
        (b) 101
        (4) 100
    s 122(1) 77, 102
    s 124(1)(b) 101
        (2) 101
    s 129(2) 38
    sch 7 . . . . 99, 101
        note 2 100
2004 Antisocial Behaviour etc (Scotland)
    Act
    part 7 (ss 68–81) 31, 91–92
    s 68 91
        (2) 92

2004 Antisocial Behaviour (*cont*)
    s 71 91
    s 74 91
    s 78 92
    s 79 92
    part 8 (ss 82–101) 31, 91, 92–95
    s 82(2) 93
    s 83 94
      (1) 93
      (6)(d) 93
      (8) 93
    s 84 93
    s 85 93
    s 87 93
    s 89 93
    s 93 94
      (1) 92
      (2)(b) 93
      (3)–(5) 94
    s 94 94
    s 101 94
      (3) 93
  Civil Partnerships Act 32, 63
  Finance Act
    ss 297–305 32
    s 297 . . . . 115, 116
    s 298 117
      (2) 117
    s 299(3) 117
    s 300 116
    s 301(5) 116
    s 302 116
    schs 39–41 32
    sch 39 part 1 (paras 1–13) 115
          para 4 116
          para 5 117
          para 11 115
          para 12 117
      part 2 (paras 14–26) . . 113, 116
          para 22 116
    sch 40 117
    sch 41 para 1 113
  National Health Service Reform
  (Scotland) Act 31
  Nature Conservation (Scotland) Act . 31
  Tenements (Scotland) Act 31, 52
    s 1 149
    s 2 . . . . 123, 124, 127
      (1) 124, 125
      (2) 125
      (3)–(5) 125
    s 3 . . . . 123, 124, 125, 127, 149
      (1) 124, 126
        (a) 136, 137
      (2) 124, 126
      (3) 126
      (4) 126, 127, 137
      (5) 125
    s 4 . . . . 128, 146
      (2) 128
      (4) 124, 130

2004 Tenements (Scotland) Act (*cont*)
    s 4(5) 131, 133
      (6) 136, 137, 143, 150
      (7) 138
      (9) 139
    s 5 133
      (10), (11) 132
    s 7 144
    s 8 . . . . 139, 144
      (2), (3) 139
    s 9(1)(a), (b) 144
      (2) 144
    s 10 139
    s 11(1), (2) 141
    s 12 150
      (1) 141
      (2) 141, 143
      (3), (5) 141
    s 13 141
    s 14 138
    s 15 138
    s 16 139
    s 17 140
      (3) 140
      (5) 140
      (8), (9) 140
    s 18 . . . . 121, 143
      (4) 143
      (5), (6) 144
    s 19 146
    s 20(1) 145
    s 22 . . . . 148, 150
      (1)–(3), (5), (8) 145
    s 23 145
    s 25 38
      (1) 134
      (2) 136
    s 26(1) 121
      (2) 123
    s 27 127
    s 28(4) 131
      (7) 138
    s 29(1) 124, 126, 127
    s 30 140
    sch 1 (Tenement Management
    Scheme) 127
      r 1 . . . . 127, 129
      r 1.2 . . . . 129, 134
        (c) 150
      r 1.3 129
        (a) 129
      r 1.5 133
      rr 2–7 127
      r 2 . . . . 130, 133, 134
      r 2.2 130
      r 2.3 . . . . 130, 134
      r 2.4 130
      r 2.5 130
      r 2.6 131
      r 2.7 131
      r 2.8 131

2004 Tenements (Scotland) Act (*cont*)
  r 2.9 131
  r 2.10 . . . .   130, 147
  r 2.11 . . . .   130, 147
  r 3 . . . . 127, 130, 131, 133
  r 3.1 131
    (a) 133, 134
    (c) 73, 137
    (d) 132
    (e) 137, 143
    (g) 138
    (h) 139
    (i) 132
  r 3.2 . . . .   134, 135
    (c) 136, 141
  r 3.3 . . . .   135, 136
  r 3.4 135
    (h) 135
  r 4 . . . .   129, 136

2004 Tenements (Scotland) Act (*cont*)
  r 4.2(a), (b) 136, 150
    (b)(i) 147
  r 4.3 . . . .   136, 147
  r 5 138
  r 6.1 131
  r 6.2 131
  r 7.2 139
  r 8 127
  r 8.2 132
  r 8.3 138
  r 9 127
  r 9.2 131
  r 9.3 131
  r 9.4 131
  sch 2 142
  sch 3 paras 1(4), 3, 4–6 145
  sch 4 38

TABLE OF ORDERS, RULES AND REGULATIONS

1980 Land Registration (Scotland) Rules, SI 1980/1413 39
1995 Fees in the Registers of Scotland Order, SI 1995/1945 38
2003 Abolition of Feudal Tenure etc (Scotland) Act 2000 (Commencement No 1) Order,
       SSI 2003/455 37
      Abolition of Feudal Tenure etc (Scotland) Act 2000 (Commencement No 3) Order,
       SSI 2003/620 38
      Abolition of Feudal Tenure etc (Scotland) Act 2000 (Commencement No 2) (Appointed
       Day) Order, SSI 2003/456 37–38
      Financial Services and Markets Act 2000 (Regulated Activities) (Amendment) (No 1)
       Order, SI 2003/1475 44
      Lands Tribunal for Scotland (Relevant Certificate) Rules, SSI 2003/451 40
      Lands Tribunal for Scotland Amendment (Fees) Rules, SSI 2003/521 40
      Title Conditions (Scotland) Act 2003 (Conservation Bodies) Order, SSI 2003/453 39
      Title Conditions (Scotland) Act 2003 (Conservation Bodies) Amendment Order,
       SSI 2003/621 39
2004 Abolition of Feudal Tenure etc (Scotland) Act 2000 (Consequential Provisions) Order,
       SSI 2004/535 . . . . 15, 38
      Abolition of Feudal Tenure etc (Scotland) (Prescribed Periods) Order, SSI 2004/477 . . . 38
      Agricultural Holdings (Fees) (Scotland) Order, SSI 2004/496 37
      Agricultural Holdings (Forms) (Scotland) Regulations, SSI 2004/497. 36
      Agricultural Holdings (Right to Buy Modifications) (Scotland) Regulations, SSI 2004/
       557 36
      Agricultural Holdings (Scotland) Act 2003 (Commencement No 4) Order, SSI 2004/511 . 36
      Antisocial Behaviour etc (Scotland) Act 2004 (Commencement and Savings) Order,
       SSI 2004/420 91
          sch 1 94
      Building (Fees) (Scotland) Regulations, SSI 2004/508 37
      Building (Procedure) (Scotland) Regulations, SSI 2004/428. 37
      Building (Scotland) Regulations, SSI 2004/406
          regs 3, 5, 6, 9–12, 13, 14, 15 37
          sch 1 37
          sch 5 37
      Building (Scotland) Act 2003 (Commencement No 1, Transitional Provisions and
       Savings) Order, SSI 2004/404 37
      Building Standards Advisory Committee (Scotland) Regulations, SSI 2004/506 37
      Community Right to Buy (Ballot) (Scotland) Regulations, SSI 2004/228
          regs 2–8 33
          schedule 33
      Community Right to Buy (Compensation) (Scotland) Regulations, SSI 2004/229
          regs 2–5 34
      Community Right to Buy (Definition of Excluded Land) (Scotland) Order, SSI 2004/296. 48
          art 2(1), (2), (3) 35
      Community Right to Buy (Forms) (Scotland) Regulations, SSI 2004/233
          schs 1–6 34
      Community Right to Buy (Register of Community Interests in Land Charges) (Scotland)
       Regulations, SSI 2004/230 34
      Community Right to Buy (Specification of Plans) (Scotland) Regulations, SSI 2004/231
          schedule 34

2004   Crofting Community Body Form of Application for Consent to Buy Croft Land etc and
           Notice of Minister's Decision (Scotland) Regulations, SSI 2004/224
               reg 2   35
               schs 1, 2   35
           Crofting Community Right to Buy (Ballot) (Scotland) Regulations, SSI 2004/227
               regs 2–8   36
           Crofting Community Right to Buy (Compensation) (Scotland) Order, SSI 2004/226 . . .   35
               art 2   36
               arts 3–6   35
           Crofting Community Right to Buy (Grant Towards Compensation Liability) (Scotland)
           Regulations, SSI 2004/225
               regs 2, 3, 4   35
               schedule   35
           Fees in the Registers of Scotland Amendment Order, SSI 2004/507   38
           Freedom of Information (Scotland) Act 2002 (Commencement No 3) Order,
               SSI 2004/203   49
           Land Reform (Scotland) Act 2003 (Commencement No 2) Order, SSI 2004/247   33
           Land Registration (Scotland) Amendment Rules, SSI 2004/476
               forms 1, 2, 3, 6   39
           Lands Tribunal for Scotland Amendment (Fees) Rules, SSI 2004/480   40
           Lands Tribunal for Scotland (Title Conditions Certificates) (Fees) Rules, SSI 2004/479 . .   40
           Register of Sasines (Application Procedure) Rules, SSI 2004/318   38
           Tenements (Scotland) Act 2004 (Commencement No 1) Order, SSI 2004/487 121
           Tenements (Scotland) Act 2004 (Consequential Provisions) Order, SSI 2004/551   38
           Tenements (Scotland) Act 2004 (Notice of Potential Liability for Costs) Amendment
               Order, SSI 2004/490 142
           Title Conditions (Scotland) Act 2003 (Conservation Bodies) Amendment Order,
               SSI 2004/400   39
           Title Conditions (Scotland) Act 2003 (Notice of Potential Liability for Costs) Amendment
               Order, SSI 2004/552.   38
           Title Conditions (Scotland) Act 2003 (Rural Housing Bodies) Order, SSI 2004/477   39
2005   Land Reform (Scotland) Act 2003 (Commencement No 3) Order, SSI 2005/17   33

TABLE OF CASES

Aberdeen (City of) Council v Clark 1999 SLT 613 107
Accountant in Bankruptcy v Mackay 2004 SLT 777 14
Adams v Thorntons WS 2003 GWD 27-771 (OH), 2004 SCLR 1016 (IH) 22
Aerpac UK Ltd v NOI Scotland Ltd, Outer House, 31 March 2004 (unreported) 3
Allan v Armstrong 2004 GWD 37-768 . . . . 17, 22, 104, 105, 106, 107
Ashworth Frazer Ltd v Gloucester City Council [2001] ! WLR 2180 108

Beard v Beveridge, Herd & Sandilands 1990 SLT 609 . . . . 24, 107
Bell v Fiddes 2004 GWD 3-50 5
Bowers v Kennedy 2000 SC 555 6
Browning Petr 1976 SLT (Sh Ct) 87 15
Burnett v Menzies Dougal 2005 SCLR 133 (Notes) 22, 63, 66, 67
Burnett's Tr v Grainger 2004 SC (HL) 19, 2004 SLT 513, 2004 SCLR 433 . . . . . 13, 78, 79, 80, 81, 84

Canmore Housing Association Ltd v Bairnsfather 2004 SLT 673 26
Caparo Industries plc v Dickman [1990] 2 AC 605 . . . . 11, 25
Caterleisure Ltd v Glasgow Prestwick International Airport Ltd 2004 GWD 37-759 . . . . . . 12, 16
Ceiling Décor Ltd v Parratt, Outer House, 5 March 2004 (unreported) 7
Clark Taylor & Co Ltd v Quality Site Development (Edinburgh) Ltd 1981 SC 111 80
Connolly v Brown 2004 GWD 18-386 26
Crampshee v North Lanarkshire Council 2004 GWD 7-149 . . . . 9, 71, 73, 74, 78
Cummins Engine Co Ltd v Inland Revenue 1981 SC 365 . . . . 16, 107

Dalton v Turcan Connell (Trustees) Ltd 2005 SCLR 159 (Notes) 27, 110, 112
Davidson v Zani 1992 SCLR 1001 106
Davie v Stark (1876) 3 R 1114 109
Dick v Clydesdale Bank 1991 SC 365 22
Duffield Morgan Ltd v Lord Advocate 2004 SLT 413 9
Dumbarton District Council v McLaughlin 2000 Hous LR 16 73

Erskine v West Lothian Council 2004 Hous LR 35 15

Gibson v Bonnington Sugar Refining Co Ltd (1869) 7 M 394 110
Gibson v Robb, Edinburgh Sheriff Court, 26 April 2004, A323/03 10
Gloag v Hamilton 2004 Hous LR 91 20
Gordon District Council v Wimpey Homes Holdings Ltd 1988 SLT 481 62

HMV Fields Properties Ltd v Bracken Self Selection Fabrics Ltd 1991 SLT 31 105
Hallam Land Management Ltd v Perratt 2004 GWD 35-720 5
Hamilton v Mundell; Hamilton v J & J Currie Ltd, Inner House, 7 Oct 2004 (unreported) . . . 7
Henderson v 3052775 Nova Scotia Ltd 2003 GWD 40-1080, 2004 GWD 40-831 28
Henderson v Merrett Syndicates Ltd [1995] 2 AC 145 25
Heritable Reversionary Co Ltd v Millar (1893) 19 R (HL) 43 80

Industrial Estates (Scotland) Ltd v Trustees for the Scottish Vintage Bus Museum, Dunfermline
  Sheriff Court, 20 Feb 2004, A241/03 . . . . 10, 71, 77, 78

Kennedy & Kennedy v MacDonald 1998 GWD 40-1653 85
Kensington Mortgage Co v Robertson 2004 SCLR 312 (Notes) 21

Killick v Second Covent Garden Property Co Ltd [1973] 1 WLR 658 108
Kingston Communications (Hull) plc v Stargas Nominees Ltd, 2003 GWD 33-946, Inner House,
    17 Dec 2004 (unreported) 17

Lashbrooke Petr 2004 SLT (Lyon Ct) 9 13

McAuslane v Highland Council 2004 Hous LR 30 15
MacDonald-Haig v Gerlings, Inverness Sheriff Court, 3 Dec 2001 (unreported) 23, 67
MacDonald-Haig v MacNeill & Critchley 2004 SLT (Sh Ct) 75 . . . . 23, 24
MacGregor v City of Edinburgh Council 2004 GWD 3-56 11
McKimmie's Trs v Armour (1899) 2 F 156 109
McLaughlan v Edward, Elgin Sheriff Court, 28 April 2004, A318/01 (unreported) 25
MacMillan Petr 1987 SLT (Sh Ct) 50 15
Mactaggart (J A) & Co v Harrower (1906) 8 F 1101 . . . . 97, 98, 99, 101
Malik v Ali 2004 SLT 1280 3
Marsden v Craighelen Lawn Tennis and Squash Club 1999 GWD 37-1820 97
Midlothian Council v Crolla 2004 GWD 38-782 8
Moggach v Milne, Elgin Sheriff Court, 22 October 2004, A451/01 (unreported) 28, 64, 65, 66
Moncrieff v Jamieson 2004 SCLR 135 (Sh Ct), 2005 SLT 225 . . . . 85, 86, 88
Murdock v McQueen 2004 GWD 39-797 . . . . 4, 59, 60

Nationwide Building Society v Walter D Allan Ltd 2004 GWD 25-539 . . . 7. 85, 86, 87, 88, 89, 90
Norman v Kerr 2004 GWD 28-589 . . . . 4, 63
North British Railway Co v Magistrates of Hawick (1862) 1 M 200 110

Optical Express (Gyle) Ltd v Marks & Spencer plc 2000 SLT 644 . . . . 106, 107

Perth and Kinross Council v Scott 2005 SLT 89 5

Ritchie v Scott (1899) 1 F 728 120
Rodger v Paton 2004 GWD 19-425 . . . . 3, 12, 13, 60, 62, 103, 104, 106
Royal Bank of Scotland plc v Lyon, Aberdeen Sheriff Court, 20 July 2004 (unreported) 21
Rutco Incorporated v Jamieson 2004 GWD 30-620 . . . . 27, 109, 111

Safeway Stores plc v Tesco Stores Ltd 2004 SC 29 112
Scotmore Developments v Anderton 1996 SC 368 109
Scottish Property Investment Co Ltd v Scottish Provident Ltd 2004 GWD 6-120 . . . 16, 107, 108
Sexton v Coia 2004 GWD 17-376, 2004 GWD 38-781 . . . . 21, 118–121
Sharp v Thomson 1994 SC 503, 1997 SC (HL) 66 . . . . 78, 79, 80
Sheltered Housing Management Ltd v Aitken (1997) (*Unreported Cases from the Sheriff Court* (eds
    Paisley and Cusine, 2000) p 225) 78

Sheltered Housing Management Ltd v Cairns 2003 SLT 578 72
Shilliday v Smith 1998 SC 725 . . . . 64, 65, 66
Skinner Petr 1976 SLT 60 15
Stodart v Dalzell (1876) 4 R 236 104

Tailors of Aberdeen v Coutts (1840) 1 Rob 296 72
Tay Valley Joinery Ltd v CF Financial Services Ltd 1987 SLT 207 81
Taylor v Irvine 1996 SCLR 937 140
Thomson v St Cuthbert's Co-operative Association Ltd 1958 SC 380 139

UPS Supply Chain Solutions v Glasgow Airport Ltd 2005 SCLR 67 19

Wallace v Simmers 1960 SC 255 103
Watson Petr 2004 GWD 31-650 14
Watts v Bell & Scott WS 2004 GWD 3-57 22
Webster v Chadburn 2003 GWD 18-562 90
West Castle Properties v Scottish Ministers 2004 SCLR 899 17
West Dunbartonshire Council v Barnes 2004 Hous LR 64 . . . . 9, 76
Whitbread Group plc v Goldapple Ltd, Outer House, 19 Nov 2004 (unreported) 19

Whitmore v Stuart and Stuart (1902) 10 SLT 290 126
Williams v Natural Life Health Foods Ltd [1998] 1 WLR 830, [1998] 2 All ER 577 25
Wilson v DM Hall & Son, Outer House, 17 Dec 2004 (unreported) 24
Wilson v Harvey 2004 SCLR 313 10
Wishaw and District Housing Association v Neary 2004 SC 463 . . . . 13, 16
Wolanski & Co Trustees Ltd v First Quench Retailing Ltd 2004 GWD 33-678 . . . . 20, 104

PART I
CASES

CASES

The full text of all decisions of the Court of Session is available on the Scottish Courts website: http://www.scotcourts.gov.uk.

MISSIVES

(1) Aerpac UK Ltd v NOI Scotland Ltd
31 March 2004, OH

A buyer was already in possession before the date of entry. When that date arrived the buyer was allowed to remain in possession despite not having paid the price. For the purposes of a collateral contract, between different parties, it became important to know whether, after the date of entry, the buyer had a 'right to occupy' the property or whether its occupancy was unlawful and could be terminated at any time. **Held:** no doubt the failure to pay the price was a breach of contract which would entitle the seller to withhold performance—in this case by requiring the buyer's removal from the property. (It might also entitle rescission.) But unless or until this was done, the buyer occupied the property under the missives and hence as rightful possessor. In effect it was a licensee. (On the personal right of occupation conferred by licences, see K G C Reid, *The Law of Property in Scotland* (1996) para 128.)

(2) Rodger v Paton
2004 GWD 19-425, OH

A seller argued that no contract had been concluded because (i) the property was insufficiently described, and (ii) no date of entry was specified. **Held:** proof allowed in respect of (i). (ii) was rejected on the basis that an express date of entry is not essential and that, in its absence, an appropriate date will be implied. See **Commentary** p 60.

   [Other aspects of this case are digested at (20) and (23).]

(3) Malik v Ali
2004 SLT 1280, IH

A house was owned by the pursuer but possessed by the defender. When the pursuer sought possession the defender averred that he had paid the price, that the house was taken in the pursuer's name only to assist her fiancé (a citizen of Pakistan) to obtain a UK visa, and that the agreement between the parties was that the house should then be transferred to the defender. He sought implement of that agreement. In reply the pursuer argued (i) that an oral agreement for the transfer of land was invalid, and (ii) that in any case it was in the circumstances a *pactum illicitum*. **Held:** proof before answer. In relation to (i), the pursuer had in fact executed (but not delivered) a disposition in favour of the defender, which was a sufficient compliance with the Requirements of Writing (Scotland) Act 1995 s 1. In relation to (ii) a proof was plainly necessary in order to determine the nature and scope of the alleged illegality.

The conclusion on (i) seems open to question. Clearly the disposition itself was valid as to form. But it had not been delivered, and delivery could not be required unless the pursuer was under a binding obligation to do so. That obligation, however, required writing, or actings which could stand in place of writing (under s 1(3), (4) of the 1995 Act). The court was reassured by the pursuer's apparent acknowledgement, in the pleadings, that if she had not paid the defender she would be bound to deliver the disposition to him (para 10). But the juridical nature, and enforceability, of such an acknowledgement were not explored.

(4) Norman v Kerr
2004 GWD 28-589, Sh Ct

A minute of agreement between a divorcing couple gave the wife an option to buy out her husband's share of the house. Later there was disagreement about the price to be paid, and the wife raised an action to enforce the option. After service of the initial writ the parties entered into negotiations by letter in which the elements of an agreement to sell were to be found. **Held** ('with some reluctance'): that the letters amounted to a binding agreement which was legally enforceable. The use of 'without prejudice' did not prevent such a result but merely indicated that the husband was not making any admissions. See **Commentary** p 63.

(5) Murdock v McQueen
2004 GWD 39-797, Sh Ct

A buyer purported to rescind missives for (i) breach of a warranty that the property was not listed, and (ii) the absence of listed building consent in respect of alterations, being a matter on which the buyer was to satisfy herself. As the transaction had proceeded almost to settlement, the sellers argued waiver and personal bar in relation to (i). **Held:** proof before answer allowed in respect of (i) only. In relation to (ii) the buyer had no remedy if she was not satisfied by the documentation which turned out to be available. On (ii) see **Commentary** p 59.

OPTIONS

(6) Hallam Land Management Ltd v Perratt
2004 GWD 35-720, IH

Hallam held an option to buy land. It could be exercised only where Hallam had obtained 'satisfactory' planning permission, except that Hallam was allowed to waive this requirement. It did so, and served a preliminary notice in respect of the option. A dispute arose as to whether the notice was valid. It was accepted by both sides (whether justifiably is perhaps open to question) that the effect of the option agreement was that the notice must specify some type of planning permission which (but for the waiver) would have been satisfactory to Hallam. In the event the notice stated that 'such Planning Permission as would have been satisfactory to us would have been Planning Permission for the existing use of the Relevant Land'. **Held:** planning permission implied development: an existing use did not require such permission. Hence the notice did not properly specify a type of planning permission and so was invalid. Accordingly, the option had not been exercised.

STATUTORY NOTICES

(7) Perth and Kinross Council v Scott
2005 SLT 89, OH

Following the collapse of a retaining wall, the roads authority served a notice under s 91(2) of the Roads (Scotland) Act 1984 requiring reinstatement within 28 days. When this was not done, the authority carried out the necessary work under its statutory powers and sought to recover the cost. The relevant provision, s 141(2), employed what is, to some, the puzzling expedient of applying an earlier provision of the Act (s 140(6), (7)) but with appropriate substitutions. The defender, ignoring the substitutions, sought to argue that the earlier provision was not capable of applying, with the result that costs under this (and many other types of) notice were irrecoverable. Lady Smith rejected what was evidently a hopeless argument and allowed a proof as to *quantum*.

SERVITUDES AND RIGHTS OF WAY

(8) Bell v Fiddes
2004 GWD 3-50, OH

This is a case of great complexity where the facts are not always evident from the very long opinion. What appears to have happened was the following. The pursuers and the defender owned neighbouring crofts which were separated from the public road by a burn. Originally access across the burn was by a ford, which was suitable for pedestrians and for off-road vehicles such as landrovers. In 1974, however, the pursuers built a bridge which led directly to their croft. A road to the east of the croft was added in 1983. It was possible to reach the defender's croft by vehicle by a combination of the bridge and the road.

At the time the bridge was built both crofts still belonged to the local estate. The pursuers bought their croft in 1979 and the defender's author bought in 1980. The 1979 disposition in favour of the pursuers reserved to the estate 'all existing rights and ways'. On the basis of this rather vague reservation the estate included in the 1980 disposition of the defender's croft an express servitude by reference to a line on a plan. The plan, however, was based on elderly OS maps which did not show the bridge. Whether for this or for other reasons the route given in the plan for the servitude did not show a crossing of the burn at the point of the bridge.

It was accepted that the defender had a servitude over the pursuers' property. The question was the route. The defender argued for access across the bridge and along the eastern road. That would allow vehicular access. The pursuers argued for vehicular access up to and including the ford and for pedestrian access thereafter.

There was much bad blood between the parties but especially, the evidence suggested, on the part of the defender. For example when the pursuers had blocked access by the use of locked gates, the defender had put superglue in the lock. There had also been various litigations; and the current action was made much more unwieldy by the fact that it took the form of a reduction of an earlier, undefended action in the sheriff court in which the defender had been granted a declarator of a servitude right of pedestrian and vehicular access along the line shown in a specially prepared plan which had now been lost. Reduction was duly granted but in the process the Lord Ordinary (Lord McEwan) took the opportunity to express views on the substantive issues.

What was the basis of the defender's servitude? Insufficient time had passed for the servitude to be constituted by prescription. As her croft was not landlocked there was no possibility of implying an access right along the lines of *Bowers v Kennedy* 2000 SC 555 (for which see *Conveyancing 2000* pp 52–54). For the same reason a servitude could not have been impliedly reserved from the 1979 disposition. That left the terms of the two dispositions themselves. The 1980 disposition did not give the defender the route that she wanted and there was no basis, in Lord McEwan's view, for varying a route which had been set out clearly by plan. A further difficulty was that the 1980 grant of servitude was *a non domino* unless it fell within the scope of the reservation from the 1979 disposition (see para 213). As for that reservation, there was a faint argument (i) that it might have reserved more than one servitude and, if so, (ii) that, given that the bridge was actually used some of the time by the defender's author, the reservation extended to a right over the bridge (para 172). Unsurprisingly this argument did not attract Lord McEwan; and even if correct there was the further difficulty that the 1979 deed could not have extended the access to a road (the eastern road) which had not yet been built. Thus the defender's servitude rested on the 1980 disposition with its (in the defender's eyes) unsatisfactory route.

(9) Nationwide Building Society v Walter D Allan Ltd
2004 GWD 25-539, OH

The pursuer and defender were neighbours. The pursuer sought interdict against parking on its land by the defender. The defender argued that it had a servitude right to park, either as a right which was ancillary to an express right of way or as a freestanding servitude. This argument was rejected and interdict granted. In particular the court held that a right to park vehicles all day six days a week in a small area was too intrusive to be allowed as a servitude. See **Commentary** p 85.

(10) Ceiling Décor Ltd v Parratt
5 March 2004, OH

The pursuer and defender owned adjacent properties at Commercial Street, Dundee. The parties were in dispute as to a stairway between the two premises. An action was raised in the Court of Session. After some days of proof, an oral settlement was agreed between the respective counsel, and accordingly the parties agreed to discharge further proof. In the settlement, the pursuer conceded that the stairway belonged to the defender, while the defender would, subject to certain conditions, grant to the pursuer a deed of servitude over the stairway. However, it subsequently turned out that the settlement could not be given effect to, because the defender denied that she had agreed to grant a servitude. The pursuer then raised the present action to have the defender ordained to implement the agreement, and in particular to grant the servitude. After hearing evidence it was **held** that the agreement reached between the counsel had indeed been approved by the defender. That, however, was not the end of the matter. The defender argued that *esto* there had been an agreement, it was not a legally binding agreement because it left too many matters open. This question was not determined at the proof but left for further procedure.

One issue in the case, on which no ruling was made, was whether it is competent to have a servitude that is limited in its scope to use as a fire escape. It is respectfully suggested that such a servitude is indeed competent.

An obligation to grant a servitude is an obligation that must be in writing: Requirements of Writing (Scotland) Act 1995 s 1(2)(a)(i). This point seems not to have been raised on behalf of the defender. No doubt there was some good reason for this. But the question of whether a written agreement is necessary is sometimes overlooked when conveyancing litigation is settled by agreement between counsel.

(11) Hamilton v Mundell; Hamilton v J & J Currie Ltd
7 October 2004, IH

A public road running through the defender's land was stopped up and ceased to be public. The pursuer, who had the residual estate title, sought declarator of ownership of the road, and that it was free of any servitude in favour of the defender. The defender argued that (i) the stopping up did not extinguish the public rights but that, in any event, (ii) a servitude of way was established by prescription as a result of possession during the period prior to the stopping up. At first instance the sheriff rejected the first argument of the defender but allowed a proof before answer in respect of the second. See *Conveyancing 2002* Case (13) and pp 52–54. An appeal against the decision in respect of the defender's second argument was allowed of consent, and the declarator granted as craved.

(12) Midlothian Council v Crolla
2004 GWD 38-782, OH

The defender owned land which was used as a shortcut to reach a park which was held as lessee by the local authority and made available to the public. When the defender blocked off the access with fences the local authority sought an interim order requiring their removal. The authority argued that, following 20 years' use, the access had become a public right of way by prescription. **Held:** application refused. The access was not a public right of way for the following reasons.

(i) It did not connect two public places. The park was not a public place. In Lord Carloway's words (para 12): 'It is not enough for a place to become public that it happens to be owned by a central or local government authority and that authority permits its use by the public for certain purposes. A place is even less likely to be determined public where it is privately owned and is furthermore leased only for a specific restricted purpose.'

(ii) Section 3(3) of the Prescription and Limitation (Scotland) Act 1973 requires that land be possessed 'peaceably'. A fence separated the access path from the park, although it seems to have been broken down in places. '[T]he existence of the fence, even in a dilapidated state, detracts from the idea of members of the public exercising a right peaceably or thinking that they were exercising any right at all' (para 13).

(iii) Section 3(3) also requires that the land is possessed 'openly'. It may not have been. The route was very short and would take only seconds to traverse.

The decision was only at an interim stage, without full pleadings or argument. Necessarily its reasoning is unrefined. Point (i) seems over-stated in relation to what is admittedly a difficult area of the law. For a full discussion see D J Cusine and R R M Paisley, *Servitudes and Rights of Way* (1998) pp 736 ff. It should not be assumed that, merely because permission could be withdrawn at will by the local authority, the public were not, until such withdrawal, using the park as of right. See K G C Reid, *The Law of Property in Scotland* (1996) para 126. Rights of use are always vulnerable to extinction for example by negative prescription, withdrawal of consent, efflux of time, or statutory interference.

Point (iii), if correct, would mean that servitudes and public rights of way could never be established over short stretches of land. It would also exclude underground servitudes, eg for pipes and services.

(13) Duffield Morgan Ltd v Lord Advocate
2004 SLT 413, OH

In 1950 the owner of Rowallan Castle in Ayrshire entered into a guardianship agreement with the Minister of Works under the Ancient Monuments Consolidation and Amendment Act 1913 (as amended). (The current legislation is the Ancient Monuments and Archaeological Areas Act 1979, and ancient monuments are now administered by Historic Scotland.) The 1950 agreement described the property which was to be subject to the guardianship arrangement but, in addition, conferred on the guardian and on the public a right of access over an access road leading to the castle. In fact the castle was not opened to the public and accordingly the access road not used by members of the public. In those circumstances the current owner of the castle argued (i) that the access right was separate from the guardianship arrangement and was akin to a public right of way, and (ii) that, in view of its non-exercise for 20 years, it had been extinguished by negative prescription. **Held:** both arguments were unsound and absolvitor granted. As a matter of construction, the effect of the 1950 agreement was to take the road into guardianship; and guardianship rights could not, it was conceded, prescribe. But in any event prescription had not operated. Under the legislation the public could take access only if the guardian agreed. The guardian had not agreed. Hence the prescriptive period had not started to run.

Whether this is the correct interpretation of the 1950 agreement is perhaps open to argument. But in any event it is not clear why a guardianship arrangement should be immune from prescription.

REAL BURDENS

(14) Crampshee v North Lanarkshire Council
2004 GWD 7-149, OH

The Council factored the pursuer's property by virtue of a manager burden. This allowed the Council to decide when, and when not, to carry out repairs. The pursuer challenged the burden as (i) contrary to public policy, (ii) too vague, and (iii) repugnant with ownership. The challenge failed. See **Commentary** p 73.

(15) West Dunbartonshire Council v Barnes
2004 Hous LR 64, Sh Ct

The Council factored the defenders' property by virtue of a manager burden. When the Council sought payment of its factoring charges, the defenders resisted on the basis that the Council had failed to provide a pro-active service of the type described in one of its booklets. **Held:** the extent of the factoring service must be taken from the manager burden itself and not from an informal booklet. Decree granted. See **Commentary** p 76.

(16) Industrial Estates (Scotland) Ltd v Trustees for the Scottish Vintage Bus Museum
20 February 2004, Dunfermline Sheriff Court, A241/03

A feu disposition imposed an obligation to contribute one half of the cost of 'security services'. **Held:** the obligation was unenforceable as a real burden for a number of reasons, including its vagueness. But since the original grantee was still owner the obligation could be enforced as a matter of contract. See **Commentary** p 71.

COMMON PROPERTY

(17) Wilson v Harvey
2004 SCLR 313, Sh Ct

Co-owners of a house entered into an agreement in terms of which one of them bound his executors on his death to sell his one-half share to the other. Subsequently he raised an action of division and sale. It was defended on the basis of the agreement which, it was said, must be read as containing an implied term preventing division and sale. **Held:** the division and sale could proceed. The agreement was in clear terms and applied only on the death of the pursuer. In terms it bound, not him, but his executor.

Division and sale, normally an absolute right of a co-owner, can be avoided by agreement of the parties. But the agreement in this case was plainly aiming at something different. In substance it bore some resemblance to a survivorship destination. If the pursuer died while still owning his half share, then the share was to pass to the survivor (albeit for money). But, as with survivorship clauses, there was nothing to prevent the transfer of his share *inter vivos* or indeed an action for division and sale.

(18) Gibson v Robb
26 April 2004, Edinburgh Sheriff Court, A323/03

The parties bought a flat to live in, do up and sell at a profit. They had previously done the same to two other properties. Title was taken in the name of both. Before completing the renovation they seem to have had a disagreement as a result of which the pursuer raised the present action, for division and sale. The defender resisted the action on the basis (i) that the parties were in partnership for the renovation of the flat, (ii) that the flat was held in trust for the partnership, and (iii) that since the flat was thus held as joint property and not as common property, division and sale was not available. The defender's averments in relation to (i) were dismissed as irrelevant, so that points (ii) and (iii) did not fall for decision.

In relation to (ii) it might be observed that it would not follow merely from the existence of a partnership that the flat was held in trust for the partnership. The question of title is different from the, largely economic, question of whether property is 'partnership property' within the meaning of s 20(1) of the Partnership Act 1890. For the defender to succeed it would be necessary to demonstrate that a trust had been duly constituted. Such a trust, however, need not be in writing, still less mentioned in the disposition and on the Register.

PROPERTY ENQUIRY CERTIFICATES

(19) MacGregor v City of Edinburgh Council
2004 GWD 3-56, OH

In 1989 the pursuers bought premises at 22–26 Lady Lawson Street, Edinburgh. They did so, they averred, in reliance on a certificate from the Council stating that the authorised use of the subjects was for a hot food carry-out shop. The certificate was wrong. The error came to light only when the premises were being marketed by the pursuers in 1998, and as a result of enquiries by potential purchasers. The pursuers had in fact operated the premises as a hot food carry-out shop. The potential purchasers did not pursue their interest. Since the original certificate had been obtained by the sellers and not by them, the pursuers sued the defender in delict. Their claim was for (i) £5,803 in respect of the cost of obtaining a certificate of established use, and (ii) £40,000 in respect of the lost sale. **Held:** proof allowed in respect of (i) but not (ii).

On the basis of cases such as *Caparo Industries plc v Dickman* [1990] 2 AC 605, the Temporary Judge (T G Coutts QC) stated the relevant law as follows (para 9):

> [T]he pursuers have to establish, since the statement was not made to them, that they were persons for whom the defenders had undertaken an 'assumption of responsibility' for the accuracy of the certificate. A defender it has been said required to be fully aware of the nature of the transaction which a pursuer has in contemplation, must know that the advice or information will be communicated to that pursuer directly or indirectly and must know that it is very likely that the pursuer will rely on that advice or information in deciding whether or not to engage in the transaction in contemplation.

The defender's case was that a request for a 'file search' of the kind made in the present case was different from a request for property enquiry certificates associated with conveyancing transactions. Accordingly the defender's officer was unaware of the pursuers' transaction.

On quantum the Temporary Judge emphasised (para 13) that, assuming the pursuers were entitled to rely on the certificate, they could only do so to the extent of their own particular transaction. He continued:

> The certificate cannot have permanent validity and the measure of damages is not, in my view, what the pursuers might have got had the position they thought existed been the position in fact. The measure of their damages is either the loss of value attributable to the absence of planning consent or the cost of rectifying that error. Loss of a prospective sale in 1998 which had not even proceeded to a note of interest does not necessarily flow directly from the mistake made by the official in 1988 and is a speculative matter.

EXECUTION OF DEEDS

(20) Rodger v Paton
2004 GWD 19-425, OH

Pre-1995 law. A contract for the sale of land was subscribed by the parties but neither witnessed nor adopted as holograph. But the buyer took possession and, it was averred, paid the price. A proof was allowed as to whether the contract had been set up by homologation or *rei interventus*.

[Other aspects of this case are digested at (2) and (23).]

(21) Caterleisure Ltd v Glasgow Prestwick International Airport Ltd
2004 GWD 37-759, OH

According to the pursuer a contract was entered into with the defender, who owns and operates Prestwick Airport, for the pursuer to provide licensed bars, catering and retail shop services. Following detailed negotiations the contract was said to have been concluded by telephone on 7 January 2001. By then the pursuer was already on site at Prestwick preparing to deliver the service, which actually began the following day, on 8 January. But on that same day the defender (following a change in the ownership of the company) withdrew from the agreement and the pursuer withdrew in turn from Prestwick. It now sued for damages.

An important part of the alleged contract was a licensing agreement which had been prepared in writing but not signed. This allowed the pursuer to use a defined area at Prestwick Airport for the provision of catering, bar and retail services. This was a licence only, terminable at will by the defender on four months' notice: clause 6 took care to provide that '[i]t is hereby agreed and declared that the Licensor does not intend to grant nor the Licensee to take a tenancy of the Licensed Area or any part or parts of the Airport'. A licence is not a real right. Nonetheless it seems to come within the definition of 'interest in land' in s 1(7) of the Requirements of Writing (Scotland) Act 1995. Until 28 November 2004 (and hence at the time of the supposed contract) that definition was:

> any estate, interest or right in or over land, including any right to occupy or to use land or to restrict the occupation or use of land, but does not include –
> (a) a tenancy;
> (b) a right to occupy or use land; or
> (c) a right to restrict the occupation or use of land.
> if the tenancy or right is not granted for more than one year ...

By s 1(2)(b) of the 1995 Act the creation of an interest in land requires formal writing. In this case there was none. Unless, therefore, its duration was for a year or less, the licence was a nullity. It was **held** that, properly read, the licence had a duration of a year or less. 'That is because', as Lord Mackay of Drumadoon explained (para 47), 'the defenders could terminate the licence agreement with effect from a date less than twelve months after 8 January 2001'. Hence the 1995 Act did not apply and a proof before answer was allowed. If the 1995 Act had applied, Lord Mackay would have allowed proof as to the actings on and after 7 January for the purposes of s 1(3), (4) of the Act, '[e]ven although the pursuers' reliance on the contract could only have been for a period of less than 48 hours' (para 48).

On the question of the break option it is instructive to compare *Wishaw and District Housing Association Ltd v Neary* 2004 SC 463 (digested as Case (30) below) where a break option in favour of the *tenant* was said not to affect the calculation of the duration of a lease.

If the events had occurred after 28 November 2004 the legal analysis might have been different (but not the result). By s 76(1) and sch 12 para 58 of the Abolition of Feudal Tenure etc (Scotland) Act 2000 the expression 'interest in land' in s 1 of the 1995 Act is replaced by 'real right in land'. But a licence is not a real right and, it seems, falls outside the 1995 Act simply on that basis.

(22) Lashbrooke Ptr
2004 SLT (Lyon Ct) 9

In signing one's name it is competent to add a territorial designation (if one has one): see Requirements of Writing (Scotland) Act 1995 s 14(5). The official arbiter of such designations is the Lord Lyon. The present case was a petition to be allowed to use the designation 'Elvin Carroll Lashbrooke of Barrowfield, Baron of Barrowfield'. Initially the Lord Lyon was reluctant to allow the territorial designation ('of Barrowfield') in a case like the present where the barony title was attached to a mere superiority interest. But, following representations from the Rothesay Herald, Lyon was persuaded to allow it. It remains to be seen what attitude will be taken to applications after 28 November 2004 now that barony titles have been severed from the land altogether by s 63 of the Abolition of Feudal Tenure etc (Scotland) Act 2000.

COMPETITION OF TITLE

(23) Rodger v Paton
2004 GWD 19-425, OH

The pursuer sought reduction of a disposition on the basis (i) that the granter had previously sold the same property to her, (ii) that she had taken possession, and (iii) that the fact of her possession was sufficient to put the grantee in bad faith. Proof before answer allowed. See **Commentary** p 103.

[Other aspects of this case are digested at (2) and (20).]

(24) Burnett's Tr v Grainger
2004 SC (HL) 19, 2004 SLT 513, 2004 SCLR 433, HL

Buyers took more than a year to record their disposition. By the time they did so, the seller had been sequestrated and the seller's trustee in sequestration had completed title to the property. The resulting litigation has been going on for more than ten years. The House of Lords has now handed down its decision upholding the position of the trustee in sequestration. This affirms the decision of the Inner House reported at 2002 SLT 699 (and digested as *Conveyancing 2002* Case (19)). See **Commentary** p 78.

(25) Accountant in Bankruptcy v Mackay
2004 SLT 777, OH

In 1978 the Scalpay Estate disponed property in Scalpay, Harris, to Mr Mackay. In November 1998 he disponed it to his wife. The disposition was 'for love, favour and affection'. In March 1999 he was sequestrated. The trustee in sequestration raised this action to reduce the disposition as a gratuitous alienation. The defence was that the debtor had held the property as trustee for his wife. It was averred that in 1978 she had paid the purchase price of the property but had decided that the property should be disponed not to her but to her husband because she had difficulty managing business matters. Hence, she averred, her husband held the property as trustee for her. It followed that even if he had still had title at the time of his sequestration, the property would not have vested in his trustee in sequestration (Bankruptcy (Scotland) Act 1985 s 33(1)(b)). The pursuer argued that the defence was irrelevant. In the first place he observed that the person to whom Mrs Mackay had allegedly paid the purchase price, a Mr McLeod, had never been the owner but was a mere occupier. (It appears that land on Harris was bought and sold on an informal basis. Mr McLeod is said to have possessed the land with the consent of the Scalpay Estate.) Hence Mr McLeod had no right that he could have transferred to Mrs Mackay. In the second place the pursuer argued that a trust of land could not be constituted without writing. These arguments were unsuccessful, and proof before answer was allowed. The fact that the 1998 disposition bore to be a donation, and not a transfer by a trustee to a beneficiary, will presumably be used by the pursuer as evidence indicating that there was no trust.

It may be noted that under the Requirements of Writing (Scotland) Act 1995 s 1, writing is required where a person makes himself trustee of property which is already his, but it is not required in other cases. So if X dispones to Y, and it is claimed that Y holds in trust for Z, the absence of writing is not fatal to that claim.

COMPLETION OF TITLE

(26) Watson Petr
2004 GWD 31-650, Sh Ct

Older deeds of trust often provided that if all the trustees died, the heir of the last would be entitled to become trustee. In such a case the heir completed title by petitioning for 'service as heir of provision in trust' and then completing title on the basis of the decree of service. The Succession (Scotland) Act 1964 abolished service for post-1964 deaths. That created a problem in the type of case just described, for there was no means for the heir of a trustee dying after 1964 to complete title: see *Skinner Petr* 1976 SLT 60 and *Browning Petr* 1976 SLT (Sh Ct) 87. As a result legislation was passed to allow service in such cases: Law Reform (Miscellaneous Provisions) (Scotland) Act 1980 s 6. But the question then arose: who is the 'heir' for this purpose? In *MacMillan Petr* 1987 SLT (Sh Ct) 50 it was held that the 'heir' is the person (or more usually set of persons) who would be entitled to succeed under s 2 of the 1964 Act. (Section 2 is roughly the same as the common law next-of-kin.) In an article at (1995) 40 *Journal of the Law Society of Scotland* 30 Adrian Ward criticised this decision, arguing persuasively that the 'heir' must be the person who would have been the heir at law if the pre-1964 law had remained in force. In the present case the Sheriff of Chancery, Iain Macphail QC, agreed with Mr Ward's argument and therefore declined to follow *MacMillan Petr*.

Section 6 of the 1980 Act was repealed on 3 December 2004 by the Abolition of Feudal Tenure etc (Scotland) Act 2000 (Consequential Provisions) Order 2004, SSI 2004/535. But it is replaced by s 26B of the Titles to Land Consolidation (Scotland) Act 1868 as inserted by the Abolition of Feudal Tenure etc (Scotland) Act 2000 s 68.

RIGHT-TO-BUY LEGISLATION

(27) McAuslane v Highland Council
2004 Hous LR 30, Lands Tr

Schedule 1 para 1(1) of the Housing (Scotland) Act 2001 provides that 'a tenancy is not a Scottish secure tenancy if the tenant (or one of joint tenants) is an employee of the landlord or of any local authority and the contract of employment requires the tenant to occupy the house for the better performance of the tenant's duties'. Only secure tenancies are subject to the 'right to buy'. In the present case the applicant was a ferry keeper and was required by his contract of employment to live in a tied house near the ferry. It was accordingly **held** that his tenancy was not a secure tenancy and that therefore the Council had been right to reject his application.

(28) Erskine v West Lothian Council
2004 Hous LR 35, Lands Tr

E and C were neighbouring Council tenants. E agreed that C could cross part of his ground, but this was not a permanent arrangement. When the Council later conveyed to C, it included in C's title a servitude right to cross the ground tenanted by E. E was not consulted about this. Later E applied to buy the house and ground that he tenanted. The Council offered to sell to him, subject to the servitude. E applied to the Lands Tribunal to have the Council ordained to offer the property to him free of the servitude. His argument was that s 64(1) of the Housing (Scotland) Act 1987 says that 'an offer to sell under s 63(2) shall contain such conditions as are reasonable, provided that: (a) the conditions shall have the effect of ensuring that the tenant has as full enjoyment and use of the house as owner as he has had as tenant'. E argued that this provision was not being complied with. The Tribunal agreed with E. The fact that the Council would find itself in a difficult position—in breach of the contract with E—was irrelevant.

LEASES

(29) Scottish Property Investment Co Ltd v Scottish Provident Ltd
2004 GWD 6-120, OH

A case where the tenant claimed that the landlord's refusal to consent to a sub-lease was unreasonable. See **Commentary** p 107.

(30) Wishaw and District Housing Association Ltd v Neary
2004 SC 463, IH

Although this case is about short assured tenancies (not usually covered in this series), it also discusses an issue of general importance, viz the manner in which the term of a lease is to be calculated. The landlord granted what bore to be a short assured tenancy. Under the applicable legislation (Housing (Scotland) Act 1988 s 32(1)), such a tenancy has to last at least six months. This lease was for a period of six months, but it also conferred on the tenant the option to terminate early. The landlord in due course served a notice to quit. The tenant declined to remove and the landlord raised an action. The defence was that the tenancy was not a short assured tenancy because the existence of the break option in favour of the tenant meant that the lease did not meet the statutory definition of a lease 'which is for a term of not less than six months'. This argument was rejected by the sheriff, then by the sheriff principal and finally, now, by an Extra Division. *Cummins Engine Co Ltd v Inland Revenue* 1981 SC 365 was followed. In that case a 99-year lease had break options in favour of the tenant and the question was whether that meant its 'term' was less than 99 years for the purposes of stamp duty. It was held that the 'term' was, notwithstanding the break options, 99 years. In both that case and the present case the break option was in favour of the tenant. No doubt the decision would have been different had it been in favour of the landlord, as in *Caterleisure Ltd v Glasgow Prestwick International Airport Ltd* 2004 GWD 37-759 (digested as Case (21)) above). Whether *Cummins* would have been decided differently in that event is less clear. But in practice break options are much more commonly in favour of the tenant than the landlord.

Though the point seems not to have been argued, one might observe that it would be odd if an additional benefit conferred on a tenant could be founded on in this way: if the tenant's argument had been sustained the effect would no doubt be that the landlords would promptly exclude break options from residential tenancies, a result damaging to the interests of tenants.

A brief note on this case by Ken Swinton is published at (2004) 72 *Scottish Law Gazette* 14.

(31) Kingston Communications (Hull) plc v Stargas Nominees Ltd
17 December 2004, IH

In 1997 Stargas Nominees Ltd granted a 25-year lease of a unit at Edinburgh's Gyle shopping centre to Kingston SCL Ltd ('KSCL'). The tenant's parent company, Kingston Communications (Hull) plc ('Kingston'), guaranteed the rent. The guarantee also provided that if the tenant became insolvent the landlord could require the guarantor to take over the lease—a common provision nowadays. In 2000 Kingston sold KSCL to Telesens AG. In 2002 KSCL went into receivership. The receivers granted what purported to be a licence to a company called Convergys EMEA Ltd to occupy the premises in exchange for payment. Meanwhile the landlord called on Kingston (i) to pay arrears of rent, and (ii) to take over the lease. Kingston refused and litigation ensued. Kingston argued that the landlord had re-let the premises to Convergys EMEA Ltd and that the lease had thus been repudiated. As a result the guarantee was no longer enforceable. This argument failed in the Outer House and the claims of the landlord were upheld. The occupation by Convergys EMEA Ltd was on the basis of a contractual arrangement with the joint receivers of KSCL and not on the basis of a lease from Stargas Nominees Ltd. See 2003 GWD 33-946 (digested as *Conveyancing 2003* Case (35)). Kingston reclaimed. The First Division affirmed the decision of the Outer House.

(32) Allan v Armstrong
2004 GWD 37-768, OH

A firm took a 25-year lease. There was a break option, but this was not contained in the lease itself. The question was whether the break option was effective as against a successor of the original landlord. See **Commentary** p 105.

[Another aspect of this case is digested at (43).]

(33) West Castle Properties Ltd v Scottish Ministers
2004 SCLR 899, OH

A 25-year lease of St Margaret's House, London Road, Edinburgh was entered into in 1977. It contained this fairly standard provision:

The Tenant HEREBY ACCEPTS ... the premises ... as in good and tenantable condition and repair and BINDS HIMSELF at his sole expense during the currency of this Lease, to keep wind and water tight, and well and substantially to repair, maintain, renew, restore, cleanse and keep in the like good tenantable condition and repair the whole premises ... in the event of any obligation binding on the Tenant under or by virtue of this Clause remaining unimplemented at the expiry ... of this Lease the Tenant shall, in the option of the Landlords, either implement such obligation or pay to the Landlords a sum equal to the cost of implementing the same ...

When the lease came to an end in 2002 the landlord claimed £4,518,475.80 by way of dilapidations. The defenders (successors of the original tenant) paid £650,000. This action was for the balance, said to be £3,917.709.10. (The arithmetic is unclear, but perhaps the explanation lies in accrued interest.) The defenders counterclaimed for return of the £650,000. At this stage of the litigation no proof had been led and the issue was how, in general, the clause should be construed. The dispute focused on whether the defenders were liable for the cost of restoring the premises to their 1977 condition. For instance, if the lifts, plumbing, roofs etc were in reasonable condition at the ish, and thus not needing repair in the near future, but nevertheless did not have the life expectancy that they had had in 1977, were the defenders liable? The pursuer and the defenders came up with radically different interpretations. The Lord Ordinary (Lord Mackay of Drumadoon) did not wholly agree with either. 'I do not consider that it would be sensible for me to attempt to frame a third formulation', he commented, but in effect he sought a middle path (para 54):

The provisions of Clause FOURTH required the defenders to carry out works that went beyond the 'repair', strictly so called, of individual parts of the premises. The terms in which Clause Fourth is framed presuppose that a particular part of the premises, or a component part of the premises such as the lift or a boiler, may suffer from some defect, such as deterioration or malfunctioning, to the degree and extent that repair, alteration or renewal has become reasonably necessary. That may be so even although the part in question remains usable for some further period of time.

To that extent he agreed with the pursuer. However, to some extent he agreed with the defenders (para 56):

The provisions of Clause FOURTH did not require the defenders to restore the premises to an 'as new' condition at the end of the Lease, by, for example, stripping out parts of the premises, such as roofs, windows, lifts, boilers and electrical equipment, which were perfectly serviceable and had periods of useful life left, merely to ensure that those component parts (once replaced) had, as at the expiry of the Lease, the same individual life expectancies as their predecessor parts had enjoyed at the commencement of the Lease.

(34) UPS Supply Chain Solutions v Glasgow Airport Ltd
2005 SCLR 67, OH

Glasgow Airport Ltd agreed to grant to UPS a 20-year lease of a unit at Glasgow Airport. This was in a contract called 'agreement for lease'. It required Glasgow Airport Ltd to carry out certain construction works. Thereafter a lease was granted. UPS then claimed that the construction works had not been properly done in the manner required by the agreement for lease and claimed £744,490 by way of damages. Glasgow Airport argued that the claim should be dismissed on the ground that the terms of the agreement for lease had been superseded by the lease itself. But the issue was one of construing the intentions of the parties as expressed in the documents that they had signed, and the court preferred the interpretation offered by UPS, namely that the agreement for lease had not been superseded.

(35) Whitbread Group plc v Goldapple Ltd
19 November 2004, OH

Goldapple owned a pub, known as the 'Hogshead', in Edinburgh's Bread Street. Whitbread held it on a 35-year lease starting in 1997. The rent was payable quarterly, on 10 February, May, August and November. The lease provided for the rent to be paid by standing order, but the practice was for it to be paid by cheque. Goldapple sought to irritate the lease for non-payment of the rent due on 10 May 2001. The case will be of interest to banking lawyers because of its analysis of the law relating to certain forms of payment, but it is also of considerable interest to commercial conveyancers.

Whitbread was involved in an internal reorganisation, part of which required the transfer of the Hogshead from Whitbread Group plc to another company in the same concern, Fairbar Ltd. The latter took possession of the Hogshead, though no consent to any assignation was obtained from Goldapple. The rent due for 10 May 2001 was not paid. On 21 May Fairbar Ltd sent a cheque direct to Goldapple's bank, RBS. Goldapple noticed that the payment was from Fairbar rather than from Whitbread and informed the latter that it was rejecting the payment as being from the wrong party. A second cheque was then sent, from Whitbread. But after posting it Whitbread noticed that the first cheque had been cleared. So it stopped the second cheque. Goldapple instructed RBS to return the money and that was done. (Actually by some mistake RBS returned it twice over, but that particular muddle is not part of the story.) When the first cheque was repaid, Whitbread made another attempt to pay the rent, on 12 June, but this time the account number it gave for Goldapple (10073383) was wrong by one digit (it should have been 10073386) and so the payment failed. Subsequently (6 July) it tried to pay the rent yet again, by CHAPS, but Goldapple had instructed RBS not to accept it, so this attempt failed too.

Meanwhile Goldapple was taking steps to irritate the lease. Under the Law Reform (Miscellaneous Provisions) (Scotland) Act 1985 irritancy for non-payment has to be preceded by an ultimatum, sometimes called a pre-irritancy notice.

Goldapple served this on 11 June, and it was followed up by a notice of irritancy on 29 June. On 6 July Goldapple raised an action of declarator of irritancy in the sheriff court. Whitbread responded by raising the present action in the Court of Session for reduction of the pre-irritancy notice, reduction of the irritancy notice, and declarator that the lease continued to exist. Whitbread was successful.

The Lord Ordinary (Lord Drummond Young) in an impressive opinion decided the following points.

(1) He rejected Whitbread's argument that the pre-irritancy notice was invalid on the ground that it merely stated that the landlord 'will be entitled to terminate the lease' rather than indicating an intention to terminate it in the event of non-payment.

(2) He rejected Whitbread's argument that the irritancy should be reduced because it was oppressive. (It may be observed that the courts have always been reluctant to apply the oppression doctrine. The present case thus fits in with the pattern.)

(3) He rejected Goldapple's argument that, since the lease provided for payment by standing order, payment by cheque was unacceptable. Since payment by cheque had been offered and accepted for some years the landlord was personally barred. If the landlord wished to insist on reverting to the method of payment laid down in the lease it would have to give reasonable notice of that fact.

(4) He rejected Goldapple's argument that Fairbar's payment was not a valid payment of the rent due by Whitbread. He held that Fairbar had paid the money as agent for Whitbread. (It is unfortunate that the attention of the court was not drawn to the authorities on this issue. The law is that one person can pay another's debt. For discussion, and full citations, see Hector MacQueen, 'Payment of Another's Debt', in David Johnston and Reinhard Zimmermann (eds), *Unjustified Enrichment: Key Issues in Comparative Perspective* (2002).)

(5) He held that Whitbread's cheque of 12 June was a valid tender of the rent. It correctly named the payee. The error in Goldapple's account number was not a sufficient ground for its rejection by RBS. Since the rejection was not Whitbread's fault, Goldapple should have given Whitbread further time.

Hence whilst Whitbread lost on points (1) and (2), it won on points (3), (4) and (5). It followed that the irritancy was invalid.

(36) Wolanski & Co Trustees Ltd v First Quench Retailing Ltd
2004 GWD 33-678, Sh Ct

Does continued acceptance of rent bar the landlord from enforcing an irritancy? See **Commentary** p 104.

(37) Gloag v Hamilton
2004 Hous LR 91, Sh Ct

The pursuer was the well-known businesswoman Ann Gloag. She bought Beaufort Castle, Inverness-shire, in 1995. At the time the defender had a tenancy of a house and garden on the estate. A dispute arose as to extent of the subjects let. Ms Gloag raised an action to determine the proper extent, and for decree to eject the tenant from the area which, according to the pursuer, the defender was occupying unlawfully. The tenancy was an oral one. After hearing evidence the sheriff found in favour of the pursuer.

HERITABLE SECURITIES
AND FLOATING CHARGES

(38) Sexton v Coia
2004 GWD 17-376, OH, 2004 GWD 38-781, OH

A dispute in which one of the issues at stake was the nature of the old *ex facie* absolute disposition. See **Commentary** p 117.

(39) Royal Bank of Scotland plc v Lyon
20 July 2004, Aberdeen Sheriff Court

In 1989 Mr and Mrs Lyon granted a standard security for all sums due or to become due to RBS. Thereafter Mr Lyon granted to RBS two guarantees for the borrowings of a company he was a director of, Video Network (Inverness) Ltd. That company went into liquidation early in 1993. In March 1993 RBS wrote to him setting out his liability under the guarantees. He did not pay, and for some years nothing seems to have happened. Eventually RBS sought to enforce its standard security under s 24 of the Conveyancing and Feudal Reform (Scotland) Act 1970. Mr Lyon's defence was that any liability under the guarantees had prescribed negatively. In the letter the bank wrote that 'the initial indications are that we will require to rely on your Guarantee. Under this Guarantee your liability as at 25 March 1993 amounts to £26,269.18'. If this was a demand for payment it would have started the running of prescription, and, by the time the action was raised, the prescriptive period would have elapsed. **Held** by Sheriff Principal Sir Stephen Young, affirming the sheriff, that the letter fell to be construed as a demand for payment, and accordingly liability had prescribed.

(40) Kensington Mortgage Co v Robertson
2004 SCLR 312 (Notes), Sh Ct

The pursuer held a standard security over the defender's property. When the defender defaulted on the secured loan, the pursuer enforced the security by sale. (In the case this was called 'repossession'. But the enforcement of a standard security is not repossession.) After sale there was still a shortfall, and the pursuer sued for this sum. The defender pled that the pursuer, in selling, had failed to obtain 'the best possible price'. The pursuer argued that this defence was irrelevant, since the duty of a heritable creditor under the Conveyancing and Feudal Reform (Scotland) Act 1970 s 25 is merely to obtain a price that 'is the best that can reasonably be obtained'. The sheriff agreed with the pursuer, citing *Dick v Clydesdale Bank* 1991 SC 365.

SOLICITORS, ESTATE AGENTS, SURVEYORS AND ARCHITECTS

(41) Watts v Bell & Scott WS
2004 GWD 3-57, OH

Watts instructed the defender to put in an offer to buy property. He intended to redevelop it. The defender submitted the offer late. The pursuer argued that if the offer had been submitted timeously it would have been successful, and he claimed loss of the anticipated profit on the redevelopment. The defender admitted liability in principle, but argued that the pursuer had not relevantly averred his claim for loss. Proof before answer allowed.

A brief note on this case by Kenneth H Forrest appears in (2004) 72 *Scottish Law Gazette* 27.

(42) Burnett v Menzies Dougal
2005 SCLR 133 (Notes), OH

This was a claim for damages against solicitors for allegedly having failed to implement instructions connected with the purchase of a property. See **Commentary** p 63.

(43) Allan v Armstrong
2004 GWD 37-768, OH

A firm took a 25-year lease. There was a break option in the missives for lease, but the option was not contained in the lease itself. The property was sold to a new landlord, which refused to accept the break option as binding on it. The firm sued its solicitors for negligence for having failed to ensure that the break option was contained in the lease itself. See **Commentary** p 105.

[Another aspect of this case is digested at (32).]

(44) Adams v Thorntons WS
2004 SCLR 1016, IH

In the quinquennial prescription there exists an important pro-creditor qualification in the shape of s 11(3) of the Prescription and Limitation (Scotland) Act 1973. This provides that the short negative prescription does not run while 'the creditor was not aware, and could not with reasonable diligence have been aware, that the loss, injury or damage ... had occurred ...'. In professional negligence claims the defender often seeks to invoke the quinquennial prescription as a defence, and when that happens the pursuer often seeks to invoke s 11(3) to overcome it. In the present case, involving a complex property development that went wrong, the pursuer's attempt to invoke s 11(3) was unsuccessful in the Outer House: see 2003 GWD 27-771 (digested as *Conveyancing 2003* Case (46)). The pursuer reclaimed and the Inner House has now affirmed the decision of the Lord Ordinary. The case is of some significance on the manner in which s 11(3) is to be interpreted.

(45) MacDonald-Haig v MacNeill & Critchley
2004 SLT (Sh Ct) 75

In 1979–80 MacDonald-Haig sold certain property to Gierlof Maas and Frederika Terpstra, reserving a pre-emption option. In 1996–97 Mr Maas and Mrs Terpstra gratuitously disponed the property to Mrs Terpstra and her son and the survivor of them. In 1999 Mrs Terpstra died. At this stage it turned out that the pre-emption right could not be enforced because (a) it was triggered only by a sale, and (b) it had contractual effect only and had not been validly constituted as a real burden, so that it could not affect singular successors. See *Macdonald-Haig v Gerlings*, Inverness Sheriff Court, 3 December 2001 (digested as *Conveyancing 2002* Case (15), and discussed at pp 63–65 of the 2002 volume).

MacDonald-Haig took the view that her law agents in 1979–80 had failed to carry out her instructions properly. She argued that if they had done so the pre-emption option would have been triggered by *any* transfer, and not only by a sale. Had it been so drafted she would, she said, have exercised the option, because the option price was a fixed one, whilst the value of the property had greatly increased. So in 2001 she raised the present action for damages against her former law agents. The defenders defended on the merits, but they also pled prescription, and it is with the prescription point that the present phase of the case was concerned.

The two main periods of negative prescription are five and 20 years. The quinquennial prescription is subject to a number of pro-creditor qualifications, such as s 11(3) of the Prescription and Limitation (Scotland) Act 1973, that do not apply to the vicennial prescription (see Case (44)). So, given the choice, an alleged debtor will choose to plead the latter rather than the former. In this case the defender pled the vicennial prescription, arguing that the prescriptive clock began to tick in 1980, and so that by 2001, when the action was raised, more than 20 years had elapsed. In prescription cases, the main area of difficulty is often identifying the *terminus a quo*, which is to say the date when the clock starts to tick. Section 11(1) of the 1973 Act, read with s 11(4), says that 'any obligation ... to make reparation for loss, injury or damage caused by an act, neglect or default shall be regarded ... as having become enforceable on the date when the loss, injury or damage occurred'. The defender argued that if there had been 'loss, injury or damage' to the pursuer it had occurred in 1979–80, which is to say more than 20 years earlier.

In the light of the leading case, *Beard v Beveridge, Herd & Sandilands* 1990 SLT 609, this defence looked solid. In *Beard* a lease was granted in 1967 with a rent review clause. The rent was to be reviewed every 21 years. (Those were the days ....) When 1987 arrived the landlords sought to have the rent reviewed, but it turned out that the clause was drafted in such a way as to make it void. The landlords sued their former law agents for damages. The action was raised more than 20 years after the granting of the lease. It was held that any liability had been extinguished by the vicennial prescription, since any 'loss, injury or damage' to the pursuers had happened in 1967. *Beard* has frequently been founded on. At para 27 of the present case the sheriff principal (Sir Stephen Young) distinguished Beard thus:

> [In *Beard*] it was obvious from the outset that, on the assumption (which could scarcely have been gainsaid) that rents would continue to rise, the pursuers would inevitably be worse off with a lease which effectively had no rent review provision than they would have been if the solicitors had done what they had been asked to do. By contrast, in the present case there was no inevitability at all about the pursuer's loss. She had a right of pre-emption which was valid and enforceable in the event that the disponees sought to sell the subjects or that Mrs Terpstra died, and only time would tell whether the disponees would discover the defect in the right of pre-emption and take advantage of it so causing loss to the pursuer.

He therefore repelled the prescription plea. *MacDonald-Haig v MacNeill & Critchley* is thus a decision of considerable importance in the law of professional negligence.

(46) Wilson v D M Hall & Son
17 December 2004, OH

Mr Wilson was a property developer. He planned a new-build development of several flats in the Firnieside area of Edinburgh. He approached Dunbar Bank for funding. The bank commissioned Messrs D M Hall to report on the proposal. Messrs D M Hall's assessment was favourable, and the bank decided to fund the project, taking a standard security. The D M Hall report contained this proviso:

> The report is provided for the stated purposes and for the sole use of the named client [Dunbar Bank]. It is confidential to the client and his professional advisers. The valuer accepts responsibility to the client alone that the report will be prepared with the skill, care and diligence reasonably to be expected of a competent chartered surveyor, but accepts no responsibility whatsoever to any person other than the client himself. Any such person relies upon the report at his own risk.

This report was not copied to Mr Wilson, but he was informed of its general tenor. After construction had begun, Messrs D M Hall upped its valuation. The new report provided:

For the avoidance of doubt, this brief letter should be read in conjunction with and as forming part of our original valuation, being subject to the same qualifications, assumptions and limitations as set out therein, where appropriate.

This was copied to Mr Wilson. When the properties were finished they were marketed roughly in line with the valuation of Messrs D M Hall. This was in March 1995. But none sold. In May 1996 Dunbar Bank began the process of enforcing its standard security.

Mr Wilson sued Messrs D M Hall for professional negligence. He claimed that they had over-valued the development and that he had relied, to his loss, on that over-valuation. There was a proof before answer, at the end of which decree of absolvitor was pronounced. Lady Paton **held**, in the first place, that whilst a surveyor acting for a lender can owe a duty of care to the borrower, on the facts of this case no such duty of care was owed. In reaching this decision she placed emphasis on the fact that this was a commercial rather than a residential loan. In the second place, she held that there was no causal link between the valuations of Messrs D M Hall and Mr Wilson's losses.

.

(47) McLaughlan v Edwards
28 April 2004, Elgin Sheriff Court, A318/01

A husband and wife contracted with a developer for the purchase of a plot of ground and the construction of a house. The house proved defective. They successfully sued the developer, but were unable to enforce the decree. So they raised the present action against the architect. Since there was no contract between the buyers and the architect, the action was based on delict. The buyers sought (i) £145,000 for alleged failure of the architect in his professional duty to design a house which would be structurally sound, dry and habitable, and (ii) £119,074.65 in respect of stage payments which they made in reliance of periodic certificates by the architect which, it was alleged, were not true and accurate. After a restricted proof on the question of whether the architect was under a duty to the buyers to take reasonable care in respect of matters (i) and (ii), the sheriff found that the duties were owed and allowed a proof before answer.

This was the appeal. The sheriff principal (Sir Stephen Young QC) upheld the decision of the sheriff, on the basis of cases such as *Caparo Industries plc v Dickman* [1990] 2 AC 605, *Henderson v Merrett Syndicates Ltd* [1995] 2 AC 145, and *Williams v Natural Life Health Foods Ltd* [1998] 1 WLR 830, [1998] 2 All ER 577. His response to the 'floodgates' argument is worth quoting in full (para 58):

[Counsel for the defender] submitted that an architect was not generally regarded as owing a duty of care to a third party who was purchasing a house from the architect's own client and she suggested that, if the arguments for the pursuers in the present case were well founded, there could be an indeterminate class of persons to whom the defender might be liable including, for example, persons who had lent money to the pursuers to purchase the house. In my opinion, the short answer to these submissions is to be found in the fact that no one else, apart from the pursuers, is said to have had detailed meetings and discussions with the defender along the lines set out in the sheriff's findings in fact, and it is the fact of these discussions and meetings having taken place which forms the backbone, so to speak, of the pursuers' claim against the defender in both its branches.

(48) Connolly v Brown
2004 GWD 18-386, OH

Mr and Mrs Connolly owned some land in West Lothian. They thought it might have development value. In 1995 they agreed with Mr Brown that he would try to find a buyer. By the end of 1997 no buyer had been found and Mr Brown suggested that he should buy it himself with an associate. Mr Brown and his associate set up a joint venture company, Hermitage Ardnaree Ltd, and this bought the property. Not long after, Hermitage Ardnaree Ltd resold to Bryant Homes for a considerably higher price. Mr Brown knew of the interest of Bryant Homes before Hermitage Ardnaree Ltd concluded missives with the Connollys, but he did not inform them. (The foregoing narrative is based on the pursuers' averments.) The Connollys sued Mr Brown for the profit he had made. They argued that either (i) he was still their agent at the time when they sold, and so he should have told them about the interest of Bryant Homes, or (ii) even if he was no longer their agent he remained under a duty of disclosure.

At debate the Lord Ordinary (Johnston) took the view that the defender had ceased to be the agent of the Connollys, but that he might nevertheless have remained under a duty of disclosure. Proof before answer was allowed. Precisely what the pursuers would need to prove is perhaps not perfectly clear. And there is another point which is perhaps unclear. According to the Lord Ordinary, 'the pursuers seek account reckoning and payment from the defender in respect of profits allegedly made by him in relation to a property transaction between him and a third party'. But this is not easy to follow, for apparently Mr Brown did *not* enter into any property transaction with Bryant Homes. It was Hermitage Ardnaree Ltd that did so, and it was that company which, it seems, reaped the profit. But it does not appear that the pursuers were seeking money from Hermitage Ardnaree Ltd. Were the pursuers perhaps seeking to claim for themselves the difference between the actual value of Mr Brown's shares in that company, and what the value would have been if the company had not entered into the transaction? No doubt there are answers to such questions, but the answers do not appear in the opinion.

BOUNDARY DISPUTES/PRESCRIPTION

(49) Canmore Housing Association Ltd v Bairnsfather
2004 SLT 673, OH

The petitioner, a housing association, had recently built a block of flats on the west side of a lane. The respondents owned and operated a garage on the same side. Both were accessed by the lane. Initially the petitioner had thought that the lane was public. Later both parties tried to buy the lane and the respondents were successful. They had now filled the lane with derelict vehicles which they used as a source of spare parts for their garage business. The petitioner sought interim interdict and an interim order under s 47(2) of the Court of Session Act 1988 for the removal of the vehicles. It argued that the vehicles were a fire hazard, that one had actually been set on fire and damaged its building, that the vehicles were being used to intimidate the petitioner, and that as a result it had so far been impossible to allow any tenants to take up residence in the flats. In short, the use of the lane constituted a nuisance. The respondents had offered to sell the lane to the petitioner for £800,000. Separately there was a dispute between the parties as to the eastern boundary of the petitioner's land and so as to whether any of the vehicles were on property belonging to the petitioner: in an earlier hearing (noted as *Conveyancing 2003* Case (50)), interim interdict was refused on that ground. **Held:** interim order refused. The Lord Ordinary (Brodie) was 'not persuaded, on the basis of one incident, that the necessary degree of risk has been established' (para 15).

(50) Dalton v Turcan Connell (Trustees) Ltd
2005 SCLR 159 (Notes), OH

This was an action of declarator of ownership of the bed (*alveus*) of part of the Water of Leith. The pursuer based her claim primarily on a feu disposition of 1972. This had a plan which was demonstrative and not taxative. The boundary in the plan followed the edge of the river and did not include any part of the *alveus*. The verbal description described the subjects as 'being on the north side of the Water of Leith'. The pursuer argued that where a river forms the boundary of a property, the presumption is that the *medium filum* of the river is the boundary. Temporary Judge T G Coutts QC took the view that this presumption was rebutted by the terms of the 1972 deed, which could not be interpreted as including any part of the *alveus*. See **Commentary** p 110.

(51) Rutco Incorporated v Jamieson
2004 GWD 30-620, OH

Action seeking declarator of the acquisition of land by prescription. The defenders, who claimed title to the same land, argued that the deed relied on by the pursuer was not a good foundation writ in that, properly construed, it did not include the land in question. **Held:** proof of possession allowed. Both the foundation writ, and a further writ referred to for description in the foundation writ, contained elements in their descriptions which were difficult to reconcile; and it was certainly possible to interpret them as excluding the land which the pursuer was seeking to acquire. But there was a range of possible interpretations, some of which would allow for the inclusion of the land. Hence the writ was habile for the purposes of prescription. See **Commentary** p 109.

MISCELLANEOUS

(52) Moggach v Milne
22 October 2004, Elgin Sheriff Court, A451/01

A couple lived in a house owned by one of them. When they became estranged, the one who did not own the house sued the other for half of its value. See **Commentary** p 64.

(53) Henderson v 3052775 Nova Scotia Ltd
2004 GWD 40-831, OH

This was an action of reduction of a disposition at the instance of the granter's liquidator. Summary decree was granted in favour of the pursuer: see 2003 GWD 40-1080 (digested as *Conveyancing 2003* Case (58)). The Inner House having recalled the summary decree and remitted the case to the Lord Ordinary for further procedure on the basis of amended pleadings, the Lord Ordinary has once again granted summary decree in favour of the pursuer.

PART II
STATUTORY DEVELOPMENTS

STATUTORY DEVELOPMENTS

The text of all Acts and statutory instruments, both of Scotland and of the United Kingdom, is available on http://www.hmso.gov.uk.

Nature Conservation (Scotland) Act 2004 (asp 6)

The Nature Conservation (Scotland) Act 2004 makes extensive changes to the Wildlife and Countryside Act 1981. For instance it repeals and replaces most of part II of the 1981 Act (Sites of Special Scientific Interest). It extends existing protections for birds, animals and plants. It amends the Protection of Badgers Act 1992. The changes are not limited to the botanical and zoological environment. For instance there are new provisions to protect fossils *in situ*. For the existing law which the new Act modifies, see Colin T Reid, *Nature Conservation Law* (2nd edn 2002).

National Health Service Reform (Scotland) Act 2004 (asp 7)

Among other things this Act dissolves NHS trusts and sets up community health partnerships ('CHPs'). One consequence, so far as conveyancing is concerned, affects health care burdens (a type of personal real burden). Section 46 of the Title Conditions (Scotland) Act 2003, as originally enacted, provides for the creation of health care burdens in favour of either an NHS trust or Scottish Ministers. The new Act amends s 46 so that, in future, only Scottish Ministers can hold health care burdens. A matching amendment is made to s 18C of the Abolition of Feudal Tenure etc (Scotland) Act 2000.

Antisocial Behaviour etc (Scotland) Act 2004 (asp 8)

Parts 7 and 8 of this Act are of considerable importance for the housing market. All clients who rent out residential property in the private sector need to know about these provisions. See **Commentary** p 91.

Tenements (Scotland) Act 2004 (asp 11)

This important Act (i) codifies the rules as to the division of ownership within a tenement, (ii) provides a new default code for management and maintenance, known as the Tenement Management Scheme, and (iii) provides for a number of other matters such as compulsory insurance, access for repairs, and costs and procedure on demolition. See **Commentary** p 121.

Finance Act 2004 (c 12)

Important changes to stamp duty land tax are made by ss 297–305 and schs 39–41 of the Finance Act 2004. See **Commentary** p 112.

Civil Partnership Act 2004 (c 33)

Once in force this Act will introduce 'civil partnerships'. These are same-sex relationships whose legal consequences are substantially the same as for marriage. It is a UK statute. However, the provisions applying to Scotland are to a large extent separate, within the Act, from those applying elsewhere in the UK. The reason is that the provisions applicable to civil partnerships seek to mirror those applicable to marriage, and matrimonial law is different in the different parts of the UK. The 2004 Act goes systematically through the legislation dealing, whether primarily or incidentally, with marriage and its consequences. Sometimes the 2004 Act amends existing legislation. For example the Succession (Scotland) Act 1964 is amended so that references to 'surviving spouses' now include references to 'surviving civil partners'. In other cases the existing legislation is separately re-enacted. For example instead of amending the Matrimonial Homes (Family Protection) (Scotland) Act 1981 so as to include civil partners, the 1981 legislation is, in effect, copied out *ad longum*, with a few minor changes, with references to civil partners and civil partnerships substituted for references to spouses and marriage. Thus while the law on occupancy rights, renunciations, consents and affidavits continues to rest on the 1981 Act as far as spouses are concerned, the law on occupancy rights, renunciations, consents and affidavits, as applicable to civil partners, rests on the 2004 Act.

It is the potential occupancy rights of civil partners that conveyancers will be chiefly concerned about. Affidavits will be needed. It would be possible to have two separate affidavits, one to deal with possible occupancy rights under the 1981 Act and the other to deal with possible occupancy rights under the 2004 Act. But there is no reason why a single affidavit should not be used to cover both statutes. In drafting such affidavits it should be borne in mind that the term that corresponds to 'spouse' is, for a same-sex relationship, 'civil partner', while the term that parallels 'matrimonial home' is, for a same-sex relationship, 'family home'. A possible combined affidavit would be:

> The subjects of sale are not a matrimonial home or a family home in relation to which a spouse or a civil partner of the seller has occupancy rights.

Likewise a dual-purpose affidavit to accompany the granting of a standard security could run:

> The security subjects are not a matrimonial home or a family home in relation to which a spouse or a civil partner of the granter has occupancy rights.

It is usual for missives to require the appropriate documentation in respect of the Matrimonial Homes (Family Protection) (Scotland) Act 1981. Missives should therefore now be revised to include references to the Civil Partnership Act 2004.

Land Reform (Scotland) Act 2003

Part 2 (community right to buy) and part 3 (crofting community right to buy) of the Land Reform (Scotland) Act 2003 were commenced on 14 June 2004; see the **Land Reform (Scotland) Act 2003 (Commencement No 2) Order 2004, SSI 2004/247**. Part 1 (access rights) was commenced on 9 February 2005; see the **Land Reform (Scotland) Act 2003 (Commencement No 3) Order 2005, SSI 2005/17**. Scottish Natural Heritage produced its final version of the Scottish Outdoor Access Code in January 2004 (see http://www.snh.gov.uk) but this requires approval both of Scottish Ministers and Parliament. On the Land Reform Act see generally *Conveyancing 2003* pp 131–141 and R Rennie, *Land Tenure in Scotland* (2004) ch 15. A number of statutory instruments have been made in respect of both part 2 and part 3.

Part 2 (community right to buy)

The **Community Right to Buy (Ballot) (Scotland) Regulations 2004, SSI 2004/228** set out the requirements on a community body which is holding a ballot under s 52 of the Act on the question of whether to proceed with a land purchase. Regulation 2 provides that there be a secret ballot and that it should be conducted in a fair and reasonable manner. Under reg 3 the community body is required to ascertain from the voters roll who is eligible to vote in the ballot. Regulations 4 and 5 give the community body the option of holding an ordinary ballot or a postal ballot, and reg 6 permits proxy votes in certain circumstances. Regulation 7 requires the community body to publish the result of the ballot in a newspaper circulating in the vicinity, and also to notify Scottish Ministers of the result and the other information specified in the form set out in the schedule to the Regulations. Scottish Ministers are also empowered to call for additional information pertaining to the ballot from the community body. Regulation 8 requires the retention by the community body of the ballot papers; where a postal ballot has been held, evidence of the sending of the ballot papers; and any proxy authorisations and notifications of intention to use a proxy, for a period of two years. That regulation also permits Scottish Ministers and specified persons to inspect the documents retained.

The **Community Right to Buy (Compensation) (Scotland) Regulations 2004, SSI 2004/229** provide the procedure by and manner in which compensation for loss or expense may be claimed by any person (other than a community body) from the Scottish Ministers under s 63 of the Act. Such compensation is payable where loss or expense has been incurred (a) in complying with the procedure or requirements of part 2 of the Act, (b) as a result of failure by a community body to comply with an order of the Lands Tribunal under s 57 of the Act, (c) in complying with a prohibition imposed under s 37(6)(c) of the Act, or (d) as a result of the operation of paragraph (a) or (b) of s 56(3) of the Act. Regulation 2 provides that a claim for compensation must be made within the time limits set out in reg 3. Regulation 3 sets out varying time limits depending on which paragraph of s 63(1) of the Act the claim is made under. Regulation 4 requires that the claim includes a statement detailing under which paragraph or paragraphs of s 63(1) of the Act the loss or expense falls, and that losses and expenses require to be fully vouched. Regulation 5 provides that Scottish Ministers shall determine the amount of compensation payable within a period of 40 days of submission of the claim, and their decision may be appealed to the Lands Tribunal under s 64 of the Act.

The **Community Right to Buy (Register of Community Interests in Land Charges) (Scotland) Regulations 2004, SSI 2004/230** specify the charges which may be made by the Keeper for supplying copies or extracts from the Register of Community Interests in Land.

The **Community Right to Buy (Specification of Plans) (Scotland) Regulations 2004, SSI 2004/231** make provision for the maps, plans or drawings which are required to accompany an application by a community body to register an interest in land. If the application is granted, the maps, plans or drawings are to be entered in the Register of Community Interests in Land. The schedule to the Regulations requires that the maps, plans or drawings use a metric scale corresponding to a scale used by the Ordnance Survey for that land, are taxative and show a north point. The maps, plans or drawings also require to show grid reference numbers, and when measurements are given these must be to two decimal places. Where a map, plan or drawing shows the location of the land in relation to the community it also requires to show the boundaries of the postcode units. Where the subject of the application is salmon fishings or mineral rights this requires to be clearly marked on the map, plan or drawing.

The **Community Right to Buy (Forms) (Scotland) Regulations 2004, SSI 2004/233** specify the forms which must be used in connection with various procedures under part 2 of the Act, as follows:

Schedule 1. Application by a community body to register an interest in land under s 37(1).

Schedule 2. Notice by a community body where the owner of land in which a community interest is sought to be registered, or a creditor in a standard security over any part of that land, may be unknown or cannot be found.

Schedule 3. Notice by the Scottish Ministers to intimate their decision on whether or not a community interest is to be registered in the Register of Community Interests in Land.

Schedule 4. Notice to a community body and the Scottish Ministers by the owner of land, or a creditor in a standard security over that land, under s 48 where there is a proposed transfer of the land.

Schedule 5. Notice by the Scottish Ministers to a community body following receipt of a notice under s 48 of the Act.

Schedule 6. Notice by the Scottish Ministers to the owner of the land following receipt of a notice under s 48.

The **Community Right to Buy (Definition of Excluded Land) (Scotland) Order 2004, SSI 2004/296** designates 'excluded land' for the purposes of s 33. Article 2(1), (2) designates settlements of more than 10,000 people (listed in the schedule) as excluded land. The boundaries of those settlements are specified in the General Register Office for Scotland report *Scottish Settlements—Urban and Rural Land in Scotland* and are delineated on maps known as *The Community Right to Buy (Definition of Excluded Land) (Scotland) Order 2004: Definitive Maps*. For the maps see http://www.scotland.gov.uk/Topics/Rural/Land/17063/8278. Article 2(3) makes clear that foreshore which is adjacent to any settlement in the schedule to the Order is excluded land.

Part 3 (crofting community right to buy)

The **Crofting Community Body Form of Application for Consent to Buy Croft Land etc and Notice of Minister's Decision (Scotland) Regulations 2004, SSI 2004/224** specify the application form to be used by a crofting community body when it is seeking the consent of Scottish Ministers to purchase eligible croft land or sporting interests (reg 2 and sch 1). The Regulations also specify in sch 2 the form to be used by Scottish Ministers when giving notification of their decision on such an application by a crofting community body. This form gives details of the rights of appeal available in relation to the decision of Scottish Ministers, and also sets out the consequences of their decision.

The **Crofting Community Right to Buy (Grant Towards Compensation Liability) (Scotland) Regulations 2004, SSI 2004/225** prescribe the procedure to be followed by a crofting community body when it wishes to apply to Scottish Ministers for a grant under s 90 of the Act. Such a grant may be applied for when a crofting community body is liable to pay compensation under s 89 to any person, including the owner, or former owner, of land or sporting interests, and that body has been unable to obtain enough money to pay, or to pay in full, the compensation. If Scottish Ministers consider that the crofting community body has taken all reasonable steps to raise money from other sources and has failed to obtain sufficient money, and that it is in the public interest to pay a grant, they may do so. Regulation 2 provides that it is the crofting community body which must apply to Scottish Ministers for a grant, and reg 3 prescribes the time limits for making an application. Regulation 4 provides that Scottish Ministers must make a decision on an application for a grant within 21 days of its receipt. The schedule to the Regulations specifies the information which must be supplied by the crofting community body when making an application.

The **Crofting Community Right to Buy (Compensation) (Scotland) Order 2004, SSI 2004/226** provides the procedure by and manner in which compensation for loss or expense may be claimed by any person, including an owner of land or sporting interests, under s 89. Such compensation is payable where loss or expense has been incurred (a) in complying with the requirements of the Act following the making of an application to purchase by the community body, (b) as a result of the withdrawal by the crofting community body of its confirmation of intention to proceed with the purchase, or its failure otherwise to complete the purchase after confirming its intention to do so, or (c) as a result of the failure of the crofting community body which made the application to complete the purchase. In these cases the compensation is payable by the crofting community body (art 2). Where loss or expense has been incurred as a result of an application under s 73 of the Act being refused, compensation for such loss or expense is payable by Scottish Ministers (art 4). Articles 3 and 4 provide for the time limits within which a claim for compensation must be made, and art 5 requires a statement detailing the head of claim in s 89(1) under which the loss or expense falls, and that losses and expenses are fully vouched. Article 6 provides that if compensation is not agreed within 60 days from the date of submission of the claim either party may refer the claim to the Land Court for resolution.

The **Crofting Community Right to Buy (Ballot) (Scotland) Regulations 2004, SSI 2004/227** set out the requirements on a crofting community body which is holding a ballot under s 75 on the question of whether to proceed with a land purchase. Regulation 2 provides that there be a secret ballot and that it should be conducted in a fair and reasonable manner. Under reg 3 the crofting community body is required to ascertain from the voters roll who is eligible to vote in the ballot, and in addition to identify tenants of crofts who are eligible voters. Regulations 4 and 5 give the crofting community body the option of holding an ordinary ballot or a postal ballot, and reg 6 permits proxy votes in certain circumstances. Regulation 7 requires the crofting community body to publish the result of the ballot in a newspaper circulating in the vicinity, and also to notify Scottish Ministers of the result and the other information requested in the schedule to the Regulations. Scottish Ministers are empowered to call for additional information pertaining to the ballot from the community body. Regulation 8 provides for the retention by the crofting community body of the ballot papers; where a postal ballot has been held, evidence of the sending of the ballot papers; and any proxy authorisations and notifications of intention to use a proxy, for a period of two years. That regulation also permits Scottish Ministers and specified persons to inspect the documents retained.

Agricultural Holdings (Scotland) Act 2003

Part 2 of the Act, which confers on tenants a pre-emptive right to buy, came into force on 15 December 2004: see the **Agricultural Holdings (Scotland) Act 2003 (Commencement No 4) Order 2004, SSI 2004/511**. For a brief guide to the Act, see *Conveyancing 2003* pp 63–64. Part 2 of the Act is itself amended by the **Agricultural Holdings (Right to Buy Modifications) (Scotland) Regulations 2004, SSI 2004/557** so as to extend the right to buy to general partners, or former general partners, in a case where the tenant was a limited partnership.

A right to buy is asserted by the registration of a notice of interest in the Register of Community Interests in Land (s 25). If, later, the owner wishes to sell, he must register a notice of proposal to transfer land (s 26). Forms of both notices are prescribed by the **Agricultural Holdings (Forms) (Scotland) Regulations 2004,**

SSI 2004/497. Fees for registration are prescribed by the **Agricultural Holdings (Fees) (Scotland) Order 2004, SSI 2004/496.** The fee for registering a tenant's interest is £40.

Building (Scotland) Act 2003

The Building (Scotland) Act 2003 replaces the Building (Scotland) Act 1959. Virtually all of the new Act comes into force on 1 May 2005: see the **Building (Scotland) Act 2003 (Commencement No 1, Transitional Provisions and Savings) Order 2004, SSI 2004/404.** The basic idea of (i) building regulations, (ii) building warrants, (iii) completion certificates, and (iv) enforcement powers continues, but there are many changes, including the introduction of 'verifiers' (to issue building warrants and completion certificates) and 'certifiers' (to certify compliance with the building regulations). For further details see *Conveyancing 2003* pp 85–88.

New building regulations, which also apply with effect from 1 May 2005, are prescribed by the **Building (Scotland) Regulations 2004, SSI 2004/406.** The basic rules are set out in sch 5. The Regulations apply to construction, conversion and demolition of buildings and also to the provision of services, fittings and equipment in or in connection with buildings (regs 9 to 12). There are certain exempted types of buildings and services (reg 3 and sch 1). There are also some descriptions of buildings and services which do not require a warrant (reg 5 and sch 3). The Regulations specify a period of five years as the life of a limited life building (reg 6). The Regulations also make provision for protective works for the safety of the public whilst work is being carried out on a building or building site (reg 13). Supplementary matters regarding the cleaning of footpaths and security of unoccupied and partly completed buildings are also covered (regs 14 and 15). See further an article by Christopher Rae in (2004) 71 *Greens Property Law Bulletin* 1.

The **Building Procedure (Scotland) Regulations 2004, SSI 2004/428** set out the procedures to be followed in connection with the submission of applications for building warrants, completion certificates and other related matters. They also detail the criteria to which Scottish Ministers are to have regard when approving schemes in terms of s 7 of the 2003 Act and the process for appointment of verifiers and certifiers. Fees are set out in the **Building (Fees) (Scotland) Regulations 2004, SSI 2004/508.**

The current Building Standards Advisory Committee is to continue (2003 Act s 31) but is subject to the new regulations: see the **Building Standards Advisory Committee (Scotland) Regulations 2004, SSI 2004/506.**

Abolition of Feudal Tenure etc (Scotland) Act 2000

The bulk of the Act came into force on 28 November 2004 (the 'appointed day'). In particular s 1, which abolishes the feudal system of land tenure, came into force on that day. All of the Act is now in force. See the Abolition of Feudal Tenure etc (Scotland) Act 2000 (Commencement No 1) Order 2003, SSI 2003/455, the Abolition of Feudal Tenure etc (Scotland) Act 2000 (Commencement No 2) (Appointed Day) Order 2003, SSI 2003/456, and the Abolition of Feudal Tenure etc (Scotland) Act 2000 (Commencement No 3) Order 2003, SSI 2003/620.

The **Abolition of Feudal Tenure etc (Scotland) (Prescribed Periods) Order 2004, SSI 2004/477** provides that, where a notice under the 2000 Act is rejected by the Keeper, the rejection can be challenged in court or by the Lands Tribunal, under s 45 of the Act, only by application within eight weeks of rejection or, if the rejection was before the appointed day, by 21 January 2005. The Order also provides that the period during which the Keeper cannot be required to remove from the Land Register real burdens extinguished by feudal abolition (s 46(1) of the 2000 Act) is 10 years beginning with the appointed day.

The **Abolition of Feudal Tenure etc (Scotland) Act 2000 (Consequential Provisions) Order 2004, SSI 2004/535** makes minor amendments to s 6 of the Land Registers (Scotland) Act 1868 and to s 142 of the Titles to Land Consolidation (Scotland) Act 1868, mainly to take account of the abolition of warrants of registration and their replacement by a statutory application form for the Register of Sasines (2000 Act s 5). In addition s 6 of the Law Reform (Miscellaneous Provisions) (Scotland) Act 1980 is repealed, but it is replaced by s 26B of the Titles to Land Consolidation (Scotland) Act 1868 as inserted by the Abolition of Feudal Tenure etc (Scotland) Act 2000 s 68.

Title Conditions (Scotland) Act 2003

The bulk of the Title Conditions Act came into force on 28 November 2003 (see s 129(2)). Only part 6 (development management scheme) is not yet in force.

Significant amendments to the Title Conditions Act are made by the Tenements (Scotland) Act 2004 (asp 11) s 25 and sch 4. Further, minor, amendments are contained in the Tenements (Scotland) Act 2004 (Consequential Provisions) Order 2004, SSI 2004/551 and the Title Conditions (Scotland) Act 2003 (Notice of Potential Liability for Costs) Amendment Order 2004, SSI 2004/552.

Fees in the Property Registers

The **Fees in the Registers of Scotland Amendment Order 2004, SSI 2004/507** amends the Fees in the Registers of Scotland Order 1995, SI 1995/1945 to take account of the abolition of the feudal system and the Title Conditions (Scotland) Act 2003. The main change is to introduce an additional fee of £22 for dual registration, ie for registration of real burdens and servitudes against the benefited property in addition to the burdened property.

New application form for Register of Sasines

A new form for applications for recording in the Register of Sasines is prescribed by the **Register of Sasines (Application Procedure) Rules 2004, SSI 2004/318**.

Amendment of Land Registration (Scotland) Rules 1980

Minor amendments are made to the Land Registration (Scotland) Rules 1980, SI 1980/1413 by the **Land Registration (Scotland) Amendment Rules 2004, SSI 2004/476**. In particular these facilitate dual registration in respect of real burdens and servitudes. Minor changes are made to forms 1, 2, 3 and 6.

Conservation bodies

Conservation bodies are bodies which are able to hold conservation burdens under s 38 of the Title Conditions (Scotland) Act 2003. Some further bodies were added to the list by the **Title Conditions (Scotland) Act 2003 (Conservation Bodies) Amendment Order 2004, SSI 2004/400**. This supplements the Title Conditions (Scotland) Act 2003 (Conservation Bodies) Order 2003, SSI 2003/453, and the Title Conditions (Scotland) Act 2003 (Conservation Bodies) Amendment Order 2003, SSI 2003/621. The current list of conservation bodies is:

All local authorities
Alba Conservation Trust
Castles of Scotland Preservation Trust
Edinburgh World Heritage Trust
Glasgow Building Preservation Trust
Glasgow Conservation Trust West
Highlands Buildings Preservation Trust
Plantlife—The Wild-Plant Conservation Charity
Scottish Natural Heritage
Solway Heritage
St Vincent Crescent Preservation Trust
Strathclyde Building Preservation Trust
Tayside Building Preservation Trust
The John Muir Trust
The National Trust for Scotland for Places of Historic Interest or Natural
    Beauty
The Royal Society for the Protection of Birds
The Scottish Wildlife Trust
The Trustees of the Landmark Trust
The Trustees of the New Lanark Conservation Trust
The Woodland Trust
United Kingdom Historic Building Preservation Trust

Rural housing bodies

Rural housing bodies are bodies which are able to hold rural housing burdens under s 43 of the Title Conditions (Scotland) Act 2003. A list of rural housing bodies was prescribed by the **Title Conditions (Scotland) Act 2003 (Rural Housing Bodies) Order 2004, SSI 2004/477**. The list is:

Albyn Housing Society Limited
Barra and Vatersay Housing Association Limited
Berneray Housing Association Limited
Buidheann Taigheadais na Meadhanan Limited
Cairn Housing Association Limited
Comhairle nan Eilean Siar
Dunbritton Housing Association Limited
Fyne Homes Limited
Isle of Jura Development Trust
Lochaber Housing Association Limited
Muirneag Housing Association Limited
Orkney Islands Council
Pentland Housing Association Limited
Taighean Ceann a Tuath na'Hearadh Limited
The Highlands Small Communities' Housing Trust
The Isle of Eigg Heritage Trust
The Isle of Gigha Heritage Trust
The North Harris Trust
Tighean Innse Gall Limited

Fees in the Lands Tribunal

The **Lands Tribunal for Scotland (Title Conditions Certificates) (Fees) Rules 2004, SSI 2004/479** fix at £25 the fee to be charged by the Lands Tribunal for the certificate which requires to be endorsed on notices of termination or minutes of waiver of community burdens to the effect that no application to the Tribunal has been made. See Title Conditions (Scotland) Act 2003 ss 23, 34, 37 and 73.

The **Lands Tribunal for Scotland Amendment (Fees) Rules 2004, SSI 2004/480** fix at £150 the fee for applications to the Tribunal (now under ss 90 and 91 of the Title Conditions (Scotland) Act 2003) for the variation and discharge of real burdens and other title conditions. This is an increase of £20. The fee for making the order at the end of the case remains unchanged at £88.

These fees rules supplement the rules made in 2003: the Lands Tribunal for Scotland (Relevant Certificate) Rules 2003, SSI 2003/451, and the Lands Tribunal for Scotland Amendment (Fees) Rules 2003, SSI 2003/521.

PART III
OTHER MATERIAL

OTHER MATERIAL

Charities and Trustee Investment (Scotland) Bill

This Bill is before the Scottish Parliament. As and when enacted it will have a significant impact on both charities and trusts (including non-charitable trusts). It extends the implied powers of trustees. For example, under current law trustees have no implied power to buy land (except for the accommodation of a beneficiary). The Bill would confer on all trusts a power to buy land. The Bill will effect numerous repeals and amendments to existing legislation, including the Trusts (Scotland) Act 1921 and the Trustee Investment Act 1961. For some critical reflections, see an article by Anne Swarbrick published in the December 2004 *Journal of the Law Society of Scotland* (p 26). The proposed test for Scottish charities is discussed by Patrick Ford in (2004) 8 *Edinburgh Law Review* 408.

Longer-term fixed-rate mortgages

In April 2003 the Chancellor of the Exchequer commissioned Professor David Miles, of Imperial College London, to 'undertake analysis of supply and demand side factors limiting the development of the longer-term fixed-rate mortgage market in the UK to establish why the share of longer-term fixed-rate mortgages is so low compared to the United States and many other EU countries' and to 'examine whether there has been any market failure that has held back the market for longer-term fixed-rate mortgages'. He was asked to produce an interim report in 2003 and a final report in time for the 2004 budget. The interim report appeared in 2003 (see *Conveyancing 2003* p 45). The final report appeared in 2004: *The UK Mortgage Market: Taking a Longer-Term View*. H M Treasury, ISBN 1 84532 004 2.

The Report notes (para 8.3) that:

- When choosing between mortgages, many borrowers attach great weight to the level of initial monthly repayments and too little to the likely overall cost of borrowing over the life of the loan.

- Many borrowers' understanding of interest rate risk is poor. The type of advice and information many people receive does not help them as much as it could in understanding these risks.

- The structure of mortgage pricing generates cross-subsidisation from many existing borrowers, a significant proportion of whom are paying standard variable rates (SVR), to new borrowers taking out discounted variable and short-term fixed-rate mortgages. This creates unfairness and makes the market less transparent than it could be. It plays to a tendency of many borrowers to focus on the initial monthly payments on a mortgage and it makes medium-term and longer-term fixed rates appear expensive.

• There are also a number of potential legislative and regulatory barriers to the cost-effective funding of longer-term fixed-rate lending and the way in which early redemption charges are structured.

The recommended approach is non-coercive. There would be two prongs: better information for consumers so that they could appreciate the benefits of longer-term fixed rates, and regulatory measures that would make it easier for lenders to provide such loan packages. Central to the process would be the Financial Services Authority which has regulatory oversight of the mortgage market.

Regulation of the mortgage market

The Financial Services and Markets Act 2000 (Regulated Activities) (Amendment) (No 1) Order 2003, SI 2003/1475 came into force on 31 October 2004. As a result law firms involved in advising on mortgages must either have 'mainstream' authorisation from the Financial Services Authority or be subject to the Law Society of Scotland's 'incidental investment regime'. See David Cullen at (2004) 49 *Journal of the Law Society of Scotland* April/44.

The FSA's rules can be found at its website, http://www.fsa.gov.uk. One set of rules of particular interest is MCOB13, which lays down a framework for the enforcement of secured loans (or 'repossession', to use the FSA's English terminology). A summary by Mark Higgins can be found at (2004) 49 *Journal of the Law Society of Scotland* Aug/64.

CML Lenders' Handbook for Scotland: new home warranties

The Council of Mortgage Lenders ('CML') first produced its *Lenders' Handbook for Scotland* in 2000, and there have been many changes since then. A further amendment has been made, with effect from 30 August 2004. For a discussion see an article by Andrew Hopkins in the July 2004 issue of the *Journal of the Law Society of Scotland* (p 54), and a note in (2004) 71 *Greens Property Law Bulletin* 5. The new paragraph 6.6.2 says:

> Before you send the certificate of title, you must obtain a copy of a new home warranty provider's cover note from the developer. The cover note must confirm that the warranty provider has carried out a final/pre-handover inspection and that the new home warranty will be provided. This will only apply where conclusion of missives occurs on or after 30 August 2004. This does not apply to self-build schemes. Check Part 2 to see what new home warranty documentation should be sent to us after settlement.

The CML official comment is:

This amendment aims to prevent borrowers moving into unfinished new properties. Conveyancers are required to have confirmation from a new home warranty provider (for example, NHBC), in the form of a cover note, that a new property has passed a final inspection and that a new home warranty will be provided. The conveyancer must receive the cover note before sending the certificate of title to the lender and requesting the mortgage funds. Faxed copies of the cover note are acceptable.

Contacting lenders

The July 2004 issue of the *Journal of the Law Society of Scotland* (p 56) contains a list of a person to contact in each of CML's Scottish lenders in cases of difficulty in obtaining discharges, loan papers, titles or settlement cheques.

Endowment mortgages

On 11 March 2004 the House of Commons Treasury Select Committee published its report, *Restoring Confidence in Long-term Savings: Endowment Mortgages*. The Report estimated that at least half of all endowment mortgage borrowers considered that their policy had been mis-sold to them. The report stated (p 3) that 'around 80% of endowment policies are now unlikely to meet their target of repaying the original mortgage, with an average shortfall across policies of £5,500. The shortfall on policies is likely to grow over time, but the current figures nevertheless suggest a collective shortfall across the endowment mortgage market that is already approaching £40 billion'. It added (p 4) that 'much of the industry is still locked into an unacceptable culture that focuses upon short term sales rather than long term customer care'. The report has much interesting information, including the following table (p 8):

Percentage Share of UK Mortgage Market

Year	Capital-and-interest	Endowment	Other
1969	88	9	3
1970	88	7	5
1971	86	8	6
1972	80	12	8
1973	72	17	11
1974	73	16	11
1975	74	16	10
1976	72	18	10

Year	Capital-and-interest	Endowment	Other
1977	71	21	8
1978	67	25	8
1979	64	27	10
1980	69	23	9
1981	74	20	6
1982	73	20	7
1983	41	54	5
1984	38	61	1
1985	42	57	1
1986	28	70	2
1987	18	80	2
1988	14	83	3
1989	18	79	3
1990	20	76	4
1991	18	77	5
1992	21	68	12
1993	26	59	15
1994	30	56	14
1995	35	46	16
1996	38	32	24
1997	41	34	26
1998	43	34	25
1999	47	28	25
2000	60	17	23
2001	72	9	19
2002	82	5	13

Standard securities in favour of Woolwich plc

From 1 December 2003 the entire mortgage book of Woolwich plc was transferred to its parent company, Barclays Bank plc. This means that discharges, assignations and restrictions of standard securities will need to run in the name of Barclays Bank and, in the case of those recorded in the Register of Sasines, will require a clause of deduction of title: see Conveyancing and Feudal Reform (Scotland) Act 1970 sch 4 note 1. The following suggested styles of deduction of title have been issued ((2004) 49 *Journal of the Law Society of Scotland* May / 53):

Security originally granted to Woolwich Building Society
Which Standard Security was last vested in the said Woolwich Building Society as aforesaid and from whom we acquired right by virtue of (one) Transfer Agreement pursuant to sections 97 to 103 inclusive of the Building Societies Act 1986 between the said Woolwich Building Society and Woolwich plc of Watling Street, Bexleyheath, Kent DA6 7RR dated 30 December 1996 (two) Confirmation of said Transfer by the Building Societies Commission dated 16 May 1997 (three) Transfer Amendment Agreement pursuant to section 97 of the Building Societies Act 1986 between the said Woolwich Building Society and the said Woolwich plc dated 28 May 1997 (four) Notice of Vesting given to the Central Office of the Registry of Friendly Societies on 23 June 1997 (five) the Barclays Group Reorganisation Act 2002 ('the Act'), and (six) resolution of the Board of us, the said Barclays Bank plc, made on 17 October 2003 pursuant to the Act.

Security originally granted to Woolwich plc
Which Standard Security was last vested in the said Woolwich plc as aforesaid and from whom we acquired right by virtue of (one) the Barclays Group Reorganisation Act 2002 ('the Act'), and (two) resolution of the Board of us, the said Barclays Bank plc, made on 17 October 2003 pursuant to the Act.

Online PECs

Property enquiry certificates from the City of Edinburgh Council can now be requested and received online: see http://www.edinburgh.gov.uk/pec.

Coal mining reports: money up front

In a change of practice the Coal Authority will only issue expedited mining reports to credit account customers or where the full fee is paid in advance. An updated Scotform (2004) has been produced to reflect these changes and can be downloaded from http://www.coalminingreports.co.uk. Fees are increased from 1 January 2005.

Delay in conclusion of missives

Expressing concern at continuing delays in concluding missives, the Professional Practice Committee of the Law Society has drawn the attention of solicitors to the 1998 Guideline on this topic: see (2004) 49 *Journal of the Law Society of Scotland* Oct / 36. The Guideline is as follows:

It is increasingly common for missives to be in an unconcluded state until shortly before or even at the date of entry. While solicitors require to have regard to the interests of their clients and to take their clients' instructions, they must have regard to the principles of good professional conduct and may not accept an improper instruction.

They should not knowingly mislead professional colleagues and must act with fellow solicitors in a spirit of trust and co-operation (*Code of Conduct for Scottish Solicitors* arts 2, 5(a) and 9).

In residential property transactions solicitors acting on behalf of both purchasers and sellers have a professional duty to conclude missives without undue delay. Clients should be advised at the outset of this duty and of the consequences.

Where a solicitor for a purchaser is instructed to submit an offer but to delay concluding a bargain until some matter outwith the selling agent's control has been resolved, eg the purchaser's own house has not been sold, a survey or specialist's report is required, or funding arrangements are to be confirmed, these circumstances should be disclosed to the selling solicitor. If the purchaser instructs the solicitor not to disclose such matters to the selling solicitor, the purchaser's solicitor should withdraw from acting. To continue acting could amount to a breach of article 9 of the *Code of Conduct* by knowingly misleading a fellow solicitor. Where a purchaser instructs his solicitor to delay concluding a bargain without giving any reason the solicitor should similarly withdraw from acting.

Where a selling client instructs a solicitor to delay concluding a bargain having given an indication that an offer is to be accepted, the reason for that delay should be disclosed to the purchaser's solicitor. If the seller instructs the solicitor not to disclose the reason, or does not give a reason for such an instruction, the solicitor should also withdraw from acting.

If a solicitor whether for seller or purchaser withdraws from acting in terms of this guideline, the confidentiality of the client should not be breached without the client's authority, but when intimating withdrawal that should be done by stating that it is in terms of this guideline.

Registers of Scotland

Hello to the Register of Community Interests in Land

The Register of Community Interests in Land ('RCIL') was born on 14 June 2004, for the registration of community interests in land under part 2 of the Land Reform (Scotland) Act 2003. On 15 December 2004 its scope was extended so as to include registrations of tenants' right to buy under part 2 of the Agricultural Holdings (Scotland) Act 2003. A useful official account of the Register is given at p 58 of the *Journal of the Law Society of Scotland* for July 2004. The RCIL can be searched free of charge on http://www.ros.gov.uk/rcil. As of 5 February 2005 there had been 13 registrations in respect of community interests in land.

A search in the RCIL is not included in standard ROS reports. Nevertheless it is likely to be needed for non-urban properties. Only towns and cities with a population of more than 10,000 are excluded from part 2 of the Land Reform Act: see the Community Right to Buy (Definition of Excluded Land) (Scotland) Order 2004, SSI 2004/296. It is understood that independent searchers now offer the service. (See further p 11 of the *Journal of the Law Society* for August 2004.) The style of *pro forma* offers should now include references to the new register. See further articles published at (2004) 49 *Journal of the Law Society of Scotland* Sept/52 (Alasdair Fox), Oct/52 (Bruce Beveridge) and (2005) 50 *Journal of the Law Society of Scotland* Jan/30 (Alistair Sim).

Goodbye to the Register of Entails

Following the extinction of the last surviving entails on 28 November 2004 the Register of Entails was formally closed immediately thereafter. See Abolition of Feudal Tenure etc (Scotland) Act 2000 s 52.

Freedom of information

By s 6(5) of the Land Registration (Scotland) Act 1979 the Keeper is required to release only copies of documents referred to in the title sheet. Other documents—prior dispositions, for example—cannot usually be obtained. The position is changed by the Freedom of Information (Scotland) Act 2002, which came fully into force on 1 January 2005: see Freedom of Information (Scotland) Act 2002 (Commencement No 3) Order 2004, SSI 2004/203. By s 1(1) of that Act, 'A person who requests information from a Scottish public authority which holds it is entitled to be given it by the authority'. The Keeper is a Scottish public authority (sch 1 para 12). Various exemptions are set out in part 2 of the Act but none is likely to apply to conveyancing deeds held at Register House. The right to information is not, however, confined to conveyancing deeds. Presumably information about the earlier states of title sheets is also covered by the 2002 Act.

Registration of company securities

Where a standard security by a company is presented for registration in the Land Register, the Keeper will, within 10 days, send a letter confirming the date of registration. But he will only do so where the words 'CONFIRMATION OF REGISTRATION IS REQUIRED' are written in block capitals on the top of the first page of the form 2 and any other application forms accompanying the application for registration. See (2004) 49 *Journal of the Law Society of Scotland* April/57. The importance of the date is that particulars of the security must be registered with the Registrar of Companies with 21 days under s 410 of the Companies Act 1985. (For a proposal by the Scottish Law Commission for the removal of this requirement see p 52 below.)

Volume of business

The *Annual Report and Accounts 2003–04* disclose that almost 500,000 transactions were registered, representing over £20 billion in value. The number is an increase of 7% on the previous year. The breakdown (p 9) is:

First registrations	70,654
Transfers of part	20,001
Dealings with whole	217,127
Register of Sasines	122,840
Chancery and Judicial Registers	44,946
Register of Inhibitions and Adjudications	18,821

The claimed accuracy rate for land certificates (p 14) is 94.7%, which falls a little short of the target of 97%. The target for 2004–05 is an ambitious 98%.

Register of Scottish Baronies

Since 28 November 2004 barony titles (ie the dignity of baron including the right to use the title 'baron') have been severed from the land: see Abolition of Feudal Tenure etc (Scotland) Act s 63. As a result they can no longer be registered in the Land Register or Sasine Register—or, officially, anywhere else (other than the Books of Council and Session or Sheriff Court Books). But a private register has now been set up, from 28 November 2004, under the direction of Alistair Rennie, a former Deputy Keeper of the Registers. The contact details are: Alistair G Rennie Associates Ltd, 98 Baronshill Avenue, Linlithgow EH49 7JG (tel 01506 844419; e-mail agrennie@baronshill.fsnet.co.uk). Baronies are now transferred by assignation and not by disposition, and the idea is that the assignation should be registered in the new register. As a matter of law, the transfer will be complete when the assignation is delivered (2000 Act s 63(2)); but the further step of registration will help reassure future purchasers that the same barony has not been sold twice, and in practice an unregistered assignation may not be accepted as a good title.

Further details of the register are given at p 57 of the *Journal of the Law Society of Scotland* for November 2004. The following in particular should be noted:

> Applications for registration will be accepted only from a solicitor with a Scottish practising certificate, who will have to sign an application form including a statement that he or she has examined the titles and is satisfied that they are sufficient to support the claim to the entitlement. An applicant will have to demonstrate that the evidence that supports the claim actually exists by submitting original deeds or extracts with the application . . . These requirements are intended to ensure that, even though the register does not guarantee the validity of a claim, it will provide a repository where claims to the Dignity of a barony and evidence adduced to support them can be identified.

Reform of land registration

The Scottish Law Commission's Discussion Paper on *Land Registration: Void and Voidable Titles* (Scot Law Com DP No 125, 2004; available on http://www. scotlawcom.gov.uk) was published in February 2004. Two further papers are due in 2005.

In the first paper the Law Commission explores some of the fundamental legal issues underpinning registration of title including the effect of registration and the protection of the acquirer. It argues in favour of new legislation which protects the acquirer a little less and the 'true' owner (ie the person from whom ownership is taken by operation of the Act) a little more. A distinction is made between 'Register error' and 'transactional error'. The former is an error already on the Register at the time of the acquisition; the latter is a new error on the Register caused by the current transaction. The Commission accepts that, as at present, an acquirer should take free of Register error, for it is of the essence of registration of title that the Register can be relied upon. But it argues that the acquirer should not take free of transactional error (eg forgery of the signature on the disposition). Instead the acquirer should be paid indemnity (if in good faith) but the property returned to the 'true' owner.

A number of other proposals are made. For example, registration should not operate 'positively', ie should not confer a good title if the deed is invalid. The present difficulties in reducing titles on the Land Register should be removed. And the 'fraud and carelessness' test for acquirers should be replaced by the more familiar and principled notion of bad faith.

For a discussion, see an article by an English specialist, Lizzie Cook, published at (2004) 8 *Edinburgh Law Review* 401.

Reform of bankruptcy and diligence

In June 2004 the Scottish Executive published draft proposals for reform of the law of bankruptcy and diligence: *Modernising Bankruptcy and Diligence in Scotland* (ISBN 0 7559 4199 3). The proposals for diligence are based on earlier work by the Scottish Law Commission. A partial draft of a Bankruptcy and Diligence etc (Scotland) Bill is included. Legislation is expected in 2005 or 2006.

On bankruptcy the principal proposal is that a bankrupt should be discharged after one year and not, as at present, after three. The proposals for diligence are more radical. Adjudication is to be abolished along with sequestration for rent and maills and duties. In the place of adjudication would be the new diligence of land attachment. Inhibition would remain, but with certain changes. The law on diligence on the dependence is to be re-cast.

The proposals are discussed briefly by Mark Higgins in the *Journal of the Law Society of Scotland* for September 2004 (p 17).

Reform of housing law

In July 2004 the Scottish Executive published draft proposals for a limited reform of housing law: *Maintaining Homes—Preserving Homes* (ISBN 0 7559 4181 0). To a considerable extent these derive from the work of the Housing Improvement Task Force, which reported in 2003: see *Conveyancing 2003* pp 96–102. Legislation is expected in 2005.

Under the proposals a single statutory housing notice would be introduced to replace the different notices in the current legislation. For the first time local authorities would have powers to anticipate the need for repairs by serving a five-year maintenance order. This would require the owners of the flats or houses concerned to put in place and implement a maintenance plan. If they failed to comply the local authority could act instead and recover the cost. The local authority could also require the appointment of a factor/manager.

The meaning of 'tolerable standard' is to be extended to cover adequate thermal insulation and safe installations for the supply, distribution and use of electrical power.

In owner-occupied tenements there is be a power in the local authority to pay the share of recalcitrant owners and then recover by means of a charging order.

The idea is that the owners should first reach agreement on repairs (typically by a majority) either under the titles or, if these are silent, under the Tenement Management Scheme provided by the Tenements (Scotland) Act 2004. If an owner then refused to pay his share other owners would issue a notice to the local authority inviting it to supply the missing funds.

Reserve power is to be taken to introduce mandatory single surveys and, possibly, purchaser's information packs. Whether the reserve powers are used will depend on the success of voluntary initiatives. A pilot of the single survey is currently underway: see http://www.singlesurveypilot.co.uk.

Various changes are proposed for private sector tenancies. For example, landlords would be under a duty to carry out a repair inspection before a tenancy began, to notify the tenant of the repair work required, and to carry it out in a reasonable time. The landlord's repairing obligation, which (as at present) would continue during the currency of the lease, would be enforceable through a new Private Sector Housing Tribunal for Scotland (replacing Rent Assessment Panels).

Reform of registration of company securities

The Scottish Law Commission published its final Report on *Registration of Rights in Security by Companies* (Scot Law Com No 197, 2004; available on http://www.scotlawcom.gov.uk) in September 2004. The Law Commission recommends disbandment of the Register of Charges. A new register should be established for floating charges. Other securities should not require additional registration merely because they are granted by companies. In particular, standard securities by companies should only require to be registered in the Land Register or Register of Sasines.

For floating charges, registration in the Register of Floating Charges would mark the moment of creation. The deed itself would be registered and not merely particulars. The new Register would be administered by the Keeper of the Registers of Scotland. Variations, assignations and discharges would likewise require to be registered. A floating charge would rank with other (fixed) securities by reference to the date of its registration (and not, as at present, its crystallisation).

House price service

Details of house prices in different parts of Scotland over a particular six-month period are now available, for a fee, on http://www.scotlandshouseprices.gov.uk. The service is provided by Registers of Scotland.

Letters of obligation and SDLT

For the meaning and scope of a 'classic' letter of obligation, see *Conveyancing 2002* pp 42–43 and (2003) 48 *Journal of the Law Society of Scotland* April/26. The Conveyancing Committee envisages possible additions to the letter of obligation in relation to SDLT where registration is to be undertaken by someone other than the person responsible for paying SDLT. Since SDLT certificates can, at present, only be sent to the person liable for paying the tax, the obligation would be (i) to deliver the certificate once it has been received, and (ii) to give notification of any requisition or response by the Revenue in relation to the SDLT application. The Committee envisages two situations where this might be necessary. One is for long leases in a case where the landlord wishes to register (including, typically, in the Books of Council and Session). The other is for standard securities if the lender and borrower are separately represented and the lender wishes to present the disposition for registration. See further (2004) 49 *Journal of the Law Society of Scotland* Jan/55. Suggested wording and procedures have been prepared by the Property Standardisation Group and may be consulted on http://www.psglegal.co.uk. (For the work of this Group, see *Conveyancing 2003* p 41 and (2004) 49 *Journal of the Law Society of Scotland* Oct/51.) In the case of leases the idea is that the matter should be dealt with in the contract rather than by means of separate undertakings.

Purchases or sales by non-solicitors

The following guidance is given by the Professional Practice Committee of the Law Society ((2004) 49 *Journal of the Law Society of Scotland* Jan/41):

> For some years now the Society have received enquiries from different parts of Scotland from solicitors who have received offers for property usually houses from agents who are not solicitors. It should be noted that missives are expressly excluded from the work reserved for solicitors in the Solicitors (Scotland) Act 1980 s 32(3). Any person is therefore entitled to prepare missives on behalf of clients. However solicitors receiving such offers should enquire which firm of solicitors will be dealing with the conveyancing and how the purchase price will be settled. They should not lend title deeds to such a person, particularly where these have been received on loan from a lender. Where the *seller* has instructed a non-solicitor business or is acting for himself, the purchasing solicitor should clarify the position regarding the letter of obligation and should consider whether it is in the clients' interests to settle on a letter of obligation which is not backed by the Master Policy. This should be dealt with in the missives.

Books

D A Brand, A J M Steven and S Wortley, *Professor McDonald's Conveyancing Manual* (7th edn) (LexisNexis 2004; ISBN 0 406 95963 3)

George L Gretton and Kenneth G C Reid, *Conveyancing* (3rd edn) (Thomson W Green 2004; ISBN 0 414 01558 4)

Kenneth G C Reid and George L Gretton, *Conveyancing 2003* (LexisNexis 2004; ISBN 0 406 97366 0)

Robert Rennie, *Opinions on Professional Negligence in Conveyancing* (Thomson W Green 2004; ISBN 0414 015 452)

Robert Rennie, *Land Tenure in Scotland* (Thomson W Green 2004; ISBN 0 414 01548 7)

John St Clair and Lord Drummond Young, *The Law of Corporate Insolvency in Scotland* (3rd edn) (Thomson W Green 2004; ISBN 0414 015 088)

Andrew J M Steven and Scott Wortley, *Avizandum Statutes on Scots Property, Trusts and Succession Law 2004–2005* (Avizandum Publishing Ltd 2004; ISBN 0 9543423 7 2)

R Zimmermann, D Visser and K Reid (eds), *Mixed Legal Systems in Comparative Perspective: Property and Obligations in Scotland and South Africa* (Oxford University Press 2004; ISBN 0 19 927100 3)

Articles

Sir Crispin Agnew of Lochnaw, 'Baronial heraldic additaments: unintended consequences of the Abolition of Feudal Tenure etc (Scotland) Act 2000?' 2004 SLT (News) 179

Hugh Angus, 'Community right to buy' (2004) 73 *Greens Property Law Bulletin* 3

Hazel Bett, 'Update on transfers of title in matrimonial disputes' (2004) 68 *Greens Property Law Bulletin* 5

Mike Blair, 'Agricultural holdings—the 2003 Act' (2004) 71 *Greens Property Law Bulletin* 3

Stewart Brymer, 'The future of conveyancing' (2003) 67 *Greens Property Law Bulletin* 5

Stewart Brymer, 'CML and contaminated land' (2004) 68 *Greens Property Law Bulletin* 1

Stewart Brymer, 'The single survey pilot: the story so far' (2004) 69 *Greens Property Law Bulletin* 1

Stewart Brymer, 'Single survey's lonely heart' (2004) 49 *Journal of the Law Society of Scotland* Oct/50

Alistair Burrow, 'The race is on (again)' (2004) 49 *Journal of the Law Society of Scotland* Oct/46 (discussing *Burnett's Tr v Grainger* 2004 SC (HL) 19)

David Cabrelli, 'Landlord's refusal of a tenant's application for consent to assignation of lease: An Update' (2004) 70 *Greens Property Law Bulletin* 1

George Clark, 'House buying and selling—do we have the English system?' (2004) 70 *Greens Property Law Bulletin* 4

Raffaele Caterina, 'Concepts and remedies in the law of possession' (2004) 8 *Edinburgh Law Review* 267

Lizzie Cook, 'Land registration: void and voidable titles' (2004) 8 *Edinburgh Law Review* 401

Lorne Crerar, 'Best foot forward' (2004) 49 *Journal of the Law Society of Scotland* March/60 (discussing the single survey)

David Cullen, 'Far from incidental' (2004) 49 *Journal of the Law Society of Scotland* April/44 (discussing the regulation of mortgage and general insurance business under the Financial Services and Markets Act 2000)

Ian C Ferguson, 'Mortgage Rights (Scotland) Act 2001: an update' (2004) 72 *Scottish Law Gazette* 70

Patrick Ford, 'The Scottish charity test: do we really need it?' (2004) 8 *Edinburgh Law Review* 408

Alasdair Fox, 'Are landlords' fears justified?' (2004) 49 *Journal of the Law Society of Scotland* March/56 (discussing Agricultural Holdings (Scotland) Act 2003 s 16)

Alasdair Fox, 'Beware all conveyancers!' (2004) 49 *Journal of the Law Society of Scotland* Sept/52 (discussing the need to search the new Register of Community Interests in Land)

George Gretton, 'Ownership and insolvency: *Burnett's Tr v Grainger*' (2004) 8 *Edinburgh Law Review* 389

George Gretton, 'From sunset to sunrise' (2004) 49 *Journal of the Law Society of Scotland* Nov/14 (discussing abolition of the feudal system)

George Gretton, Robert Rennie, Roddy Paisley and Stewart Brymer, 'Waste paper?' (2004) 49 *Journal of the Law Society of Scotland* May/54 (discussing ARTL)

Nicholas J M Grier, 'Baronial titles revisited' 2004 SLT (News) 233

Mark Higgins, 'FSA's net widens' (2004) 49 *Journal of the Law Society of Scotland* Aug/64 (discussing FSA regulation of arrears and repossessions)

Mark Higgins, 'Forgive us our debts' (2004) 49 *Journal of the Law Society of Scotland* Sept/17 (discussing the Scottish Executive's proposals for the reform of bankruptcy and diligence)

Andrew Hopkins, 'New build: getting the loan funds' (2004) 49 *Journal of the Law Society of Scotland* July/54 (discussing changes to the CML *Lenders' Handbook* in respect of new houses)

Mignonne Khazaka, 'Asbestos control' (2004) 71 *Greens Property Law Bulletin* 4

Linsey Lewin, 'Housing Improvement Task Force' (2004) 49 *Journal of the Law Society of Scotland* Jan/58, Feb/56, April/60, July/59. And on the same issue see the note in (2004) 72 *Scottish Law Gazette* 62

Angus McAllister, 'Leasing to a tenant's business competitor' 2004 *Juridical Review* 133

Donna McKenzie Skene, 'The shock of the old: *Burnett's Tr v Grainger*' 2004 SLT (News) 65

Donna McKenzie Skene and Anne-Michelle Slater, 'Liability and access to the countryside' 2004 *Juridical Review* 353

John McNeil, 'Abolition of the feudal system: the new law of real burdens' (2004) 49 *Journal of the Law Society of Scotland* Jan/56, Feb/54, March/62, May/52, June/56

George Menzies, 'Walk this way?' (2004) 49 *Journal of the Law Society of Scotland* Oct/26 (discussing part 1 of the Land Reform (Scotland) Act 2003)

Russell Paterson, 'Beware of Companies House disclaimers' (2004) 49 *Journal of the Law Society of Scotland* May/49

Christopher Rae, 'The new building regulations' (2004) 71 *Greens Property Law Bulletin* 1

Robert Rennie, 'Solicitors' negligence: dealing with tricky twosomes' 2004 SLT (News) 33

Robert Rennie, 'Widening the duty of care' 2004 SLT (News) 245

Robert Rennie, 'Last piece of the jigsaw' (2004) 49 *Journal of the Law Society of Scotland* March/26 (discussing the Tenements (Scotland) Bill)

Robert Rennie, 'How much law, anyway?' (2004) 49 *Journal of the Law Society of Scotland* Aug/60

Roy Roxburgh, 'Nightmares about trust clauses' (2004) 49 *Journal of the Law Society of Scotland* June/12 (discussing the use of trust clauses following *Burnett's Tr v Grainger* 2004 SC (HL) 19); and see Aug/10 for a rejoinder

Jonathan Seddon, 'Assignations, third party rights and no loss arguments' (2003) 67 *Greens Property Law Bulletin* 1

Jonathan Seddon, 'Certificates of practical completion and leases' (2004) 68 *Greens Property Law Bulletin* 3

Alistair Sim, 'Critical dates—who is watching the clock?' (2004) 73 *Greens Property Law Bulletin* 1

Andrew Steven and Alan Barr, 'The Land Reform (Scotland) Act 2003 (Part 2)' (2003) 67 *Greens Property Law Bulletin* 3

Anne Swarbrick, 'A defining era' (2004) 49 *Journal of the Law Society of Scotland* Dec/26 (discussing the Charities and Trustees Investment (Scotland) Bill)

Ken Swinton, 'ARTL, remortgages and free-standing securities' (2004) 72 *Scottish Law Gazette* 7

Ken Swinton, 'Money Laundering Regulations 2003' (2004) 72 *Scottish Law Gazette* 23

Ken Swinton, '*Burnett's Trustee v Grainger*' (2004) 72 *Scottish Law Gazette* 41

Ken Swinton, '"Equally between them"?' (2004) 72 *Scottish Law Gazette* 82

Ken Swinton, 'The Tenements (Scotland) Bill' (2004) 72 *Scottish Law Gazette* 134

Ken Swinton, 'In search of meadows new—secured consumer loans' (2004) 72 *Scottish Law Gazette* 161

Sandy Telfer, 'Extending public sewerage networks' (2004) 72 *Greens Property Law Bulletin* 1.

Richard Turnbull, 'Third party rights of appeal' (2004) 72 *Greens Property Law Bulletin* 4.

C G van der Merwe, 'The Tenement (Scotland) Act 2004: a brief evaluation' 2004 SLT (News) 211

Niall R Whitty, 'Unjustified enrichment and *Burnett's Trustee v Grainger*' (2004) 8 *Edinburgh Law Review* 395

PART IV
COMMENTARY

COMMENTARY

MISSIVES OF SALE

Self-satisfaction

Murdock v McQueen[1] considers a short but important point on which there is no previous authority. An offer was made requiring the exhibition of consents for all work undertaken on the property since 1974. The qualified acceptance responded as follows:

> This condition will be deleted, under explanation that all documentation in connection with our clients' alteration of the Subjects … is exhibited in full satisfaction of this Clause. Your client will have to satisfy herself beyond what is contained in the documentation exhibited.

When, later, some of the documentation was found to be missing, a question arose as to the meaning of the qualification. That the buyer was not 'satisfied' was plain. But did that allow a remedy against the sellers?[2] The qualification is not easy to interpret. It opens with a forthright deletion of the original condition, which seems designed to exonerate the sellers.[3] But it closes with a statement that the buyer is to satisfy herself, which seems to leave open the question of what is to happen if she is not satisfied. The sheriff (G J Evans) decided that the contract had not been breached. In his view the buyer

> misinterprets the use of the word 'satisfy' in the qualified deletion by giving it too positive a meaning whereas it was, in my view, being used in context in a more neutral way. When the qualified deletion provided that 'your client will require to satisfy herself as to the position beyond what is contained in the documentation exhibited', it means no more than that the Defender [the buyer] will have to make her own inquiries full stop. It does not mean that in addition the result of those inquiries has to be to her positive satisfaction.

Two conclusions can be drawn from this decision. The first is the potential ambiguity of the self-satisfaction formula: if the buyer is *not* satisfied, what then?

---

1 2004 GWD 39-797.
2 The buyer purported to rescind.
3 But why 'will be' deleted rather than 'is' deleted? This might seem to carry the uncomfortable idea that the condition is to remain in force for some further, undisclosed, period before eventually falling. Indeed that interpretation gains support from the reference, later in the same sentence, to 'full satisfaction of this Clause' (for what otherwise is there to be satisfied?).

It should not be taken from *Murdock* that the formula will always leave a buyer without a claim. That depends on the overall wording. As the sheriff pointed out, it would have been open to the buyer to qualify the clause

> by providing that while she accepted the qualified deletion ... she did so only on the footing that she would require X days to satisfy herself thereon and she reserved the right to resile if at the end of that time, she was satisfied that certain items ... were not covered by the documentation.

Indeed even an 'X days' qualification might have been enough on its own, for there would be no point in allowing a certain number of days if no rights accrued to the buyer during this period. The important message for practice is to use the self-satisfaction formula with care, so that its meaning is clear.

The second conclusion is to avoid the self-satisfaction formula where the seller is seeking to repel liability. From a legal point of view it is plainly unnecessary. The result in *Murdock* would have been the same but uncontentious if the clause had stopped with the first five words ('this condition will be deleted'). In cases like this, the self-satisfaction formula is used merely to soften the blow so as to make outright rejection seem less stark than it really is. That is almost always a mistake. The proper place for blow-softening is in the covering letter. A qualified acceptance is a contractual document and not an exercise in etiquette.

D-I-Y missives

It is easy to criticise drafting with the benefit of hindsight. Could the layman do better? In *Rodger v Paton*[1] the buyer was already in possession and the parties chose to dispense with legal advice. The agreement between them was drawn up in succinct form:

Mr Robert Paton
6 Store Lane
Rothesay
1/12/90

Re Shop Premises and Garden Ground of approximately 1 Acre at 14 Westland's Road, Rothesay

I , Robert Paton of 6 Store Lane, Rothesay, hereby agree to sell to Mrs C B Rodger of Ivybank Villa, Westland's Road, Rothesay. the Shop premises and piece of ground at 14 Westland's Road, Rothesay for the Sum of £36,000,00. **THIRTY SIX THOUSAND POUND'S**.

The above monie's are to be paid in monthly installments of £200. (fixed) with no allowances for inflation or any other cause whatsover. *1st; payment to commence on the 1/2/91 and to run for 180 months thereafter. I agree that I will have no right of access to the shop or land at any time for any reason, and also I will have no say whatsoever as to what may or may not be done with the land or shop.

---

1 2004 GWD 19-425.

In the event of more than three consecutive monthly payments being outstanding I shall have the right through the Court's to sell the Property and land for the best price obtainable with a minimum of three months national advertising and to take the best offer thereof, and any surplus monies thereof will be returned to Mrs Rodger after the deduction of my REASONABLE expenses and dispersements.

Mrs Rodger may settle up the outstanding monies at any time after 1995 without penalty.

I state categorically and unreservedly that the SHOP and Land are mine to sell and that they are free from any debt or lien or any other type of legal hold that may affect the clean title which I hold. I also state that the title is completely clear in my favour as at the time of this agreement and that there is no possible outstanding retrospective actions that could be enforced.

If for any reason whatsoever I cannot pass on clean title to Mrs Rodger on payment of the monies or if for any reason whatsoever Mrs rodger is unable to get clean title, then I agree to be held liable for damages and disbursements to mrs Rodger the amount of which will be settled and agree by an independent arbitrator whose decision shall be binding and FINAL to both parties.

Both parties signed. But as can happen with even the most carefully drawn contracts, events overtook the original provisions. The seller's title, it seems, was not beyond reproach. A reduced price was agreed and paid; and the revised arrangements were recorded in the following way:

BY HAND Ivybank Villa

Westlands Road
Rothesay
PA20 0HQ
5/3/93

Re Shop Premises and Garden Ground at 14 Westlands Road, Rothesay: Final Settlement of Agreement Dated 1/12/1990

I, Robert Paton of 6 Store Lane, Rothesay, due to numerous difficulties in my supplying CLEAN TITLE to the above Land, and with reference to all the correspondence on this matter hereby accept the payment of £10,000 (Ten Thousand Pounds Cash) as being FULL and FINAL SETTLEMENT of the above dated AGREEMENT.

As and when I am able to pass on Clean Title to Mrs Rodger I shall do so at the earliest possible time.

In light of this agreement Mrs Rodger shall have no re-dress if my Inhibitor presses for the Sale of Land.

Given all the difficulties I hereby accept this reduced payment.

Again both parties signed, this time with witnesses.

Purists may be unsettled by the mis-spellings and by the outbreaks of apostrophes and block capitals. Nonetheless there is much to admire in these documents. The parties are named and designed. The property is described. The price is fixed, and may be paid either in instalments over a stipulated period or by lump sum. And the seller warrants his good and marketable title, undertaking to pay damages if things go wrong. Naturally there are imperfections. It is not clear, for example, what 'surplus monies' are to be returned to the buyer in the event of a sale 'through the Court's'. Not many solicitors would be satisfied with an obligation to pass on 'Clean Title' only 'as and when' the seller is able. There is no express obligation to deliver a disposition.

In the event no disposition was ever delivered. Instead the seller disponed the property to someone else.[1] When the buyer sought to found on the above documents, the seller argued that they were defective in a number of respects. Only two need be mentioned here.

The first was the description of the property. It goes without saying that in missives the property must be sufficiently described. That does not mean a full conveyancing description. But if the property cannot be identified even after recourse to extrinsic evidence, then there is no agreement as to the subjects of sale and hence no contract at all.[2] At first sight it seems beyond argument that the property in the present case was sufficiently described. There was a postal address, a mention of the type of property (shop premises), an approximate acreage for the garden, and the clear implication that title is held in the name of the seller (the property being 'mine to sell'). If such a description is too vague, then most descriptions in missives would fail the test. To make matters clearer still the buyer was already in possession of the property. The difficulty concerned the size of the garden. The document promised 'approximately 1 Acre'. In fact it appears to have amounted only to about half that extent. Was that fatal to the validity of the description? Quite properly, the Lord Ordinary (Hardie) thought not:[3]

> This is not a case where the ambiguity, if any, as to the identification of the subjects is so obvious that it cannot be said that the parties were in agreement as to the extent of the subjects of sale. Before determining this issue, I consider that the pursuer [the buyer] should be afforded the opportunity of leading evidence to identify the subjects.

The second defect was more easily disposed of. No date of entry was mentioned. Therefore, argued the seller, no binding contract had been reached. The authorities against that view are, however, clear and well known.[4] A date of entry is not needed in a contract for the sale of land. If none is given, then one will be implied by the court. *Rodger* usefully provides further authority as to how this will be done:[5]

> [I]n cases where settlement has been effected, in the absence of a stated date of entry, the date of settlement is implied to be the date of entry. In the present case the pursuer avers that in March 1993 she paid £10,000 in cash to the first defender in full and final settlement of the purchase price ... If the pursuer can establish these averments, the date of entry would be implied as the date of settlement, being the date on which the first defender [the seller] acknowledged receipt of the final instalment of the price.

---

1 For this aspect of the case, see p 103.
2 G L Gretton and K G C Reid, *Conveyancing* (3rd edn 2004) para 4-03.
3 Paragraph 18.
4 In particular *Gordon District Council v Wimpey Homes Holdings Ltd* 1988 SLT 481. For a discussion see G L Gretton and K G C Reid, *Conveyancing* (3rd edn 2004) para 4-13.
5 Paragraph 20.

In another case from 2004, *Norman v Kerr*,[1] the date of entry was said to be that date occurring after a 'reasonable period'.

COHABITATION BLUES

Two recent cases

Two people meet, exchange glances, reciprocate civilities, and go home and dream of each other. Perhaps they live together happily ever after. Or perhaps they don't. If they don't, there may be many ensuing legal problems. One is the house including the mortgage. If the parties are married,[2] then family law provides an overarching system which, in principle at least, should be able to resolve disputes in a fair way. But if the parties are unmarried, the law for most purposes treats them as strangers.[3] There does not exist a special body of law to resolve their disputes: such disputes must be resolved by the general law. This issue is a relatively new one. Thirty years ago it was almost unknown for an unmarried couple to buy a house together. Today it is common. Because cohabitants do not have the framework of family law to assist them if they become estranged, the time may now have come to offer such clients co-purchase contracts: indeed some law firms already do this. Such contracts are in the interests of the clients, and indirectly in the interests of the law firm, because they reduce the danger that later on one of the clients will be able to claim that the law firm failed to give proper advice or failed to implement instructions. Indeed, while co-purchase agreements are mainly aimed at cohabitants, they could also be appropriate for married clients.

Two cases from 2004 are illustrative of how smiles can turn to tears. The first is *Burnett v Menzies Dougal*.[4] Verona Burnett and Alistair Burnett bought 46 Swanston Avenue, Edinburgh. At the time they were unmarried. The defenders acted for them. The price was £90,000. Verona contributed about £70,000 of this. The balance of about £20,000 came from a loan from Halifax plc. This was secured by standard security. No doubt both parties were jointly and severally liable on the loan. Title was taken four-fifths to Verona and one-fifth to Alistair. This was in 1997. In 1998 they married. In 1999 they separated. Verona stayed in the house. Alistair then proposed that Verona should buy his one-fifth share at a price equivalent to one fifth of the value of the property. By that time the property was worth about £115,000, and so on that basis the price for the one-fifth share would be about £23,000. Verona agreed to this proposal. She paid £23,000 and Alistair disponed his share. Verona also assumed sole responsibility for the Halifax loan, which at that time stood at £20,315.[5]

---

1 2004 GWD 28-589.

2 Or civil partners, once the Civil Partnerships Act 2004 comes into force.

3 There are a number of exceptions. For example, s 18 of the Matrimonial Homes (Family Protection) (Scotland) Act 1981 confers certain rights on cohabitants. But those rights are very limited in scope.

4 2005 SCLR 133 (Notes).

5 The story as outlined here is taken from the pursuer's pleadings as given in the Opinion of Temporary Judge R F Macdonald. There was no proof and so the facts were never judicially determined. Some parts of the story are less than clear.

Verona then sued the defenders for £20,315, alleging that they had been negligent. She averred that the agreement between herself and Alistair at the time of the purchase had been that he would be solely responsible for the Halifax loan and she would have had an option to buy his one-fifth share at a fair value. She claimed that they had instructed the defenders to draw up a formal agreement to that effect. Because the defenders had failed to do so, she had been forced, she said, to take on sole responsibility for the loan herself. She produced a copy of a note seemingly unsigned that, she said, recorded the agreement. She said that it had been written by Alistair and had been handed by him to the defenders:

> SIDE AGREEMENT BETWEEN A & V STATING THAT IN THE EVENT OF THEM SPLITTING-UP OR HOUSE BEING SOLD V'S SHARE OF NET PROCEEDS WILL BE 4/5 AND A'S SHARE WILL BE 1/5 LESS TOTAL BALANCE OF MORTGAGE THEN OUTSTANDING. PLUS OPTION TO V TO BUY A'S 1/5 SHARE AT INDEPENDENT VALUATION, PRICE BEING USED TO REDUCE/REPAY MORTGAGE, ANY SHORTFALL OR SURPLUS BEING FOR A'S ACCOUNT. AGREEMENT REQUIRED BECAUSE V IS SCARED OF MORTGAGES & AFRAID THAT SOMEHOW I MIGHT DO SOMETHING TO REDUCE THE VALUE OF HER SHARE OR EVEN BANKRUPT HER! UNDER THE ABOVE ARRANGEMENTS, A & V ARE BOTH TAKING THE RISK THAT IF THE MARRIAGE BREAKS UP THE HOUSE MAY HAVE TO BE SOLD.

For the purposes of the litigation, the most important part of this note was the provision which in effect says that Alistair would have sole responsibility for the mortgage loan. The defenders attacked the pursuer's pleadings as lacking in relevancy and specification. They were successful: the action was dismissed. It is, indeed, not easy to perceive the basis of the claim. Either Verona and Alistair had agreed that Alistair would be solely liable for the loan or they had not. If they had not, then Verona's whole case fell to the ground. But if they had, why did she not insist that that agreement be honoured by him, instead of settling with him on entirely different terms? If she could prove such an agreement in a question with the law agents (which is precisely what she was seeking to do) then she could equally have proved it in a question with Alistair.

The decision to dismiss the action on the basis of the pleadings is thus an understandable one. However, it does rather seem, from the standpoint of the uninformed outsider, as if Alistair somehow gained £23,000 from the property without having made any significant financial contribution himself. If that is what happened (and it must be stressed that the account here given is based only on the pursuer's averments) then one must wonder why. And that brings one back to the central puzzle of the case, which is why Verona agreed to take on the whole liability for the loan. There is no way of answering that on the information available.

The second case is *Moggach v Milne*.[1] To explain the purported legal basis for the pursuer's claim one has to go back to *Shilliday v Smith*.[2] In *Shilliday* a couple

---

1 22 October 2004, Elgin Sheriff Court, A451/01.
2 1998 SC 725.

became engaged. The man owned a house. The plan was that they would live there when they were married. The woman spent money improving it. But the wedding never happened. They parted. She sued him for the money she had spent. Her action was not based on any contract. Rather it was based on the *condictio causa data causa non secuta*. She had, she argued, expended money for his benefit in the expectation of an event that did not materialise, and so under the *condictio* she was entitled to her money back. The Inner House upheld this argument. *Shilliday* has become a leading case in the law of unjustified enrichment. In *Moggach* the pursuer based his action on *Shilliday*.

The pursuer's averments were, the sheriff principal, Sir Stephen Young, commented, 'not exactly a model of clarity'. But it seems that the pursuer's case was that he and the defender had been co-owners of one house, in Culloden, and that they then sold that house and used some of the net proceeds to buy another house, in Duffus.[1] He and his partner agreed that the new house too should be in joint names. But for reasons that are not explained in the pursuer's pleadings, it was bought in the defender's name only. The pursuer averred that he spent much time and money on improvements to the new property. The value of these improvements was said to be £24,000. The property was worth £85,000. The pursuer claimed one half of this (said, curiously, to equal £50,000) on the footing of the law of unjustified enrichment.

The defender's position was that although the first house (in Culloden) had indeed been owned in equal shares, the parties had in fact contributed unequally to the original purchase price. Most of the price had been paid by her. When it was sold the parties had accordingly agreed to an unequal division of the proceeds. She had used her share to buy the new house, in Duffus. The pursuer had been paid his share of the proceeds of the sale of the first house. He had not contributed to the price of the new house. Nor had he spent time and money improving it.

Despite the inadequacies of the pursuer's pleadings, the sheriff principal allowed proof before answer. It is, indeed, not easy to follow the pursuer's case in a number of respects. For instance, why is half of £85,000 equal to £50,000? The sheriff principal commented: 'It might have been thought that the sum sued for would be £42,500. It was explained that £50,000 had been selected instead to allow for the possibility that the value of the house had increased further since the action was raised.'[2] But this explanation is no explanation. Why should a pursuer be able to select a sum apparently at random? What if there were a bear market and the value of the property were to fall to say £70,000? Then the pursuer would get £50,000 and the defender £20,000—hardly an equal division. But more fundamentally, the pursuer seems to have been presenting two quite different cases. One was a claim, based on *Shilliday*, for the value of his expenditure, allegedly £24,000. But then this claim was seemingly disregarded in favour of an

---

1 The Duffus house was less expensive than the Culloden house. What happened to the rest of the proceeds of sale of the Culloden house is something the pursuer seems not to have made any averments about.
2 Paragraph 7.

entirely different one, to half the value of the property. It is difficult to see how a claim could be based on *Shilliday* and the *condictio causa data causa non secuta*. The *condictio* gives a right to the return of money (or property) that has been transferred on some basis that has failed to materialise. But the pursuer's claim for £50,000 was not a claim for the *return* of anything. It seems, however, that the relevancy of this claim was not seriously challenged.

Co-purchase agreements

The copy note that Verona Burnett produced was an embryonic co-purchase agreement. As mentioned above, some firms already offer these to unmarried clients. But the literature on the subject is sparse, and published styles seem to be non-existent, so we venture to offer some suggestions. All the points below can be considered simply in the light of making sure of clients' instructions. Where there are joint clients there must be joint instructions, and advice must be given to both, although in a speedy and under-remunerated conveyancing transaction this may be difficult to ensure[1] and, even if ensured, difficult to document on file.[2] Since joint instructions presuppose a mutual agreement between the clients, it makes sense to document that agreement. A formal document puts that agreement down on paper, so that neither party can later deny it in a dispute with the other. The incidental benefit to the law firm is evident.

Who is contributing what?

It is wise to check the sources of funds as between the parties and to record this in the co-purchase agreement. In *Moggach*, title to the first property was held equally between the parties and yet the defender asserted that the contributions to the price had in fact been unequal, with the result that, on sale, an unequal division of the proceeds was appropriate. One suspects that this sort of situation is quite common. Clients may later disagree about who contributed what. Hence there is a value in getting it down in writing at the outset.

Sometimes one sees a co-purchase agreement that says: 'Brad is contributing £100,000, Jennifer is contributing £75,000 and the balance of £50,000 is from Abracadabra Bank plc.' This is inexact in respect of the loan. If both are equally responsible for the loan, then, as between themselves, £25,000 is lent to Brad and £25,000 to Jennifer, and they are then using the money to pay the price. So Brad is contributing £125,000 and Jennifer is contributing £100,000. Abracadabra Bank plc is contributing nothing to the price. This is not a *ménage à trois*.

---

1 In *Burnett v Menzies Dougal* 2005 SCLR 133 (Notes) the pursuer claimed that 'the pursuer had very few direct dealings with [the partner]. Matters upon which [the partner] required instructions were discussed between the pursuer and Mr Burnett, who then issued instructions to [the partner], usually by telephone.' Whether this was the case or not, it is indeed the sort of thing that does often happen, and the risks are apparent.

2 It should be borne in mind that what cannot be proved from the file may turn out to be incapable of proof at all.

What ownership shares do the clients want?

It is wise to check what share of ownership the parties wish to have. Many clients do not know what the possibilities are here. Most clients have little or no idea of what is meant by ownership shares.[1]

Some clients think that the share of co-ownership is not determined by the title but by other factors. For example they assume that if title is in the name of A and B, and A contributed 70% of the price, then A will automatically have 70% of the ownership. Many clients do not realise that the title can expressly provide that the ownership share is 70/30 or whatever. The twenty-something newlyweds, with stars in their eyes, may choose equal shares regardless of price contribution. The forty-somethings, both on their second marriage, and with children by their first marriages, may want the ownership share to track the price contribution.

Should an inequality of contribution be deemed a loan?

Often if there is inequality of contribution to the price the parties will wish this to be reflected in the ownership shares. But there is also another way. Jack and Jill buy a house for £160,000. Jack contributes £40,000 and Jill contributes £120,000. They may want ownership shares to be equal coupled with an agreement that, when the property is sold, Jill will take the first £80,000 with the balance split equally. In other words, what is happening, in effect, is that Jill is lending Jack £40,000. After the loan she has £80,000 cash, and he has the same, and so their contribution to the purchase price is equal. Sometimes something like this is what the parties have agreed but it is not discussed with their law agent because the right questions have not been asked.

Sometimes such agreements say that the money is repayable only on a 'sale'. This is inadequate.[2] Would a sale by a heritable creditor count? What happens if there is a gratuitous transfer? What happens if one party dies? In short: what events will trigger repayment of the loan? This is for discussion, but the natural solution is to provide that payment is due if there is a 'transfer'. Another issue is whether interest is to run. Without interest, the value of the loan could be badly eroded by inflation.

Usually an arrangement of this sort is less favourable to Jill than a 75% ownership share, because property prices tend to go up. But if there is a bear market the loan route will be more favourable.

If, as will usually be the case, the parties are borrowing part of the price, a similar effect can be achieved by agreeing that Jack will be solely responsible for the loan. Which leads on to the next point.

---

1 Thus in *Burnett v Menzies Dougal* 2005 SCLR 133 (Notes) the note said that 'in the event of them splitting-up or house being sold V's share of net proceeds will be 4/5 and A's share will be 1/5'. This shows how clients, if they think of the subject at all, may think of ownership shares not as conveyancers think of them but as 'rights to proceeds of sale'.

2 Cf the wording of the deed in *Macdonald-Haig v Gerlings*, 3 December 2001, Inverness Sheriff Court, digested as *Conveyancing 2002* Case (15).

Liability for the mortgage loan

If there is a secured loan, it is wise to check who will be responsible for repaying it. As between the clients and the bank, liability is solidary (joint and several). But the parties are free to choose their liability as between themselves.

For instance, Jack and Jill buy a house together for £200,000. Jill has £100,000 cash. The other £100,000 is borrowed. They are both earning and they have both been through messy divorces. They might decide that although the loan is a joint one, as between themselves the loan is exclusively Jack's responsibility. In that case they are each paying half the price and so they will probably wish to have equal ownership shares. By contrast, suppose that they wish to consider the loan as one they are to be equally responsible for. In that case Jill would be contributing £150,000 (£100,000, plus her half of the borrowed money) and Jack would be contributing £50,000 (his half of the borrowed money), so that they might wish the ownership shares to be 75% to Jill and 25% to Jack.

Take another example. Suppose that Rachel and Ross are buying a house with a loan. Ross is working while Rachel is at home with the young children. The ownership shares are 50%. They have not made any agreement about the loan and so the law implies that, as between themselves, they are equally liable. Over a period of five years Ross pays the monthly mortgage payments. Then the relationship breaks up. In principle Ross can demand from Rachel half of all that he has paid, for he has been paying *her* debt as well as his own: this is the right of relief.[1] That would seem unfair. Hence in cases where the liability is shared as it usually will be it may be wise to have an agreement that so long as the parties continue to cohabit any payment by either in relation to the mortgage will be deemed to have been made equally by both.

Sexually transmitted debt

The parties obtain a loan from a bank. Depending on the wording of the deed, it may mean that each party is liable jointly and severally with the other party for any debt due to the bank. Thus suppose that Ross grants a guarantee to the bank for his company's borrowings. The result may be that Rachel is, without being aware of it, also liable on that guarantee.[2] The clients need to be warned in advance that this might be a danger, and that it can be avoided by ensuring that any future liabilities are unconnected with the bank that provided the mortgage finance. It may also be desirable for the parties to agree with each other not to incur any liability, whether actual or contingent, to the mortgage lender except with the consent of the other. However, the effectiveness of such an agreement is limited. Suppose that Ross so agrees, but then breaches the agreement. What

---

1   If they were married, Ross's claim would normally be barred because his payment of Rachel's debt would be regarded as made in pursuance of the mutual obligations of support owed by spouses. But as between cohabitants there are no such obligations.

2   This depends on the terms of the standard security. For some discussion see *Conveyancing 2003* p 79.

is Rachel's remedy? She will need a remedy only if he is insolvent, but if he is insolvent no remedy will be effective.

However, in many cases an agreement of this sort may not be possible. To take one example: the parties may be getting an offset mortgage in which the mortgage loan is simply part of the current account. In that case every time one of them withdraws something from the account the mortgage debt is increased.

Special destination

A survivorship destination should not be inserted without the instructions of both clients. Power of evacuation[1] has been an issue which has often caused problems. The deed itself can state expressly whether or not the destination can be evacuated. That being so, it seems perhaps unsatisfactory that the matter is so often left to the default rules of the common law. We would suggest that a clause about evacuability always be added.[2] Whatever it may be that the clients desire, it needs to be documented in the co-purchase agreement.

Drafting

Drafting is a risky business. But here is a possible style. No doubt it could be improved, and it may well be that more points should be added. In this case Adam and Eve are buying a £200,000 house. Adam has no cash but Eve has £100,000. They are borrowing £100,000.

> Whereas Adam and Eve are purchasing, or intend to purchase,[3] the dwellinghouse at 1234 Eden Lane, Paradiseburgh, they agree as follows:
>
> (a) The price is £200,000.[4]
> (b) Adam is contributing £50,000 (from the loan mentioned below) and Eve is contributing £150,000 (of which £50,000 is from the loan mentioned below).
> (c) Their ownership shares are to be 25% to Adam and 75% to Eve. [Or: Notwithstanding the unequal contributions to the price, the ownership shares are to be equal.]
> (d) There is to be a survivorship destination, which is to be evacuable/unevacuable by either party.[5] [Or: There is to be no survivorship destination.[6]]
> (e) They are borrowing £100,000 from Wolverhampton Bank plc. As between themselves their liability is equal. But any payment made by either, whether of

---

1 Ie evacuation *mortis causa*. It appears that it is always possible to evacuate a destination by transfer of one's share *inter vivos*: see G L Gretton and K G C Reid, *Conveyancing* (3rd edn 2004) para 23-14.

2 It can be done quite simply. After the words 'and to the survivor of them and to the executors and assignees of the survivor' add in brackets: 'which foregoing destination is/is not evacuable by either party'.

3 This formula covers both concluded and open missives.

4 It may be desirable to add to the basic price such extras as SDLT, registration dues and conveyancing expenses.

5 Another possibility is that it is to be evacuable by one party but not the other. Indeed, that is the rule which the common law will in some circumstances imply.

6 If the parties have so agreed, it is sensible to document that fact, to avoid future claims that there ought to have been such a destination.

capital or interest, while they live together, shall be deemed a payment made equally by both.[1]

(f) Neither shall incur any liability (including any contingent liability, for instance by a guarantee) to any lender holding a security over the said property,[2] without the other's consent.

(g) The parties consent that this agreement be registered for preservation in the Books of Council and Session.

In witness whereof ...

If the agreement is that the disparity of contribution is not to be handled by an unequal share of ownership, but by one party's accepting sole liability for the loan, the following might be suitable.

Whereas Donna and Donald are purchasing, or intend to purchase, the dwellinghouse at .... , they agree as follows:

(a) The price is £200,000.

(b) Donald is contributing £100,000 (from the loan mentioned below) and Donna is contributing £100,000.

(c) Their ownership shares are to be equal.

(d) Whilst the parties are jointly and severally liable on the loan from Wolverhampton Bank plc, as between the parties Donald is solely liable for both capital and interest.

(e) [Other provisions.]

(f) The parties consent that this agreement be registered for preservation in the Books of Council and Session.

In witness whereof...

Suppose there is no loan, that the parties are making unequal contributions, and that they wish this to be reflected not in an unequal ownership share but by 'top-slicing' eventual sales proceeds. This might be done thus:

Whereas Donna and Donald are purchasing, or intend to purchase, the dwellinghouse at .... , they agree as follows:

(a) The price is £200,000.

(b) Donald is contributing £100,000 and Donna is contributing £100,000.

(c) Their ownership shares are to be equal.

(d) Of the £100,000 to be contributed by Donald, £50,000 is a loan to him from Donna. This is to be repayable to her when his share, or any part of it, is transferred, whether gratuitously or onerously, and whether voluntarily or involuntarily. Interest is not payable. [Or: Interest at ...% per annum compounded annually at Martinmas is payable on the date when the capital is repayable.]

(e) [Other provisions.]

(f) The parties consent that this agreement be registered for preservation in the Books of Council and Session.

In witness whereof...

---

1 It may be desirable to expand this to cover premiums on mortgage-linked life policies. It may also be desirable to bring in house insurance, house repairs and renovations.

2 This formulation is to cover the possibility of a remortgage.

Ideally the agreement would be registered for preservation in the Books of Council and Session, but the clients may not wish to pay for that. It is at any rate sensible to include a clause of consent to registration. The alternative is to keep the agreement with the land certificate, with a copy sent to each client and another on the file.

REAL BURDENS

Security services

Industrial Estates (Scotland) Ltd v Trustees for the Scottish Vintage Bus Museum[1] was decided under the old law but is also an instructive authority for the new. The facts were these. The pursuer owned the M90 Commerce Park at Lathalmond Fife extending to some 100 acres. In 1995 it feued around half of the site to the defenders. The defenders used the property to repair, maintain and exhibit vintage buses. Among the conditions in the feu disposition was the following:

> The Feuars shall reimburse the Superiors and pay on demand a one-half share of the cost of providing the services aftermentioned so far as they are common to or used in common by the subjects hereby disponed and the remainder of the M90 Commerce Park including without prejudice to the foregoing generality security services, cleaning and clearing snow or ice from the access road and so far as located at the edges of the access road, street lighting.

The Park was surrounded by a perimeter fence. Initially the security was provided by a resident officer at the gatehouse. Later this arrangement was replaced by a barrier and by two CCTV cameras which were monitored (along with cameras serving other properties of the pursuer) at the pursuer's head office. The new arrangements were much more expensive than the old and the defenders refused to pay for them. Hence this action.

The sheriff[2] held that the condition was not a valid real burden, for a variety of reasons:

(1) the money to be paid by the feuar was unascertained;
(2) the services were shared with the other half of the Park, which was not itself subject to an obligation to pay the cost;
(3) the obligation was not praedial; and
(4) the obligation was too vague.

The first objection (money unascertained) reflects a contested view of the, admittedly unsatisfactory, case law on the point. As it happens, another case from 2004—*Crampshee v North Lanarkshire Council*[3]—took the opposite view, treating such an obligation as 'simply a pecuniary commutation of what could

---

1 20 February 2004, Dunfermline Sheriff Court, A241/03.
2 Sheriff I C Simpson.
3 2004 GWD 7-149, discussed further below.

undoubtedly be a real burden'.[1] The point need not detain us, however, because it has been displaced, with retrospective effect, by s 5(1)(a) of the Title Conditions (Scotland) Act 2003.[2] Whatever the law may have been before, it is now clear that the actual amount due need not be specified in a real burden.

The second objection (no matching burden on the rest of the Park) is puzzling and does not seem to be based on any authority. Certainly there is nothing in the Title Conditions Act which lends it support. In fact it is relatively common to impose real burdens which, at least at the time they are imposed, meet only part of the cost in question. That would be the case, for example, where a house is divided and part sold and part retained. The inference is that the owner of the retained property will meet the rest of the cost; but in any event the burdened owner cannot be made to pay more than his title provides.[3] So there is nothing in this point to disturb the effectiveness of the burden.

It is not clear whether the third objection (not praedial) was seen as an independent ground or merely as part of the first objection.[4] As an independent ground it is unconvincing. It is true, of course, that the praedial rule is carried forward to the new law by the Title Conditions Act, s 3(1) providing that 'A real burden must relate in some way to the burdened property'. But, as s 3(2) adds, the relationship need only be indirect. Examples of such an indirect relationship were given by the Scottish Law Commission in the report which gave rise to the Act:[5]

> So it is possible to impose as a real burden an obligation to maintain a boundary fence even if the fence is situated on the benefited property, or an obligation to maintain a common facility which lies some distance from the burdened property.

An obligation to contribute to security for a park of which the burdened property forms one half seems, equally, to 'relate' to that property.

The last objection (too vague) is both the most difficult and the most important. The terms of a real burden must be set out in the four corners of the deed. In other words, the burdened owner must have reasonable notice of the obligation which is being placed upon him or her. In the sheriff's view, the condition in the feu disposition failed to achieve that standard:[6]

> Security services are not defined in the deed and there is no defined mechanism for assessing what they might encompass at any given time. They might be extensive and

---

1 Lord Carloway at para 20. A similar view was taken in *Sheltered Housing Management Ltd v Cairns* 2003 SLT 578, another Outer House case. For a discussion see *Conveyancing 2002* pp 65–67.
2 'It shall not be an objection to the validity of a real burden (whenever created) that an amount payable in respect of an obligation to defray some cost is not specified in the constitutive deed'.
3 At least under the burden. Of course further liability may arise if the person owns the thing in question.
4 The doubt arises because in a passage from *Tailors of Aberdeen v Coutts* (1840) 1 Rob 296, 340 and quoted in the sheriff's opinion, Lord Brougham appears to suggest that an obligation to pay an unascertained amount would be allowed as a real burden if it was 'immediately connected with the subject granted'.
5 Scottish Law Commission, Report on *Real Burdens* (Scot Law Com No 181, 2000; available on http: // www.scotlawcom.gov.uk) para 2.12.
6 Paragraph 19.

very expensive or negligible and very cheap. I do not think it can be right to claim, as the pursuers' solicitor did, that parties could always have recourse to the court to rein in excessive claims in respect of security services.

It is always difficult to know when a condition drifts over the line from being sufficiently certain to being unreasonably uncertain. But the sheriff's view here is probably correct. The condition arguably amounted to a blank cheque, allowing the pursuer to decide on whatever level of security it wished and then to recover half the cost from the defenders. Acquirers of the burdened property could not be sure as to the extent of their future liability. There is of course a drafting point here. A real burden cannot spell out every last detail, but it must at least give a clear idea of the obligation being imposed. Too much detail does no harm. Too little may be fatal. The motto must be: when in doubt don't leave it out.

Factoring services

Manager burdens

It has become almost standard for deeds of conditions to provide for factoring. Broadly this can be done in one of two ways. One is to allow the owners to appoint their own factor, typically by a majority decision. And even in the absence of express provision in the titles owners in a development now have this right by statute.[1] That is an important change in the law. The other is for the developer or his nominee to be named in the deed as factor. Under the Title Conditions Act a burden providing for this second alternative is known as a manager burden. Quite often the two methods are found in combination: the developer factors the property until all the units are sold after which the owners make their own arrangements.

At common law manager burdens were controversial. Sometimes they were challenged as unlawful monopolies, though such challenges seem always to have failed.[2] *Crampshee v North Lanarkshire Council*[3] is another example of an unsuccessful challenge on this ground. The position is, however, authoritatively resolved by the Title Conditions Act. Section 3(7) provides that:

Except in so far as expressly permitted by this Act, a real burden must not have the effect of creating a monopoly (as for example, by providing for a particular person to be or to appoint

(a) the manager of property; or
(b) the supplier of any services in relation to property.)

But manager burdens are then expressly permitted by s 63 of the Act, subject to stringent restrictions. Normally a manager burden is limited to five years,

---

1 Title Conditions (Scotland) Act 2003 ss 28 (subject to the titles) and 64 (overriding the titles); Tenements (Scotland) Act 2004 sch 1 r 3.1(c).
2 See *Dumbarton District Council v McLaughlin* 2000 Hous LR 16, discussed in *Conveyancing 2000* pp 70–73.
3 2004 GWD 7-149.

with the owners being free to make their own appointment once the five-year period has expired. For former council houses, however, the period is 30 years and for sheltered housing a mere three years. In all cases the developer loses his rights on ceasing to own any units in the development even if this is within the statutory period.

But while a manager burden is permitted in principle, it may still fail in practice if it does not conform to the normal rules for the creation of real burdens—rules which are now set out in ss 1–6 of the Title Conditions Act. Thus the manager burden in *Crampshee v North Lanarkshire Council* was challenged as void from uncertainty and as repugnant with ownership. Both grounds merit further discussion.

Void from uncertainty

If the main issue with security services (discussed above) is the extent of the *services* to be provided, the main issue with factoring services is likely to be the extent of the *powers* conferred on the factor. These must be reasonably certain. A deed which appoints a factor and says nothing about what the factor can or cannot do risks invalidity on grounds of uncertainty.[1]

In terms of the deed of conditions in *Crampshee* the owners were taken bound to pay for the maintenance of certain common parts ('maintenance' itself being defined). The deed further provided that:

> It shall be in the option of the Superiors to act as Factors in any or all of the said blocks of flats and, in the event of the Superiors' exercise of such option, their powers in the exercise of such office shall be in their sole discretion.

The pursuer, who owned one of the flats in the development, took exception to the words 'sole discretion':[2]

> It appeared to allow the factor a discretionary power, without limit, to carry out repairs and renewals, including improvements. For a real burden to be created, the clause had to be precise enough to allow a disponee to understand what the scope of the burden was … Where there was a doubt about the nature of a burden, which could not be resolved within the four corners of a deed, the burden could not be a real one. In this case, it was not possible for a purchaser of the flat to tell what the powers of the factor would be and thus what restrictions were being placed upon his ownership of the flat.

Closer analysis did not support this argument. Under the deed the owners were bound to pay only for 'maintenance'. If the factor went beyond this, any

---

1 It is of course arguable that the idea of a factor is itself reasonably clear, and that, in the absence of express powers, the factor must simply do as instructed by the owners (or, in many cases, a majority of owners). But much will depend on the wording used, and on the terms of other provisions in the deed.

2 The argument is presented as summarised by Lord Carloway at para 6 of his Opinion.

sums expended would be irrecoverable. Hence his powers were in effect limited to instructing maintenance. The position was put in this way by Lord Carloway:[1]

> Given that the obligation of maintenance is sufficiently specific to constitute a real burden, the question is whether the creation of a factor with powers to act 'in their sole discretion' takes the burden into territory too vague for enforcement against singular successors. It does not. The factor is simply a person charged with the maintenance of the property. In carrying out his duties, he may have a discretion in the manner in which he carries out his task, but he cannot impose a greater obligation on the proprietors than is already defined in the deed. He cannot carry out works beyond what is necessary maintenance and then expect payment from a proprietor who has not consented to works beyond those defined in the titles.

Repugnancy with ownership

A factor's powers might be certain yet unreasonably extensive. Following the previous case law the Title Conditions Act provides that a real burden must not be 'repugnant with ownership'.[2] This means that it must not go too far. The owner of the burdened property will be restricted, of course, but the restrictions must not take away the normal incidents of ownership. Arguably one of those incidents is the right to manage one's property. In some cases a manager burden might bring about an unreasonable shift in power from owners to factor. In *Crampshee* the factors were restricted to maintenance, it is true, but within that broad category they could do what they wanted. It was for them to decide if and when work should be carried out. Since most property could do with maintenance most of the time, a hyperactive factor could easily run up substantial bills for work which the owners considered unnecessary or premature. Conversely an inactive factor could bring about serious decline in the fabric of the building. The pursuer in *Crampshee* regarded the factors as hyperactive. They had embarked on an 'Estate Regeneration Programme' which involved (or so it was averred) the removal and replacement of rendering, the installation of cavity wall insulation, the replacement of roof tiles, the manufacture of a new roof projection with fascia, the renewal of external walls, railings and paved areas, and the provision of new door screens for the close. The pursuer's share for this work was nearly £6,000.

The court concluded that the manager burden was not repugnant with ownership, although without giving reasons. That conclusion may possibly be justified on the basis that the surrender of power to the factor is, under the Title Conditions Act, temporary, although the period may be as long as 30 years. A different conclusion might be necessary if the factor's powers extended not only to common parts but also to individual houses, as often occurs in the case of sheltered housing.[3] We return to the issue of repugnancy with ownership later, in the context of servitudes.[4]

---

1 Paragraph 17.
2 Title Conditions (Scotland) Act 2003 s 3(6).
3 But in sheltered housing the surrender is only for three years.
4 At pp 87.

Informal guidance

Under-active factors are perhaps the more common experience. In *West Dunbartonshire Council v Barnes*[1] the defenders had a house in a block of four. As a former council house it was factored by the local council under a manager burden. The Council sued for their factoring charges. The defence was that the service provided was inadequate and not as promised. The booklet prepared for the use of tenants and owners had promised so much more. The defenders outlined the Council's alleged shortcomings as follows:[2]

> [I]t has failed to provide a pro-active factoring service, has not carried out the property inspections which it undertook to carry out, has not advised the defenders properly of proposed repairs, has not provided the defenders with a written estimate of common repair costs, cost breakdown and job descriptions, has not liaised with the defenders in connection with common repairs, has not carried out post-inspection of common repairs and has not responded to the defenders' enquiries about common repairs promptly.

In the face of these disappointments the defenders were not disposed to pay the Council the £150 demanded by way of fee.

The sheriff[3] rejected the argument that the Council's duties were those set out in an informal booklet:[4]

> The bullet points in the booklet may be regarded as a list of promises, or aspirations, or pious hopes or earnests of good intention, but they are not undertakings contractually binding on the pursuers.

The result is not surprising. A real burden must be set out in full within the four corners of the deed, as was done in the present case. It cannot then be supplemented by some extrinsic document.

Drafting mishaps

In the thicket of words it is easy to stumble. In *West Dunbartonshire Council v Barnes* (discussed above) the proposed arrangement as set out in the feu disposition was a standard one. The building was a four-in-a-block. For as long as the Council continued to own one of the houses it was to act as factor. That was the manager burden. Once all the houses were sold it was for the owners to appoint their own factor. Remuneration of the factor was dealt with by clause 9(b):

> The remuneration of the factor and the terms and conditions of his appointment shall be determined from time to time by the persons entitled to appoint him.

Where the factor was appointed by owners, clause 9(b) worked in a straight-forward way. But where the factor was the Council, so that its appointment

---

1 2004 Hous LR 64.
2 Paragraph 3.
3 Sheriff T Scott.
4 Paragraph 37.

stemmed from the feu disposition itself, it seemed that the clause did not apply at all; for there were no 'persons entitled to appoint' such a factor and hence no one to fix the remuneration. In the absence of such a person the Council must apparently provide its factoring services for nothing.[1]

It is easy to see how mistakes of this kind occur. Drafting is often carried out with particular situations in mind. In preparing clause 9(b) the draftsman was thinking of a factor appointed by the owners and overlooked the fact that, for the initial years, the factor would be the Council.

Feudal abolition

In each of the three cases discussed in this section the burdens (or purported burdens) were imposed in or in association with a feu disposition. On the assumption that they were effective feudal burdens it is a useful mental exercise to consider their fate now, after the appointed day.[2]

There is no difficulty with the manager burdens, considered in two of the cases. A manager burden survives feudal abolition as such[3] but will come to an end after the period laid down by s 63 of the Title Conditions Act (discussed above)—normally five years but, in the case of former council houses, as much as 30 years.

The position is more difficult in *Industrial Estates (Scotland) Ltd v Trustees for the Scottish Vintage Bus Museum*. With the abolition of the feudal system, the pursuer would lose all right of enforcement as superior. But, if the burden had been valid in the first place (which on balance it was not), the ex-superior would be likely to have acquired enforcement rights as a neighbour, ie in its capacity as owner of the other half of the park. That would plainly be true if it had served and registered a notice under s 18 of the Abolition of Feudal Tenure etc (Scotland) Act 2000. But even without such a notice, enforcement rights would probably arise under s 56(2) of the Title Conditions Act. Section 56 applies to facility burdens. A facility burden is defined as[4]

> a real burden which regulates the maintenance, management, reinstatement or use of heritable property which constitutes, and is intended to constitute, a facility of benefit to other land …

The whole security system was intended to benefit other land (ie land belonging to the pursuer and to the defenders); and some or all of it was heritable property, although in the case of the CCTV cameras this may be stretching a point. If and to the extent that the burden is a facility burden, it is enforceable by the owners of any land to which the facility is of benefit.

---

1 Paragraph 48. In fact the sheriff then proceeded to avoid this result (para 49) by making use of what he seems to have regarded (perhaps wrongly) as a concession by the defenders.
2 Ie 28 November 2004, the day appointed for feudal abolition.
3 Title Conditions (Scotland) Act 2003 s 63(9).
4 Title Conditions (Scotland) Act 2003 s 122(1).

Enforcement by contract

In two of the three cases, the original grantee continued to own the property.[1] Thus, whatever the enforceability of the condition as a real burden, it was enforceable as a matter of ordinary contract law. This is because a conveyance is, among other things, a contract between the original parties to it. In *Industrial Estates (Scotland) Ltd*, where the condition failed as a real burden, this was crucial to the outcome of the case.[2] Thus, for as long as the defenders continued to own the land they were bound to contribute one half of the security costs. Only their successors would be free of the obligation. The result here is of some importance. There are significant numbers of feus, particularly in commercial properties, where the original grantees remain as owners of the property. In that case the whole terms of the feu grant are enforceable against them. The position is unaffected by the abolition of the feudal system, for the legislation takes care to preserve contractual rights.[3] But contractual liability can probably be avoided by conveying the property to someone else, such as an associated company;[4] and in some cases the extent of liability may make this a step worth taking.

PASSING OF PROPERTY AND THE QUESTION OF TRUST CLAUSES

Burnett's Tr v Grainger: the House of Lords decides

On 11 May 1994 Lord Penrose, sitting in the Outer House, issued his decision in a case called *Sharp v Thomson*.[5] Ten years later, on 4 March 2004, the House of Lords issued its decision in *Burnett's Tr v Grainger*.[6] The *Sharp v Thomson* saga has been of the greatest theoretical interest, but its importance to practitioners may be less apparent.

First, the case. Mrs Burnett sold her house to the Rev Harvey and Mrs Grainger. The price was paid and possession was given, and the disposition was delivered on 8 November 1990. For reasons which do not appear in the reports, the disposition was not recorded in the Register of Sasines until 27 January 1992. By the time this had happened, not only had Mrs Burnett been

---

1 The exception is *Crampshee v North Lanarkshire Council*.
2 An earlier example is *Sheltered Housing Management Ltd v Aitken* (1997) *Unreported Property Cases* (eds Paisley and Cusine) 225.
3 Except in respect of feuduty: see Abolition of Feudal Tenure etc (Scotland) Act 2000 s 75.
4 This is because it is likely (but not certain) that liability ends with ownership: for a discussion, see Scottish Law Commission, Report on *Real Burdens* (Scot Law Com No 181, 2000; available on http://www.scotlawcom.gov.uk) paras 3.40 and 3.41.
5 1994 SC 503. The subsequent progress of the case can be found at 1997 SC (HL) 66.
6 2004 SC (HL) 19. For the earlier stages see 2000 SLT (Sh Ct) 116 and 2002 SLT 699. For commentary on the earlier stages see *Conveyancing 2000* pp 93–97 and *Conveyancing 2002* pp 92–97. There has not so far been very much commentary on the House of Lords decision. G L Gretton, 'Ownership and Insolvency: *Burnett's Tr v Grainger*' (2004) 8 *Edinburgh Law Review* 389 cites what there is. For a review of the extensive literature on the whole subject as at 2001, and for careful analysis of the issues, see Scottish Law Commission, Discussion Paper on *Sharp v Thomson* (Scot Law Com DP No 114 (2001); available on http://www.scotlawcom.gov.uk).

sequestrated but her trustee in sequestration had completed title to the property by recording a notice of title. The disposition in favour of the Graingers did not contain a trust clause. That is not surprising given that the disposition dates from 1990. Indeed, the *Burnett's Tr* disaster was happening at about the same time as the *Sharp* disaster, but it took more than ten years to grind through the judicial system.[1] The trustee in sequestration raised an action of declarator that he was the owner of the property. In the sheriff court he was unsuccessful on the basis that *Sharp v Thomson* protected the buyers. He appealed. The Inner House reversed, holding that this was a classic case of a 'race to the register', as to which the law was clear. The trustee had won the race. The Inner House observed that the *ratio* of the House of Lords' decision in *Sharp v Thomson* was obscure—something that seems to be fairly widely conceded—and accordingly felt free to interpret that decision narrowly, as applying only to floating charges. This time it was the defenders' turn to appeal. Nobody was sure which way the House of Lords would go, especially given that in the House of Lords the Scottish judges are always in a minority. In fact the Inner House's decision was affirmed. The trustee had won.

Where does that leave the law? It confirms the established idea that the real right of ownership passes on registration, and that until registration a grantee has no real right at all. That being so, an unregistered grantee is at risk. Since the seller still has the real right of ownership, there is the risk that the seller's creditors will take the property, either through diligence, or through sequestration or liquidation. It is only from a floating charge that the grantee is protected: that was decided in *Sharp v Thomson* itself, and that decision has not been overruled. What has happened to *Sharp v Thomson* is that it has been reduced to being a special case.

In a sense this news is no news. It emphasises the vital importance of timeously completing title. But conveyancers knew that anyway. But even no news can be news. After all, the House of Lords could easily have decided that English law, or something like English law, should be applied. Indeed, two of the judges, Lord Hoffmann and Lord Hobhouse, made it fairly clear that they would have wished to do precisely that. Had they had their way, on 5 March 2004 conveyancers would have woken up to a world remade.

The practical implications, such as they are, concern trust clauses.

Trust clauses: to use or not to use?

Trust clauses in dispositions had their origin back in the late 1970s when civil service strikes shut the registers on more than one occasion. The idea is to place the property out of the reach of the seller's creditors, without registration.[2] Although the general principle is that an insolvent person's assets are available

---

1 Justice delayed is justice denied. Perhaps there were good reasons why the case took so long, but, if so, they do not appear from the reports.
2 Of course the intention is that registration will follow, but a registered buyer has nothing to fear from the seller's creditors.

to the creditors, there is an exception for assets held in trust.[1] If Sally Seller holds the property in trust for Bertie Buyer, her creditors cannot touch it. So perhaps he need not take a taxi to Register House. Perhaps he can saunter and dawdle. If the trust clause is effective, that is indeed the case up to a point. The trust clause would, if effective, protect Bertie from Sally's creditors, though it would not protect him from a deed granted by Sally, such as a disposition or a standard security.

Trust clauses largely disappeared during the 1980s, but after the Outer House decision in *Sharp v Thomson* in 1994 they became common again, and have remained common ever since. The decision of the House of Lords in *Burnett's Tr v Grainger* may further encourage their use, for two reasons. One is that any idea that *Sharp v Thomson* might have introduced some general doctrine about 'beneficial interest' has now disappeared. A buyer who does not register is unprotected from the seller's creditors. The second reason is that there are *dicta* in *Burnett's Tr v Grainger* to the effect that trust clauses work. In other words, *Burnett's Tr v Grainger* simultaneously underlines the danger and offers a remedy. It is thus not surprising that in an article on *Burnett's Tr* Ken Swinton concluded with these words, printed in bold type: 'Insert a trust clause in every disposition.'[2]

The case for using trust clauses seems strong. Either they work or they do not work. If they work, well and good. And if they do not work, nothing is lost. But in fact matters are not quite so simple, for even if trust clauses work they may have unwanted side-effects.

Do trust clauses work?

The main argument for the ineffectiveness of trust clauses is that a trust does not necessarily come into existence merely because the parties have so agreed.[3] A trust is not like a contract. It confers on one party, the trustee, a new legal capacity, a capacity that has numerous ramifications, including effects on third parties.

On one view the law will recognise a trust only if it has some *bona fide* purpose. If its sole purpose is to circumvent the law of insolvency, it will be regarded as abusive and will be disallowed. As the Inner House said in a 1981 case, if the law were to permit the use of trusts merely to defeat the rights of creditors 'the damage which would be done to the objectives of the law of bankruptcy and of liquidation would be incalculable'.[4] The idea that a stroke of the pen in a purely

---

1 This rule is sometimes supposed to have been established in *Heritable Reversionary Co Ltd* v *Millar* (1893) 19 R (HL) 43. That is not so. The rule goes back to the seventeenth century. What *Heritable Reversionary Co* did was to remove an important exception, which was that the rule did not apply to latent trusts of land. Thus at common law (ie before the judicial legislation of *Heritable Reversionary Co*) trust clauses in dispositions could not work because they are latent. For sequestration the rule is now statutory: Bankruptcy (Scotland) Act 1985 s 33(1)(b).

2 'Burnett's Trustee v Grainger: A Race not a Match' (2004) 72 *Scottish Law Gazette* 41, 43. For other discussions of trust clauses, see Andrew Steven and Scott Wortley, 'The Perils of a Trusting Disposition' 1996 SLT (News) 365; James Chalmers, 'In Defence of the Trusting Conveyancer' 2002 SLT (News) 231; Roy Roxburgh, 'Nightmares about Trust Clauses' (2004) 49 *Journal of the Law Society of Scotland* June/12; Ian Tweedie (2004) 49 *Journal of the Law Society of Scotland* August/10.

3 And the other requirements have been met, such as the existence of trust assets.

4 *Clark Taylor & Co Ltd v Quality Site Development (Edinburgh) Ltd* 1981 SC 111, 116.

private deed can put property out of the reach of lawful creditors is certainly a disturbing one. While, however, there is much to be said for a principle that only *bona fide* trusts will be recognised, it is not certain whether Scots law adopts it. Other cases could be cited in which judges seem to have had no qualms about allowing trusts to be used in this way.[1] The issue has never been properly debated in any appellate court. There are merely *dicta*. In *Burnett's Tr v Grainger* there are further *dicta* which are supportive of this sort of use of the trust. Anything said in the House of Lords merits the deepest respect. But no argument was heard on the point. We still do not know when Scots law will recognise the existence of a trust and when it will not.

There are also technical considerations. A trust must have purposes. Yet it is not clear what are the purposes of a trust of this sort. They cannot be merely 'to hold', for that is not a possible trust purpose. 'Holding' is something that trustees have to do as a *pre-condition* for carrying out the trust purposes. (One might as well say that the 'purpose' of a company is to be registered in the Companies Register.) A trustee has to hold *for some purposes*. What? To convey on demand? But the seller has *already* granted the necessary deed. To allow the buyer the use of the property as against the seller? But the buyer has that right anyway because the transaction has already settled. So precisely *what* rights is the trust clause giving to the buyer? If the answer is 'none' it seems that this cannot be a trust at all.[2]

A drafting problem

A drafting difficulty exists in many, though not all, trust clauses. A fairly typical clause might run:

> And notwithstanding that I have sold the subjects to the said ABC and have received payment of the price in exchange for delivery of the disposition, I hereby declare that so far as I remain registered as proprietor in the said subjects before ABC's title has been registered in the Land Register in pursuance of these presents I shall hold the said subjects as trustee for behoof of the said ABC.

Suppose that a clause of this sort[3] had been used in the disposition by Mrs Burnett in favour of the Graingers. When the trustee in sequestration completed title, the trust would presumably have come to an end, because the condition expressed in the words 'in so far as I remain registered as proprietor in the said subjects' would no longer apply. Hence, it may be argued, the clause would have failed to benefit the Graingers.

The clause could, and should, be reworded to circumvent this problem:

> And notwithstanding that I have sold the subjects to the said ABC and have received payment of the price in exchange for delivery of the disposition, I hereby declare that

---

1 Such as *Tay Valley Joinery Ltd v C F Financial Services Ltd* 1987 SLT 207.
2 In reality there is a single trust purpose: to keep the property out of the hands of the seller's lawful creditors. But no one dares put that in writing. This is a truth which cannot safely be uttered.
3 The clause given here is a modern one. Back in 1990 slightly different wording would have been used, with references to infeftment, to recording, and to the GRS.

until ABC's title has been registered in the Land Register in pursuance of these presents I shall hold the said subjects as trustee for behoof of the said ABC.

Adverse implications for the buyer?

If trust clauses do succeed in setting up a valid trust, there may be undesirable consequences for the buyer and, much more significantly, for the seller. First, the buyer. An unregistered buyer runs two main risks. The first is that the seller will become insolvent. The second is that he or she might grant a deed—a disposition, say, or a standard security—to another party. A trust clause, if it works, protects the buyer from the first risk. But it is arguable that it exacerbates the second. In the absence of a trust clause, a later deed granted by the seller would be voidable if the grantee knew of the earlier deed.[1] So a buyer has some protection. What, however, if there is a trust clause? The problem here is that s 2 of the Trusts (Scotland) Act 1961 says that if a person takes a deed such as a disposition or a standard security from a trustee, that person's title cannot be challenged on the ground that the deed was granted in breach of trust. So if Sally Seller grants to Bertie Buyer a disposition with a trust clause, and the next week she grants a standard security to Slimy Sid, who registers first, the inference is that Slimy Sid's position is protected by s 2, even though he knew that the deed in his favour was granted in breach of trust. Hence the trust clause has removed the protection that Bertie would otherwise have had. James Chalmers has disputed this conclusion, on the ground that, while the standard security might not be challengeable as a breach of Sally's trust obligations, it could still be challenged as a breach of her duties as seller.[2] This may or may not be right. The underlying problem is that a trust clause is trying to mix oil and water: sale and trust, which in themselves are quite different. One party is supposed to be simultaneously trustee and seller, and the other beneficiary and buyer. If one says that Sally is granting the security 'as seller' and not 'as trustee', how can one then say that her trustee in sequestration would have to treat her title as being one held by her 'as trustee' and not 'as seller'?

Although a trust clause, if it works at all, may expose the buyer to such risks, the practical importance of the danger should not be exaggerated. In many cases where the seller grants a deed to a third party, that third party will be in good faith, and so would prevail over the buyer anyway. From a buyer's standpoint, the benefits of protection against the seller's insolvency probably outweigh the heightened risks of a deed to a third party. So one can conclude that trust clauses should indeed be used as far as the interests of the *buyer* are concerned.

Adverse implications for the seller?

It is no light matter to take up office as trustee, and it is perhaps curious that law agents acting for sellers are so willing to commit their clients to that office. And they commonly do so, one fears, without instructions. It may be that the office created by a trust clause in a disposition involves such slight duties that there is

---

1 This is the 'offside goals rule': see K G C Reid, *The Law of Property in Scotland* (1996) paras 695 ff.
2 James Chalmers, 'In Defence of the Trusting Conveyancer' 2002 SLT (News) 231.

nothing to worry about. But it is not, in fact, clear that that is the case. The issue has not been explored. For example, it is the duty of a trustee to insure the trust's heritable property.[1] It is true that risk will have passed, but that merely means that the seller has no duty to insure in his capacity *as seller*. But in his new capacity *as trustee* he is under a duty to insure. He will be presumptively liable if he does not and the property is damaged by fire.[2] There might be an argument that under the special circumstances the duty to insure does not exist. But should a seller be taking such risks merely to help a buyer who fails to register? This particular issue can be resolved by adding a further sub-clause to the disposition saying that the seller is under no duty to insure the property:

> And further providing that notwithstanding that I hold the said subjects in trust as aforesaid I am and shall be under no duty to insure the same against fire or other risks.

But there must always be a concern that Sally Seller, by assuming office as trustee, might be exposing herself to other problems. Trust law is a large subject, spanning both common law and many statutes. In that woodpile there might be other scorpions—not only the insurance scorpion. Take another example. A trustee has a duty to litigate to protect the trust estate.[3] So if there is a neighbour dispute, the seller, even after settlement, would thus be under a duty, for example, to raise an action to interdict a threatened encroachment. Perhaps that duty too could be excluded by adding a further clause to the disposition. But however many sub-clauses one adds, one can never be sure that there are no other scorpions. One could respond to the open-endedness of the difficulty by using a catch-all sub-clause:

> And further providing that notwithstanding that I hold the said subjects in trust as aforesaid I shall be exempt from all the duties, whether statutory or non-statutory, of a trustee.

But what would a court make of that? Perhaps it would accept it as it stands. Or it might take the view that a trust in which there are no duties is impossible.[4] If it took such a view, it might jump in one of two ways. It might hold that the disclaimer, being repugnant to the essence of a trust, is to be regarded as *pro non scripto*. The result would be that the seller would be subject to the whole range of trust duties—bad news for the seller. Or it might hold that the effect of the disclaimer is to invalidate the trust—bad news for the buyer.[5]

In genuine trusts there is also the risk of scorpions; and sometimes trust deeds qualify the trustees' duties. But in genuine trusts no one seeks to delete almost the whole of trust law, for such a deletion would be absurd. In a genuine trust the trustees will positively *want* to insure the heritable property against fire, to resist unlawful encroachments by neighbours, and so on.

---

1 W A Wilson and A G M Duncan, *Trusts Trustees and Executors* (2nd edn 1995) para 23-15.
2 In most cases the buyer would be insured. But the buyer's insurers, after paying up, would have a subrogation claim against the seller.
3 W A Wilson and A G M Duncan, *Trusts Trustees and Executors* (2nd edn 1995) para 23-16.
4 Without duties and (see above) without purposes.
5 Of course, these issues only arise if trust clauses are valid.

Adverse implications for the seller's law agents?

It has been argued that there may be problems for the seller's law agents because the trust clause has the effect of creating a new client.[1]

The balance of advantage

The discussion so far can be encapsulated in Disraeli's epigram that 'every woman should marry—and no man'.[2] Every buyer should have a trust clause—and no seller. Yet this over-states its value to the buyer. As we have seen, there are risks attached to trust clauses even for the buyer. In return the benefits are surprisingly small. A trust clause is of use only if the seller becomes insolvent *after or around the time of settlement*.[3] There is then a race to the Register between the buyer and the trustee in sequestration or liquidator.[4] It is a race in which, in the normal course of events, there can be only one winner; for in practice no trustee in sequestration or liquidator could get a title on the Register within the 21 days allowed to the buyer under a classic letter of obligation.[5] Indeed, where a trustee in sequestration does complete title it tends to take several months—as in *Burnett's Tr* itself. The trust clause thus offers a protection which, in ordinary conveyancing, will never be needed. Admittedly the position is made more difficult by delays in registration caused by delays in obtaining an SDLT certificate. It is to be hoped that, in time, a more robust system will eliminate such delays. But in any event an SDLT delay will only rarely be so prolonged as to put a buyer's title at risk. If it did, questions as to the liability of the Inland Revenue would arise.

Conclusions

It is difficult to arrive at conclusions with confidence in this difficult area. But tentatively:

(a) Whether trust clauses work has not yet been tested in court. The arguments against their validity are weighty.

If they do work, then:

(b) They protect the buyer from the largely theoretical danger that, if the seller becomes insolvent at or after settlement, the trustee in sequestration or liquidator will achieve registration ahead of the buyer.

(c) They probably weaken the buyer's protection against deeds granted by the seller to other parties. However, the possible benefits to a buyer probably outweigh the possible drawbacks.

---

1 Roy Roxburgh, 'Nightmares about Trust Clauses' (2004) 49 *Journal of the Law Society of Scotland* June/12.
2 *Lothair* (1870) ch 30.
3 Insolvency earlier than this will be picked up by the usual searches with the result that settlement will not take place.
4 In fact liquidators seldom complete title in their own name. But it can be done: see Titles to Land Consolidation (Scotland) Act 1868 s 25 and Insolvency Act 1986 s 145.
5 Scottish Law Commission, Discussion Paper on *Sharp v Thomson* (Scot Law Com DP No 114, 2001) paras 4.8 and 4.24.

(d) The styles currently in use may be inadequate.

(e) Trust clauses create risks for the seller without conferring any benefits.

(f) Hence while it probably makes sense for buyers' agents to ask for them, it is difficult to see any reason why sellers' agents should agree.

(g) If a trust clause is used, the seller's agents should qualify the duties incumbent on the seller in his capacity as trustee.

(h) It may be questioned whether a seller's law agents should agree to a trust clause without instructions.

SERVITUDES

Parking—again

In *Nationwide Building Society v Walter D Allan Ltd*[1] the pursuer and defender owned adjoining premises in Peterhead. Both premises were used for commercial purposes. At the rear of the pursuer's premises was a small area of ground belonging to the pursuer and capable of providing parking for about half a dozen cars. The defender, or so it was averred, had used this area for more than 20 years during normal business hours (8 am to 6 pm from Monday to Saturday) for the parking of two cars. The pursuer denied the right to park and sought interdict against the defender from parking for any time longer than was necessary to permit the loading or unloading of goods or the alighting from or boarding of persons into vehicles. The defender claimed a servitude. Interdict was granted. In the course of a careful and valuable Opinion, Lady Smith concluded that the extent of the right claimed by the defender was not consistent with a mere servitude. In the language of the Title Conditions (Scotland) Act 2003 (although not of the court) it was 'repugnant with ownership'.[2]

In so far as it is recognised at all, a servitude of parking can take one of two forms. It can be a freestanding right, existing independently of any other right; or it can be a right ancillary to a servitude right of way. In *Nationwide* the defender argued for each in the alternative.

Ancillary to a servitude of way

The defender had an express servitude of access and this, it argued, included a right to park by necessary implication. The principle of parking as an ancillary right is now accepted by the courts.[3] As Lady Smith said:[4]

---

1 2004 GWD 25-539.

2 Title Conditions (Scotland) Act 2003 s 76(2).

3 At the time the case was argued, the previous authority was at the level of the sheriff court: see in particular *Kennedy & Kennedy v MacDonald* 1998 GWD 40-1653, and *Moncreiff v Jamieson* 2004 SCLR 135. But the position was confirmed by the Inner House on 4 February 2005 in the appeal in *Moncreiff* (albeit with reluctance on the part of one of the judges, Lord Hamilton: see para 70). See *Moncrieff v Jamieson* 2005 SLT 225.

4 Paragraph 17.

[I]t seems not to be in doubt that there will, from time to time, be cases where it is implicit from the facts and circumstances of a particular grant of a servitude right of access that the owner of the dominant tenement will be entitled to park a vehicle on the servient tenement.

That leaves open the question of how such an ancillary right might come about. If the servitude of way was constituted in writing then the ancillary right of parking could equally be so specified. Otherwise the facts and circumstances might be such that the right to park arose by implication. The typical case is where the access road leads to the benefited property and there is no possibility of parking on the benefited property itself. Thus unless the benefited owner is to turn round and come straight back, the servitude of way must carry with it the right to park at least for a limited period. Such a limited right was indeed conceded by the pursuer in the present case, where the interdict was not to extend to loading and unloading. A more extensive right can also sometimes be recognised.[1]

The position is more difficult still if the servitude of way was constituted only by prescription. The effect of rule *tantum praescriptum quantum possessum* may be that prescriptive possession of the way would need to be supplemented by prescriptive possession of the parking.[2]

Freestanding right

Can a servitude of parking exist on its own? Is it possible, in other words, for an owner who has no need of a servitude to reach either his own land or the land on which it is proposed to park yet to have a servitude of parking? In *Nationwide* — where the defenders argued that such a right had been established by prescription—Lady Smith takes the answer to be no.[3] But her view is *obiter* and the case law is equivocal.[4]

The position is altered to some extent by s 76 of the Title Conditions Act, which came into force on 28 November 2004. Section 76 abolishes the rule that a servitude must be of a type known to the law, but this is qualified abolition only. It does not apply to any servitude created before 28 November 2004. And it does not apply to a servitude created on or after that date unless it is created expressly by writing and registration. It does not, in other words, apply to servitudes created by prescription (as was averred to have been the case in *Nationwide*) or to servitudes arising by implication in a conveyance. Further, s 76 does not allow *all* rights to be created as servitudes. For a servitude must be praedial, ie must burden one property for the benefit of another; it must be positive in nature, ie must involve making use of

---

1 *Moncreiff v Jamieson* 2005 SLT 225. The implications of this case will be considered in *Conveyancing 2005*.
2 Such possession was averred to have occurred in *Nationwide*.
3 'I cannot conclude that Scots law recognises, in principle, a servitude right of parking independent of any right of access' (para 26).
4 See generally D J Cusine and R R M Paisley, *Servitudes and Rights of Way* (1998) paras 3.45 ff. The most recent case of all is generally sympathetic to a freestanding servitude: see *Moncreiff v Jamieson* 2004 SCLR 135 affd, 2005 SLT 225.

the burdened property;[1] and it must not be repugnant with ownership.[2] Parking satisfies the first two of these. Whether it satisfies the third will depend on the facts and circumstances and is discussed further below.

For completeness it may be added that until 28 November 2004 a right of parking could be constituted as a real burden.[3] Since the Title Conditions Act came into force, however, real burdens have been restricted to negative burdens and affirmative burdens and so can no longer be used for rights of parking.[4]

It may be helpful to represent the current position in tabular form:

Can a freestanding right of parking be created?

Date of creation	Express servitude	Implied servitude	Servitude by prescription	Real burden
Before 28 November 2004	perhaps	perhaps	perhaps[5]	Yes
On or after 28 November 2004	yes	perhaps	perhaps	No

Repugnancy with ownership

The main reason for rejecting parking as a servitude in *Nationwide* was that the right was so extensive as to be repugnant with ownership. The principle is both familiar and, since the appointed day, statutory.[6] A servitude must leave something to the owner. Otherwise it is not a mere burden on ownership but is tantamount to ownership itself. And that the law will not recognise. Lady Smith expressed the position in this way:[7]

> If what is asserted is so extensive as to deprive the landowner, in practice, of the reasonable use of his own property, it will not be sustained. Determination of the issue will depend on the particular facts and circumstances of each case. Retention of reasonable use of the servient proprietor's own land in the countryside is bound to

1 Negative servitudes were abolished by the Title Conditions (Scotland) Act 2003 s 79. Further, a servitude cannot impose an affirmative obligation on the owner of the burdened property. For that a real burden is needed.
2 Title Conditions (Scotland) Act 2003 s 76(2) but, as the cases on parking show, the common law appears to have been the same.
3 D J Cusine and R R M Paisley, *Servitudes and Rights of Way* (1998) para 3.46.
4 Title Conditions (Scotland) Act 2003 s 2. But a right to enter property can be constituted as a real burden if it is ancillary to an affirmative or negative burden.
5 In *Nationwide* Lady Smith appears to suggest (at para 29) that, even if a right of parking could be created expressly, it would not follow that it could be created by prescription. That indeed is the law for servitudes created on or after 28 November 2004, but it seems doubtful if it was the law before.
6 At least in relation to express servitudes: see Title Conditions (Scotland) Act 2003 s 76(2).
7 Paragraph 23.

involve different considerations from those which arise in the urban context. In the present case, it is abundantly clear that the parking right asserted by the defenders would, in effect, deprive the pursuers of virtually all practical use of their property. Space at the rear of their premises is at a premium. Like the defenders, they are a commercial entity which carries on business during normal working hours from Monday to Saturday each week. To suggest that retaining the use of parking spaces outwith those hours would afford the pursuers reasonable use of their own land is like suggesting that reasonable use could be made of a car that has no petrol tank. The rights retained would ... be illusory.

The courts in England have approached the issue in much the same way, and some English cases were cited and discussed in *Nationwide*.[1]

But while the law is thus settled, its application is fraught with difficulty. How 'extensive' must a right of parking be before it is disallowed? Here three factors seem mainly relevant:

(1) the length of time each day for which parking is allowed;
(2) the number of vehicles which may be parked; and
(3) the extent of the area over which parking is allowed.

The first factor is straightforward. Temporary parking would not be intrusive. Parking for most of the day, for most days of the week—the position in *Nationwide*— is potentially intrusive but might be balanced by the other two factors.

The second factor is also straightforward. A right to park one vehicle is less demanding than a right to park five. Both are less demanding than the right which was apparently asserted in *Nationwide*, namely the right to park as many vehicles as the servitude holder wished.

The final factor is crucial yet elusive. An initial distinction is between:

• a right to park anywhere in the burdened owner's land; and
• a right to park only in one particular part of that land.

Whether an *unrestricted* right of parking is acceptable will depend on the size of the land. In *Nationwide* the land was small and the right accordingly disallowed. Plainly the position would be different if the land was extensive, particularly if parking were to be available only for a limited number of vehicles.[2]

It might be supposed that a *restricted* right would be less intrusive and so more readily allowed. But that depends on how much account is taken of the land over which no servitude right is to subsist. Suppose for example that the land extends to one hectare and it is proposed that parking should be confined to a small, marked area. In practice that is less intrusive than a right to park anywhere within the hectare. But in theory it can be presented as *more* intrusive. For the property which is burdened by the servitude is not the whole hectare but merely

---

1 For an insightful account of the position in England and Wales, see K Gray and S F Gray, *Elements of Land Law* (4th edn 2004) paras 8.77 and 8.88.
2 See *Moncreiff v Jamieson* 2005 SLT 225, where a right to park was recognised. Lord Marnoch's view (para 23) was that: 'I do not consider that the recognition of a right to park would significantly displace the third defender from the enjoyment of his own lands and property.'

the small area on which parking is allowed; and with respect to that small area, the right is so extensive as virtually to exclude the owner. The point is not merely presentational. In the future the land might come to be divided and sold in parts. If the right were a right to park anywhere, division would make no difference and each part would be subject to the original servitude. But if the right were confined to one small area, and that area were sold on its own, its acquirer would receive property which was virtually unusable. The result is a paradox. A right confined to a small area may, at least in the long run, be more repugnant with ownership than one which can be exercised anywhere. How a court might weigh these respective rights is less easy to say.

Creating new servitudes of parking

Since 28 November 2004 it has been possible to create new, freestanding, servitudes of parking. But, as has been seen, the right will fail as a servitude if it is repugnant with ownership. Repugnancy is indeed a risk that affects all servitudes, but particularly the new, individually-crafted ones which can now be created for the first time. No doubt the courts will offer further guidance in due course. For the moment caution and restraint seem wise, for greed may be punished with invalidity. And in the particular context of servitudes of parking the prospects of success will be best if the area for parking is large and the right small, limited both by number of vehicles and by permitted hours.

Prescriptive acquisition: possession as of right

Another aspect of *Nationwide Building Society v Walter D Allan Ltd*[1] merits discussion. In claiming that it had acquired a servitude by prescription, the defender averred 20 years' possession. Strictly, however, that is not enough. The possession must also be of the right type: it must be possession as of right and not merely by the consent or tolerance of the owner of the land in question. To suppose that mere possession suffices may be, as the pursuer pointed out, a 'common misconception'.[2] If so it was a misconception which the court was anxious to correct:[3]

> Servitudes emanate from grants. They are given, not taken. The grant may, through the operation of prescription, be implied but it follows that, to prove prescriptive acquisition of a servitude right, the person claiming must show not only use but use in a way that has amounted to a clear assertion communicated to the landowner that he was doing so as of right. If it is not insisted upon then there would be a real risk of burdening a person's land with a servitude in circumstances where, whilst he may have been content to tolerate use by a particular neighbour, he would not be content to tolerate use by all neighbouring proprietors in all time coming.

---

1 2004 GWD 25-539.
2 Paragraph 15.
3 Paragraph 35.

The first part of this *dictum* seems to toy with the curious doctrine of 'lost grant' that is, the doctrine of English law that the prescriptive acquisition of an easement is explicable by the legal fiction of an earlier grant which has since been lost. That doctrine, little admired in its country of origin, is no part of Scots law.[1] In other respects the *dictum* is unexceptionable. Indeed it recalls remarks in *Webster v Chadburn*.[2]

But there are limits to what can sensibly be required of a person seeking to establish a servitude. It is one thing to ask for an acknowledgement in the pleadings that possession must be of right. It is quite another thing to require decisive proof of the matter, because the evidence is likely to be thin, equivocal and, it may be, contradictory. The court must listen to the evidence and make up its mind; but if too much is required no servitude could ever be established by prescription.

The evidential difficulties spring from the law. To say that possession is of right is to say that it must be *nec precario*, that is to say without the consent of owner of the land.[3] In consequence it seems that any of the following will disqualify possession for the purposes of prescription:

(1) The landowner consents expressly to the possession.
(2) The landowner consents by implication to the possession—in other words the possession is by tolerance.
(3) The landowner is believed by the possessor to consent—even where no consent is in fact given.

But the proof of a negative—as (1) and (2) seems to require—is a task beyond a litigant. The law must therefore be indulgent.

In practice the main difficulty is caused by (2). There must be no tolerance by the landowner. The opposite of tolerance is intolerance or, in this context, indifference also. Typically the landowner has done nothing and said nothing; and the possession has continued for 20 years. What then? Has the landowner been tolerant or merely indifferent? In the absence of other evidence the tendency has been to look to the volume and extent of the possession.[4] Once possession becomes too intrusive or prolonged the landowner is treated as having crossed the threshold from tolerance to indifference. The accommodating neighbour has become the owner careless of his rights. In *Nationwide* the possession was substantial and, on that ground at least, the requirements for prescription would appear to have been met.[5]

---

1 Despite some *obiter dicta* to the contrary: see D J Cusine and R R M Paisley, *Servitudes and Rights of Way* (1998) para 10.03. Indeed the *nec precario* rule presupposes that there was *no* grant.
2 2003 GWD 18-562. See *Conveyancing 2003* pp 65–68.
3 The rule in England and Wales is much the same, and cases from that jurisdiction are likely to be of assistance. See K Gray and S F Gray, *Elements of Land Law* (4th edn 2004) paras 8.184–8.187.
4 D J Cusine and R R M Paisley, *Servitudes and Rights of Way* (1998) paras 1.70 and 10.19. It is because possession by the public is usually more intrusive than possession by a neighbour that tolerance is rarely found in cases involving public rights of way. In this respect at least the court was justified in distinguishing such cases (para 39). But the underlying principle is the same.
5 As was seen earlier, however, the servitude failed on other grounds.

ANTISOCIAL BEHAVIOUR ETC
(SCOTLAND) ACT 2004

Conveyancers might suppose that the Antisocial Behaviour etc (Scotland) Act 2004 (asp 8) deals only with criminal law. In fact it has important provisions for the housing market. Part 8 provides, roughly speaking, that it is unlawful to let out residential property unless the local authority approves of you. Part 7 provides for penalties against a landlord whose property is occupied by antisocial tenants. Both parts come into force on 15 November 2005.[1]

Part 7 comes into play only if there are antisocial tenants in the property and so is of limited importance to the conveyancer. But conveyancers need to be aware of it, and it is essential background to Part 8.

Part 7: penalising landlords for antisocial tenants

Section 68 says that if 'it appears to a local authority' that an occupant of tenanted property is 'engaging in antisocial behaviour' then the local authority can serve on the landlord an 'antisocial behaviour notice', which is a notice 'requiring the landlord of the relevant house to take, before the expiry of such period as may be specified in the notice, such action for the purpose of dealing with the antisocial behaviour as may be so specified'. It is not necessary that the occupant has actually been convicted of anything: all that is required is that it 'appears' to the local authority that 'antisocial behaviour' has occurred. Nor, apparently, is it necessary that the alleged antisocial behaviour has any direct connection with the property. One might suppose that the legislation is aimed at the characters who deal in drugs from the property, or who play loud music in the middle of the night, and no doubt it is. But it is also broader than that, applying where the antisocial behaviour is 'at, or *in the locality* of' the property. One wonders how local 'locality' is.

If the landlord fails to comply with the notice, there can be four consequences. The first two are of particular interest for property lawyers.

(1) No rent is payable if the court so orders, following an application by the local authority.[2] It seems odd that the antisocial should be thus rewarded for their bad behaviour.[3]

(2) The local authority can take over the management of the property for up to a year.[4] This once again requires a court order: a 'management control order'. The effect is to transfer to the local authority 'the rights and obligations of the landlord under the tenancy'. That means confiscation of the rental income.

---

1 Antisocial Behaviour etc (Scotland) Act 2004 (Commencement and Savings) Order 2004, SSI 2004/420.

2 Antisocial Behaviour etc (Scotland) Act 2004 s 71.

3 If they are receiving housing benefit the beneficiary will be the public purse.

4 AB(S)A 2004 s 74.

(3) 'The local authority may take such steps as it considers necessary to deal with the antisocial behaviour described in the notice.'[1] These 'steps'—one wonders what they might be—will be at the expense of the landlord.

(4) Failure to comply with an antisocial behaviour notice is an offence.[2]

We will not go into the definitional scheme except to mention that the machinery can be activated not only if the antisocial behaviour is by the tenant but also if it is by an occupant or even by a visitor.[3] That covers the all-too-common case where the tenancy is in the name of an adult who has children who are out of control. The provisions also apply to owners who take in lodgers.

How workable will all this be? One difficulty is what is meant by 'action' for dealing with the alleged antisocial behaviour. Such action has to be specified in the notice which is served on the landlord. What can be specified? One awaits with interest the first antisocial behaviour notice. In practice a landlord would often have only two ways of clamping down. The first would be to terminate the tenancy and evict the occupants, and the second would be persuasion. Unless backed by force, persuasion may often be ineffective, but one does not anticipate that the notices will require the use of force. That leaves termination and eviction. Eviction can be a slow business even if the landlord pursues the matter actively. A more fundamental difficulty is that there may be no right to terminate. As already pointed out, the legislation does not require that the alleged antisocial behaviour occurs at the property itself. On what basis is the landlord to evict a tenant whose misbehaviour does not happen in the property? Perhaps the conclusion to be drawn is that in such a case no notice would be served because there would be no 'action' for dealing with the behaviour that the local authority could impose on the landlord. Nevertheless here, as elsewhere in this Act, one feels some doubt as to how thoroughly the provisions were thought through before they were enacted.

Critics might argue that antisocial behaviour ought to be addressed by the criminal justice system, and that for government to penalise private parties for its own failures is unacceptable. We will not comment on that argument, but the question of whether part 7, and especially its confiscatory aspects, is wholly compatible with the European Human Rights Convention[4] might be open to debate.

Part 8: compulsory registration of private landlords

Part 8 sets up a registration system for private landlords. It makes it an offence to be an unregistered private landlord. Section 93(1) provides that

Where—

(a) a relevant person owns a house within the area of a local authority which is subject to

---

1 AB(S)A 2004 s 78.
2 AB(S)A 2004 s 79.
3 AB(S)A 2004 s 68(2).
4 And especially article 1 of the First Protocol.

(i) a lease; or

(ii) an occupancy arrangement,

by virtue of which an unconnected person may use the house as a dwelling; and

(b) the relevant person is not registered by that authority,

the relevant person shall be guilty of an offence.

Registration is done by each local authority. The basic idea comes from the 2003 report of the Housing Improvement Action Task Force.[1]

Part 8 does not apply where the landlord is a local authority, or a registered social landlord, or Scottish Homes.[2] Nor does it apply where the landlord and tenant are 'connected', ie in the same family.[3] Another important exception is properties let for holidays.[4]

Each local authority will keep a register of registered landlords for its area.[5] Registration is by landlord, not by property. However, in the application for registration applicants must give details of any properties in the area that they are renting out[6] and must notify the local authority thereafter of any changes.[7] So for instance if XYZ Ltd buys a new property to let it out, it must tell the local authority. Or if it sells a property it must tell the local authority. The system is operated by each local authority in its own area. Thus a client who owns, and lets out, flats in different local authority areas will have to go through the procedure for each such area. The register is public and may become a useful source of information to neighbours wishing to discover the identity of the landlord.[8]

A person cannot be registered unless judged to be a 'fit and proper person to act as landlord'.[9] Certain factors are mentioned which are to be taken into account in assessing prospective landlords, namely whether they have ever breached the criminal law, whether they ever have exhibited racism or sexism, and whether they have ever contravened any provision of 'the law relating to housing or landlord and tenant law'.[10] Deregistration can happen if the local authority no longer considers the landlord to be a fit and proper person.[11]

What is the compulsitor for registration? As already mentioned, it is a criminal offence for an unregistered person to let out residential property. It is even a criminal offence if an unregistered person 'communicates with another person with a view to entering into a lease'.[12] That would presumably include putting a postcard stuck in a newsagent's window saying 'flat to let'. Further, the local

---

1 See *Conveyancing 2003* p 96.

2 They are not 'relevant persons': see AB(S)A 2004 s 83(8).

3 AB(S)A 2004 s 83(8). Section 101(3) provides that 'any reference to a person's being a member of another's family shall be construed in accordance with section 108(1) and (2) of the Housing (Scotland) Act 2001 (asp 10)'. The latter has a broad definition.

4 AB(S)A 2004 s 83(6)(d).

5 Rather inconveniently the register seems to have no name.

6 AB(S)A 2004 s 83(1).

7 AB(S)A 2004 s 87.

8 AB(S)A 2004 s 82(2).

9 AB(S)A 2004 s 84.

10 AB(S)A 2004 s 85.

11 AB(S)A 2004 s 89.

12 AB(S)A 2004 s 93(2)(b).

authority can serve a notice terminating the landlord's right to collect rent.[1] Unlike the parallel sanction in part 7, this does not require any court order.[2] These sanctions cannot, however, be applied if the landlord has applied for registration and the application is still pending.[3]

The legislation presumably has its eye on short-term urban lets. But in fact it makes no distinction between urban and rural properties. Nor is any distinction made between short and long leases. It would seem to apply to owners of properties subject to crofting tenure and to owners of properties that are leased on 1000-year leases.[4] As well as leases it applies to 'occupancy arrangements' and hence, it seems, to owners who have, or wish to have, a lodger. An 'occupancy arrangement' is defined as meaning 'any arrangement under which a person having the lawful right to occupy a house permits another, by way of contract or otherwise, to occupy the house or, as the case may be, part of it'.[5]

Although most of part 8 does not come into force until 15 November 2005, an application for registration may be made now.[6] The Act does not say what an existing landlord is to do if his application for registration is refused. Presumably he must evict the tenant or sell. The first may be impossible and even if possible would take time, as would sale. In the meantime he seems to be a criminal. The same issues will presumably arise, after the Act is up and running, where a landlord is deregistered. They will also arise where an unregistered person inherits tenanted property.

The Act is silent on cases where the property has been taken over by a representative of the landlord, such as an executor, trustee in sequestration, liquidator, guardian or judicial factor. Must such persons be registered as a fit and proper person before appointment? It might be argued that the answer must be negative since they are not heritable proprietors unless they complete title. That raises the question as to whether the legislation is limited to heritable proprietors. The Act at certain places (such as s 93) seems to assume that the landlord is the owner; yet it would be odd if a rogue landlord could defy the policy of the legislation on the ground of an uncompleted title, or on the ground that his title was itself a leasehold one. Perhaps representative parties are automatically covered by the registration of the person they represent, but the legislation does not so provide. Parallel issues arise for heritable creditors in possession. Questions must also arise about trusts: can the trust be registered, or must each trustee be registered?

---

1 AB(S) A 2004 s 94.

2 Incidentally, it would be interesting to know why the penalty for a landlord who tolerates antisocial tenants was not simply de-registration, since the consequences of de-registration are actually quite similar to the remedies in part 7.

3 AB(S)A 2004 s 93(3)–(5).

4 Since the Land Tenure Reform (Scotland) Act 1974 the maximum length of lease for residential property has been 20 years.

5 AB(S)A 2004 s 101.

6 Section 83 came into force on 28 October 2004 to the effect of allowing applications to be made. See Antisocial Behaviour etc (Scotland) Act 2004 (Commencement and Savings) Order 2004, SSI 2004/420 sch 1.

No doubt there are answers to such questions. In law, every question must have an answer. If an issue is litigated the court must provide an answer. In law there is, in principle, no indeterminacy, so that uncertainty must be subjective rather than objective. But such philosophical reflections are, perhaps, cold comfort. One is left with the impression of legislation that has been enacted before being completely thought through. The very fact that part 8 has hitched a lift in a statute which is about quite different matters is indicative.

Enforcement may be an issue. How will the provisions be made known to everyone affected? Even if made known, how extensive will compliance be? For instance the provisions appear to apply to anyone who has a lodger. Is every such person really going to register? Perhaps. If not, there is going to be a mass criminalisation of honest citizens.

The practical implications for conveyancers are considerable. Clients who are landlords need to be informed of the new law. So do clients who have lodgers which is to say potentially most clients. The buy-to-let market will be affected, and there can be little doubt but that lenders in that market will insist that the borrower be registered.

PRESERVATION NOTICES

Old notices

Under the Abolition of Feudal Tenure etc (Scotland) Act 2000 it was competent for superiors to preserve the right to enforce real burdens if certain conditions were satisfied. The main provision was s 18 which allowed enforcement rights to be reallotted to other property owned by the superior provided that it contained a building used as a place of human habitation and resort which lay within 100 metres of the feu. No such notices could be registered after 28 November 2004.

Registers of Scotland have kindly made available the final figures for notices registered under the Act. They are as follows:

Type of notice	Number registered
Section 18 reallotment	1960[1]
Section 18A personal pre-emption (or redemption) burden	642
Section 18B economic development burden	31
Section 18C health care burden	2

1 This is the figure for applications to the Register of Sasines. A further 719 applications were made to the Land Register, but, since s 18 notices require registration against both the benefited and the burdened property, it is likely that in most cases the notice was also registered in the Register of Sasines and so is covered by the figure given. But to that figure must be added the, probably small, number of notices in respect of which both properties were on the Land Register.

Type of notice	Number registered
Section 19 agreement	10
Section 20 Lands Tribunal blocking notice	1
Section 27 conservation burdens	263
Section 27A conservation burdens (third party)	5
Section 33 development value burdens	50
Section 65A sporting rights	65

Although 13 months were allowed for registration, 65% of all notices were registered only in the final week and 30% on the final day.[1] The overall numbers are small. Of the 2 million or so title units in Scotland only about 2000—a mere 0.1%—are affected by former feudal burdens which have been reallotted under s 18. The figures for other types of notice are smaller still, although the total of 642 notices in respect of rights of pre-emption (or redemption) is, relatively speaking, quite high.

It should not be assumed that all notices are valid.[2] The 2000 Act exempted the Keeper from certain checks which he might otherwise have felt bound to make (eg whether the superior's building does indeed lie within 100 metres of the feu).[3] It should also be borne in mind that some notices were prepared in haste and others in a spirit of optimism as to the enforceability of the burdens in question. Notices believed to be invalid can be challenged before the Lands Tribunal or in other ways.[4]

New notices

With the appointed day (28 November 2004), the era of notices ends, but also starts again. Notices under the 2000 Act cease to be competent, of course. But in their place are two new notices under the Title Conditions (Scotland) Act 2003: notices of preservation and notices of converted servitude. Admittedly there is less rush than before, for the two notices can be registered at any time before 28 November 2014. Nonetheless it is necessary to start thinking about them right away.

---

1 (2005) *Journal of the Law Society of Scotland* Jan/48.
2 For a non-exhaustive list of possible defects, see K G C Reid, *The Abolition of Feudal Tenure in Scotland* (2003) para 11.15.
3 Abolition of Feudal Tenure etc (Scotland) Act 2000 s 43.
4 Abolition of Feudal Tenure etc (Scotland) Act 2000 s 44. See further K G C Reid, *The Abolition of Feudal Tenure in Scotland* (2003) paras 11.17–11.20.

Notices of preservation

Of the two new notices, the notice of preservation is by far the more important.[1] It is best to begin with some background.

The rule in *Mactaggart*

Under the law which was in force before 28 November 2004 it was possible, and indeed common, for the right to enforce a real burden to arise by implication—without express words in the deed. This was the so-called implied *jus quaesitum tertio*. All existing implied rights were abolished on the appointed day only to be substantially recreated by ss 52 and 53 of the Title Conditions Act. There was one exception to the abolition (and recreation): this was implied rights arising as a result of the rule in *J A Mactaggart & Co v Harrower*.[2]

The rule in *Mactaggart* is—or, more properly, was—as follows:[3]

Where –

(a) A, the owner of land, transferred part of that land to B;
(b) the transfer was by disposition;
(c) the disposition was recorded before 28 November 2004; and
(d) the disposition imposed real burdens without making provision as to enforcement,

it was implied that the benefited property in the real burdens was such property as, at the time of registration of the disposition, was still retained by A.

Once land became a benefited property in this way it was subject to the same rules as any other benefited property. Thus the burdens are enforceable not merely by A, the original disponer, but by A's successors as owner, without the need for assignation of the right.[4] If the benefited property comes to be divided, the effect depends on the date of the division. For divisions occurring before the appointed day, each divided part remains a benefited property; for divisions on or after that day, only the part retained remains the benefited property unless the disposition provides otherwise.[5]

The rule in *Mactaggart* is confined to real burdens created before the appointed day. For burdens created on or after that day it is necessary to nominate and identify the benefited property and to register the deed against that property (as well as against the burdened property).[6] Further, the exemption for rights created by *Mactaggart* is temporary. All[7] such rights will be extinguished on 28 November

---

1 See also D A Brand, A J M Steven and S Wortley, *Professor McDonald's Conveyancing Manual* (7th edn 2004) paras 17.10–17.14; R Rennie, *Land Tenure in Scotland* (2004) paras 8-13–8-15.
2 (1906) 8 F 1101.
3 K G C Reid, *The Law of Property in Scotland* (1996) paras 403 and 404.
4 For a contrary view, see *Marsden v Craighelen Lawn Tennis and Squash Club* 1999 GWD 37-1820, discussed in *Conveyancing 1999* pp 59–61.
5 Title Conditions (Scotland) Act 2003 s 12.
6 TC(S)A 2003 s 4.
7 Other than rights in respect of facility or service burdens, both of which are preserved by TC(S)A 2003 s 56. For example an obligation to maintain a boundary fence would remain enforceable on this ground.

2014 except where, before that date, a notice of preservation is registered under s 50 of the Title Conditions Act by an owner of the benefited property.[1]

Ten years may sound a long time. But notices are likely to be registered only when a particular title comes to a conveyancer's attention, which in practice means when the benefited property is being acquired. And since a property may be bought and sold only once (if indeed at all) in the course of 10 years, the buyer's solicitor must seize the chance as it arises. The problem thus resolves into a practical one: how can s 50 cases be identified?

Identifying s 50 cases

When acting in a purchase, a solicitor will, naturally, take stock of the real burdens affecting the property in question—of the burdens, in other words, in respect of which the property is a *burdened* property. If it was customary to overlook the burdens in respect of which the property might be a *benefited* property, this was because such information was not readily available. Until the appointed day real burdens were registered only against burdened properties. If the property being acquired was a benefited property (whether by express provision or by implication), there might be nothing registered against that property to say so.[2] Further enquiries would be onerous and, often, fruitless; and the value of the information to the client was unlikely to justify the expense.

Section 50 changes matters somewhat. If a s 50 notice is not registered in a case where it is required, the right to enforce the burdens will be lost. On one view the matter is self-sorting. If the burdens are known about, a notice will be registered; and if they are not known about there is little pain in the prospective loss. The trouble is that eligible burdens will rarely be known about, yet in some cases the loss will be serious. And if the cases can be identified now there is an important long-term gain. The question is how identification can be achieved.

The rule in *Mactaggart* only operates in respect of what may be termed *rump titles*, that is to say, titles to land left behind when the rest was sold off. Further, at least in the form mediated by the Title Conditions Act, it does not apply to common scheme cases.[3] Thus, in the typical case where land is divided into two, with one plot (plot A) sold and the other (plot B) retained to be sold later, there is a distinction between the situation where:

(1) plot B is sold subject to the same burdens as plot A;
(2) plot B is sold without burdens or subject to different burdens.

In the first case there is a common scheme of burdens affecting both plots, and the question of enforcement rights is regulated by ss 52 and 53. At any rate no notice can be registered under s 50. In the second case plot B is, by virtue of

---

1 TC(S)A 2003 s 49(2). If a notice of converted servitude (discussed below) is needed, it can additionally be used to perform the function of a notice of preservation. See s 80(5)(f).
2 Information would, however, be available if the burdens were imposed by deed of conditions.
3 TC(S)A 2003 s 50(6).

the rule in *Mactaggart*, the benefited property. A s 50 notice is both competent and necessary.

Conveyancers need to become alert to rump title cases. The initial question is: is the property now being bought the rump (or part of the rump) of a formerly larger property? If so, a s 50 notice is needed if –

- the property or properties previously split off were conveyed by disposition (as opposed to feu disposition)
- the disposition was recorded before the appointed day
- the disposition imposed real burdens without making provision as to their enforcement
- the title to the property being acquired does not contain the same, or similar, burdens.

This is a daunting list. For properties on the Land Register the history of the title is particularly difficult to discover. And in all cases it will be necessary to look at titles of other properties, sometimes on a speculative basis. To assemble the necessary information will thus take time and trouble. If, as often, one of the conditions will turn out not to have been satisfied, the work will have been for nothing. At the outset the clients must of course be asked whether they wish to incur the expense. No doubt the answer will often be no. Sometimes, however, the nature of the property itself may indicate that s 50 might apply. That will be true, for example, where a second house has been built on what was formerly part of the garden of the house now being acquired. A less conclusive case is where the property being acquired is a sub-divided part of a formerly single house. At least in situations like this, the case for further investigation is reasonably strong.

The notice itself

The form of notice is laid down in schedule 7 to the Title Conditions Act. It closely resembles notices under the 2000 Act. A completed notice might look like this:[1]

NOTICE OF PRESERVATION

Name and address of person sending notice:

James Alexander Macfarlane
47 Church Lane
Lanark ML11 6LH

Description of burdened property:

47A Church Lane, Lanark registered in the Land Register under title number LAN 57312.

---

1 But it is always necessary to consult the statutory style and the notes for completion.

Description of benefited property:[1]

47 Church Lane, Lanark, being the subjects described in Disposition by Andrew Rennie in favour of Catherine Anne Smith dated 9 September 1912 and recorded in the Division of the General Register of Sasines for the County of Lanark on 15 September 1912, under exception of the said subjects registered in the Land Register under title number LAN 57312.

Terms of real burdens:

The real burdens set out in Disposition by Robert Campbell Wilson in favour of Norman Adams and Serena Joanna Knowles or Adams dated 12 February 1952 and registered in the said Division of the General Register of Sasines on 19 February 1952.

Explanation of why the property described as a benefited property is such a property:

The property so described was the property still retained by Robert Campbell Wilson following the registration of the said Disposition in favour of Norman Adams and Serena Joanna Knowles or Adams. It is thus the benefited property by legal implication.

Service:

A copy of this notice has been sent by recorded delivery on 8 December 2005 to the owner of the burdened property at 47A Church Lane, Lanark ML11 6LH.

I swear that the information contained in the notice is, to the best of my knowledge and belief, true.

Signature of person sending the notice:

Signature of notary public:

Date:

The notice runs in the name of the owner of the benefited property or, if more than one, of any such owner.[2] It is not necessary that there is a title completed by registration provided that the necessary links in title are listed in an additional box.[3] The same notice can be used for more than one burden, and for more than one benefited or burdened property, so long as the burdens writ is the same.[4]

---

1 If the person sending the notice does not have a completed title to the benefited property, it is necessary to narrate the midcouples in a separate box. See sch 7 note 2.

2 TC(S)A 2003 s 50(1) ('an owner').

3 TC(S)A 2003 s 50(2)(c).

4 TC(S)A 2003 s 115(4).

The only box likely to cause difficulty is the fifth. The Act requires that the notice 'set out the grounds, both factual and legal, for describing as a benefited property' the land so identified.[1] It is thought that there is only one 'legal' ground, namely the rule in *Mactaggart*. It is competent, but presumably unnecessary, to give the name and citation of the case.[2] The style given above simply describes the rule. The 'factual' ground is that the property in question was left behind after the burdened property was disponed and the burdens imposed.

Before the last two boxes are completed a copy of the notice must be served on the owner of the burdened property.[3] Service can be by post, by delivery, or by electronic means such as e-mail.[4] Unless the name of the owner is known it is sufficient to send the notice to the burdened property addressed to 'The Owner' or similar.[5] If the name *is* known and there is more than one owner, it is arguable, but not certain, that a separate copy must be served on each.[6] On service the notice must be accompanied by the explanatory note set out in schedule 7.[7] This may be reproduced at the end of the notice or, if preferred, on a separate piece of paper. The note is as follows:

Explanatory Note

This notice is sent by a person who asserts that the use of your property is affected by the real burdens whose terms are described in the notice and that that person is one of the people entitled to the benefit of the real burdens and can, if necessary, enforce them against you. In this notice your property (or some part of it) is referred to as the 'burdened property' and the property belonging to that person is referred to as the 'benefited property'.

The grounds for the assertion are given in the notice. By section 50 of the Title Conditions (Scotland) Act 2003 (asp 9) that person's rights will be lost unless this notice is registered in the Land Register or Register of Sasines by not later than 28 November 2014. Registration preserves the rights and means that the burdens can continue to be enforced by that person and by anyone succeeding as owner of that person's property.

This notice does not require you to take any action; but if you think there is a mistake in it, or if you wish to challenge it, you are advised to contact your solicitor or other adviser. A notice can be challenged even after it has been registered.

The notice is completed by entering the details of service, and by signature before a notary public, the owner of the benefited property having sworn or affirmed that to the best of his knowledge or belief all the information contained in the notice is true.[8] The notary must also sign[9] and should, as a matter of good

---

1 TC(S)A 2003 s 50(2)(e).
2 D A Brand, A J M Steven and S Wortley, *Professor McDonald's Conveyancing Manual* (7th edn 2004) para 17.12(4).
3 Unless 'not reasonably practicable to do so': see TC(S)A 2003 s 115(2).
4 TC(S)A 2003 s 124(2).
5 TC(S)A 2003 s 124(1)(b).
6 For the, perhaps comparable, position of notices under the 2000 Act, see K G C Reid, *The Abolition of Feudal Tenure in Scotland* (2003) paras 11.7 and 12.1 note 6.
7 TC(S)A 2003 s 115(2)(b).
8 TC(S)A 2003 s 50(4).
9 TC(S)A 2003 sch 7 note 7.

practice, be named and designed.[1] Swearing or affirming a statement that is known to be false or is believed not to be true is an offence under the False Oaths (Scotland) Act 1933. Normally the oath must be given personally and not, for example, through a solicitor; but a company or other juristic person is represented by a person authorised to sign documents on its behalf,[2] and a person without legal capacity by an appropriate person.[3] An oath outside Scotland may be given before any person duly authorised by the country in question to administer oaths or receive affirmations.[4] The final step is to register the notice, in the Land Register or Register of Sasines. The Keeper has indicated that the land certificate need not accompany the application.[5] Section 50 requires registration against both the burdened property and the benefited property, in the usual way.[6]

Effect of notice

Registration of a notice of preservation does not create new rights, but it prevents the loss of existing rights. Whether a notice is registered or not, the property retains its status as a benefited property until 28 November 2014. Thereafter that status will survive only if it has been preserved by a notice registered before that day.[7]

Section 50 notices are potentially troublesome and arduous. But there are important long-term gains for transparency of the Registers. After 28 November 2014 enforcement rights for most real burdens will appear on the Register.[8]

Notices of converted servitude

Notices of converted servitude will be much rarer, and it is possible to be brief.[9] One of the effects of the Title Conditions Act was the abandonment of the category of negative servitudes. In future all restrictions must be created as real burdens and not as servitudes;[10] and all existing negative servitudes were automatically converted into real burdens on the appointed day.[11]

Unlike real burdens, negative servitudes were not always visible to an acquirer of the burdened property. They might be registered only against the benefited property or, in a few cases, they might not be registered at all. Section 80 of the

---

1 See a note by the Keeper at (2004) 49 *Journal of the Law Society of Scotland* Nov/55. The notary is not, however, a witness, and a witness is not required: see Requirements of Writing (Scotland) Act 1995 s 6(3)(a).
2 See generally the Requirements of Writing (Scotland) Act 1995, sch 2.
3 TC(S)A 2003 s 50(5).
4 TC(S)A 2003 s 122(1) (definition of 'notary public').
5 See (2004) 49 *Journal of the Law Society of Scotland* Nov/55.
6 TC(S)A 2003 s 50(1), (3).
7 TC(S)A 2003 s 50(1).
8 For rights arising by implication under ss 52, 53 and 56 of the TC(S)A 2003 the Keeper is directed, by s 58, to note their existence.
9 See also D A Brand, A J M Steven and S Wortley, *Professor McDonald's Conveyancing Manual* (7th edn 2004) paras 17.15–17.19; R Rennie, *Land Tenure in Scotland* (2004) para 11-09.
10 TC(S)A 2003 s 79.
11 TC(S)A 2003 s 80(1).

Title Conditions Act seeks to remedy the situation. Where a converted servitude[1] is not currently registered or noted against the burdened property, the owner of the benefited property must register a notice of converted servitude. If this is not done by 28 November 2014 the servitude is extinguished. The form of notice is set out in schedule 9. The form and procedure are close to those already described for notices of preservation.

Happily, notices of converted servitude do not give rise to the problems of recognition which afflict notices of preservation. Either the title of a property will disclose the benefit of a (former) negative servitude or, as almost always, it will not. In the first case it is necessary to check whether the servitude is also noted in the title of the burdened property and to register a notice of converted servitude if it is not. In the second case no action is needed for, except where the servitude is not registered at all (which is so rare that it can be discounted in practice), the servitude will already be registered or noted in the title of the burdened property. Thus action is needed only in the case where one knows of the servitude from one's own title. Unknown servitudes survive anyway.

OFFSIDE GOALS, POSSESSION AND BAD FAITH

A wise buyer considers possession and not merely title. And indeed the application forms for registration ask whether there is 'any person in possession or occupation of the subjects or any part of them adversely to the interest of the applicant'.

Possession by a third party is not always a problem for a buyer. The buyer may be deliberately buying pre-let property. Even in other cases there may be an innocent explanation for the third-party possession. The possessor may be a relative or friend of the seller, allowed to occupy at will but without a legal right to do so. The possessor, in short, may be a licensee, the holder of a merely personal right. It is well settled that a right of this kind does not transmit against successors.[2]

Real rights, of course, do transmit. But most real rights require registration for their constitution, so that if the Register is silent there is nothing to fear. To this principle the main exception is the short lease. Hence if a third party is in possession, enquiries are likely to focus on the possible existence of such a lease.

The idea that real rights bind successors and that personal rights do not—and that real rights can generally be detected from the Register—is of the very essence of our system of conveyancing. *Rodger v Paton*[3] is a reminder that things may not always be so simple. In that case it was averred both that the seller had previously contracted to sell the property to a third party and that the third party had taken

---

1 Ie a former servitude which was automatically converted into a real burden by the TC(S)A 2003 s 80(1).
2 *Wallace v Simmers* 1960 SC 255.
3 2004 GWD 19-425. Another aspect of this case was discussed earlier, at p 000. It is not clear from the judgment whether the property was on the Land Register or the Register of Sasines, but the principles are the same in each case.

possession. The right of the third party, it was true, was merely personal in nature. It was a right against the seller and not against the buyer. But a buyer who knows of a prior right to acquire the property is bound by it. That is the so-called rule against offside goals: if the buyer proceeds with the purchase his title is disallowed in the same way as a goal is disallowed as offside. The offside goals rule depends on bad faith; but the mere fact of adverse possession may be sufficient to trigger bad faith.[1] In *Rodger* a proof was allowed on the point.

Whether the offside goals rule is a good one is controversial. Certainly there are some things that can be said in its favour. But the more generously it is applied, the more it threatens the security of title given by a public system of registers; and the more it blurs the distinction between real rights and personal rights.[2] It remains to be seen what is and is not proved in *Rodger*, but it should not be assumed that possession is enough to put a purchaser on notice of the possible existence of a rival right to purchase. In *Stodart v Dalzell*,[3] the leading case on this point, there were factors other than possession at issue, and the possession itself involved the construction of part of a building and was of long duration. Given the policy aims of registration of title, a modern court should hesitate before going any further.[4]

LEASES

Irritancy and acceptance of rent

Does continued acceptance of rent bar the landlord from enforcing an irritancy? That was the issue at stake in *Wolanski & Co Trustees Ltd v First Quench Retailing Ltd*.[5]

The landlord and the tenant were in dispute as to what sums were due by the latter to the former. Under the Law Reform (Miscellaneous Revisions) (Scotland) Act 1985, irritancy for non-payment has to be preceded by an ultimatum, sometimes called a pre-irritancy notice. In September 2002 the landlord served a pre-irritancy notice, followed, on 8 October 2002, by a notice of irritancy. Despite this, the tenant continued to tender, and the landlord continued to accept, the quarterly rent, and this carried on until November 2003. Presumably the tenant remained in occupation. The landlord then raised an action for declarator of irritancy. The tenant defended the case on the merits, but also pled that even if an irritancy had been incurred (which was denied), the landlord was personally barred from insisting on it because of the continued acceptance of rent.

---

1 For a discussion see K G C Reid, *The Law of Property in Scotland* (1996) para 699.
2 In this connection see also the discussion of *Allan v Armstrong* 2004 GWD 37-768 at p 105.
3 (1876) 4 R 236.
4 Even if the disposition is reduced, however, the buyer, if in possession, will retain the property unless he is judged to have been fraudulent or careless. See Land Registration (Scotland) Act 1979 s 9(3)(a)(iii). It is not clear that carelessness equates to the bad faith required for the offside goals rule. See Scottish Law Commission, Discussion Paper on *Land Registration: Void and Voidable Titles* (Scot Law Com DP No 125 (2004); available on http:// www.scotlawcom.gov.uk) para 6.10.
5 2004 GWD 33-678.

The Sheriff (C A L Scott), after a careful review of the authorities, took the view that the mere fact of continued acceptance of rent does not create personal bar against the landlord, and held that a proof would be needed of the whole circumstances. This is consistent with the approach of the Inner House in *HMV Fields Properties Ltd v Bracken Self Selection Fabrics Ltd*,[1] in which it was held, on the particular facts of that case, that acceptance of rent did not bar the enforcement of irritancy.

Modern academic writing has been developing a more robust structure for the law of personal bar.[2] This requires that for a person (A) to be barred from the exercise of a right (such as a right to irritate), A must have behaved in a manner which is inconsistent with the exercise of the right in circumstances which create unfairness for another person (B). In many cases B will be able to establish that element of unfairness because of reliance—because B has relied upon A's conduct and would suffer prejudice if the right were now to be exercised. The problem in landlord and tenant cases is that the tenant wishes to preserve the *status quo*—to bar the landlord from changing or even terminating the landlord–tenant relationship; and it is meaningless to look for reliance or change of position when what the tenant wants most of all is to carry on exactly as before.[3] In practice if reliance is not in issue, a landlord who accepts rent after irritancy will not find it easy to rebut a plea of personal bar. As Lord Coulsfield said in *HMV Fields*, 'acceptance of rent is, in all normal circumstances, an act so unequivocal that it must be taken to amount to a waiver of an irritancy'.[4]

Is a successor landlord bound?

In *Allan v Armstrong*[5] a firm of architects took premises on a 25-year lease from Dunedin Property Investment Co Ltd (DPI). There were missives of let followed by a lease. The missives provided for a break option in favour of both the landlord and the tenant, but the lease was silent on the point. The missives contained a two-year non-supersession clause but thereafter DPI agreed that 'the missives will remain in full force and effect until the date immediately following the tenth anniversary of the date of entry'. Later still DPI sold the property to Midland Bank Pension Fund (MBPF). When the tenth anniversary came, the tenant sought to exercise the break option, but MBPF claimed that the option was not binding on it. At this point the partners of the now-dissolved firm of architects sued their solicitors for negligence.

It would perhaps have been more convenient if the pursuer had first litigated with the landlord on the effectiveness of the break option. Since it had not done so, the present action had to determine the hypothetical question of what the outcome of that litigation would have been if it had taken place.

---

1 1991 SLT 31.
2 Elspeth Reid, 'Personal Bar: Case-Law in Search of Principle' (2003) 7 *Edinburgh Law Review* 340 esp at 348–389.
3 Ibid p 357.
4 1991 SLT 31, 37K.
5 2004 GWD 37-768.

The defender pled (i) that its client had been told that there might be problems enforcing the break option against a singular successor of the landlord but that the client had decided to go ahead anyway, (ii) that MBPF had been aware of the provisions of the missives when it bought the property and accordingly was bound by their terms, and (iii)—seemingly on an alternative basis to the previous argument—that the break option was indeed not binding on MBPF, but it would not have been binding even if it had been part of the lease because a break option is not *inter naturalia* of a lease and so cannot bind singular successors. Temporary Judge T G Coutts ordered a proof before answer to determine whether or not MBPF knew about the terms of the missives.

The case raises some difficult issues. When property is subject to a lease and the owner sells, the new owner is normally bound by the lease. That has been so ever since the Leases Act 1449. But the new owner is not necessarily bound by all the provisions of the lease. Only such provisions as are 'natural' (*inter naturalia*) are binding on a singular successor.[1] If the lease provides that the landlord is to dance a jig every Christmas Day that is not a provision which belongs to the 'nature' of a lease and so will not bind a new owner. Although the question of whether a break option is *inter naturalia* has never been litigated, we would suggest that it must be. A break option is simply a provision about the length of the lease. It is difficult to think of anything more central to a lease than that.

But the break option was not in the lease itself but in a collateral document; and in general a successor is bound by the lease alone. He is bound by real rights and not by personal rights. In *Optical Express (Gyle) Ltd v Marks & Spencer plc*[2] one of the points at issue was whether a back letter could be regarded as a variation of the lease, the implication being that if it was not then a successor would not be bound. If that is the right approach then presumably missive terms could never bind a successor because missive terms are prior to the lease and so could hardly be regarded as varying it.

In *Allan v Armstrong* the defender sought to meet these difficulties by recourse to the so-called 'offside goals rule'. This is the rule that a real right granted in breach of a pre-existing contract or other obligation is voidable at the instance of the creditor in that obligation if the grantee knew of the obligation.[3] There was indeed a close precedent from the sheriff court. In *Davidson v Zani*[4] the tenant had an option to purchase. Such a provision is almost certainly not *inter naturalia* of a lease. Nevertheless it was held that the singular successor of the owner knew of the provision and was bound by it, on the basis of the offside goals rule. It is respectfully suggested that *Davidson v Zani* was wrongly decided. The offside goals rule can be activated only if a real right is granted in breach of a pre-existing obligation. But the real right granted in that case—by disposition of the landlord's interest—did not breach a pre-existing obligation. The option was not such an

1 On the *inter naturalia* doctrine see Angus McAllister, *Scottish Law of Leases* (3rd edn 2002) paras 2.31 ff.
2 2000 SLT 644, discussed in *Conveyancing 2000* pp 56–60.
3 Or did not give value. See K G C Reid, *The Law of Property in Scotland* (1996) paras 695 ff. *Rodger v Paton* 2004 GWD 19-425 may be an example. See p 103 above.
4 1992 SCLR 1001.

obligation. The analysis in *Allan v Armstrong* is the same. The lease imposed no prohibition on transfer of the landlord's interest. The break clause was not such a prohibition. It could not bind a successor merely because the successor knew of its existence.[1]

The unreasonably unconsenting landlord

Once upon a time the question of whether a lessee could assign or sub-let was dealt with in one of three ways. In the first place, the lease might be silent on the point, in which case the default rules of common law would apply. In the second place it might forbid assignation and sub-letting. In the third place it might allow them. In all three cases one knew reasonably accurately where one was. But relatively recently in legal history—probably in the 1960s but perhaps slightly earlier—a new form of alienation clause began to become common. It probably began in Glasgow but in any event spread quickly. It came from England. It provided that the lessee could not assign or sub-let without the consent of the landlord, but also provided that the landlord's consent was not to be unreasonably withheld. It was thus a compromise. Since reasonableness lay at the heart of the alienation clause, plenty of scope for dispute arose. But since the clause was of English origin, there was at least the benefit of the English case law.

One tends to associate this type of alienation clause with the 25-year commercial lease—another English import. But in fact in *Scottish Property Investment Co Ltd v Scottish Provident Ltd*[2] the lease (which was entered into in 1970) was for 98 years.[3] The property was an office block at the corner of 8 St Andrew Square and 21 South St David Street, Edinburgh. The alienation clause bound the lessee:

> ... not to assign transfer[4] sub-let or part with or share the possession of the subjects or any part thereof without the previous consent in writing of the Landlords and in any event not to assign[5] less than the lease of the whole of the leased premises PROVIDED that such consent shall not be unreasonably withheld in the case of a respectable and responsible sub-tenant or assignee.

In 2003 the tenant asked the landlord to consent to a sub-let of part of the building. The landlord refused, on the ground that the proposed sub-tenant wished to use the premises for purposes not permitted by the user clause in

---

1 Similarly, the argument based on the offside goals rule failed in *Optical Express (Gyle) Ltd v Marks & Spencer plc* 2000 SLT 644. See A J M Steven, 'Keeping the Goalposts in Sight' 2000 SLT (News) 143.
2 2004 GWD 6-120. See David Cabrelli, 'Landlord's refusal of a tenant's application for consent to assignation of lease: an update' (2004) 70 *Greens Property Law Bulletin* 1.
3 The future legal historian will have much fun tracing developments in lease practice in the second half of the twentieth century. This was also the time when the modern rent review clause was developing. For instance, in the same year (1970) that the present lease was granted, Aberdeen City Council was granting commercial leases with rent reviews every 21 years: see *City of Aberdeen Council v Clark* 1999 SLT 613. Another example of a 21-year rent review, dating from 1967, can be found in *Beard v Beveridge, Herd & Sandilands* 1990 SLT 609. For a 20-year review period in a lease granted as late as 1977 see *Cummins Engine Co Ltd v Inland Revenue* 1982 SLT 170.
4 The nature of the contrast between 'assign' and 'transfer' is perhaps not immediately obvious.
5 No mention here of 'transfer' or of 'sub-letting'.

the lease. The tenant then claimed that the refusal was unreasonable, that the refusal was a material breach of contract, and intimated that it was rescinding the contract of lease. The tenant then raised the present action for declarator of the foregoing.

In *Killick v Second Covent Garden Property Co Ltd*,[1] the Court of Appeal had held that it is never reasonable for a landlord to withhold consent on the ground that the proposed assignee intends to breach the user clause. The reason was that the user clause would be just as enforceable against the assignee as it was against the previous lessee, so that the landlord's rights would be unaffected. The same reasoning applies, *mutatis mutandis*, to sub-letting. The *Killick* decision was thus favourable to the pursuer. But in *Ashworth Frazer Ltd v Gloucester City Council*,[2] the House of Lords overruled *Killick*. The House of Lords held that in such circumstances a refusal of consent *may* be unreasonable, but is not *automatically* unreasonable. There is, said the House, no rule of law to the effect that refusal on this ground is an unreasonable refusal. The reasonableness of refusal of consent is always a question of fact. Although an English decision of the House of Lords is not a binding precedent in a case of this sort, it is of considerable persuasive value. The Lord Ordinary (Mackay of Drumadoon) preferred the approach of *Ashworth Frazer* to that of *Killick*, and accordingly held that a proof would be necessary on the question of reasonableness.

In fact the user clause in the lease was obscure. It said:

> The subjects hereby let are let for the purpose only of banking and office premises in connection with the tenants' business of Bankers and Financiers and all matters necessary therefor or such purposes as the Landlords in their absolute discretion may from time to time approve.

It is apparent that this provision was oddly drafted. If it had just said that 'the subjects hereby let are let for the purpose only of banking and office premises' then that would still have left the problem of whether the property could be used either for banking *or* for offices or whether both uses had to be combined. But, even worse, it added 'in connection with the tenants' business of Bankers and Financiers'. This seems to mean the business of the *original* lessees. But assignees or sub-tenants would presumably be carrying on their *own* business. Even if that business happened to be of that of 'Bankers and Financiers' it would still not be the business of the original lessees.

Rescinding a lease for material breach

At this stage of *Scottish Property Investment Co Ltd v Scottish Provident Ltd* the issue of the right to rescind was not considered. The idea of rescinding a lease is not one that is universally familiar. Yet a lease is a contract. Indeed it is one of the so-called 'nominate contracts' based ultimately on the contract of *locatio-conductio*

---

1 [1973] 1 WLR 658.
2 [2001] 1 WLR 2180.

of Roman law. It is a general principle of the law of contract that material breach justifies rescission. This principle applies to leases as it does to other contracts. Authority is sparse but does exist: see for example *Davie v Stark*[1] and *McKimmie's Trs v Armour*.[2] Whether unreasonable refusal to consent to an assignation or sub-lease would constitute a breach justifying rescission is another matter. The point has never been decided, but in *Scotmore Developments v Anderton*[3] the Inner House said, in an *obiter dictum*, that 'we are inclined to the view' that it would indeed justify rescission.

DESCRIPTIONS, BOUNDARIES AND PRESCRIPTION

Descriptions: conflicting elements

In Sasine titles land may be described in different ways: by words, by plan, by measurements of boundaries, by superficial area. If more than one method is used, the results are likely to be mutually reinforcing. Where they are not—where two elements in the description are in irreconcilable conflict[4]—the position is usually resolved in practice by a statement as to the status of the plan. If the plan is stated to be demonstrative it must give way to other elements; if, as is unusual, it is stated to be taxative, it prevails over other elements.[5] But what happens if no statement is made as to the plan and yet the elements conflict? Two new cases provide useful illustrations of the difficulties and of possible solutions.

Plans v words

In *Rutco Incorporated v Jamieson*[6] a feu disposition described land as:

> ALL and WHOLE the lands and estate of Gannochy in the Parishes of Edzell and Lethnot and Navar and County of Angus all as delineated and contained within the boundaries coloured purple on the plan annexed and signed as relative hereto … but excepting from the said lands and estate that part thereof belonging to the Trustees acting under a Deed of Trust granted by me dated Thirty First March and registered in the Books of Council and Session on Twenty Sixth July both in the year nineteen hundred and fifty one and conveyed or about to be conveyed by the said last mentioned Trustees to the said Herbert Frederick Brudenell Foster, Anthony Biddulph and Gordon

---

1 (1876) 3 R 1114.
2 (1899) 2 F 156. See further Martin Hogg, 'To Irritate or to Rescind? Two Paths for the Landlord?' 1999 SLT (News) 1, and Angus McAllister, *Scottish Law of Leases* (3rd edn 2002) para 4.22.
3 1996 SC 368.
4 The choice between two elements arises only where the conflict cannot be reconciled. For instance, if the verbal description can be read in two ways, but the plan is consistent with only one of them, the fact that the plan is declared to be demonstrative does not matter: in such a case the plan is decisive.
5 The former rule was given effect in respect of one of the deeds considered in *Rutco Incorporated v Jamieson* 2004 GWD 30-620. Thus Lord Kingarth (para 17): 'That plan, of course, was declared to be demonstrative only, and would not take precedence over words of description, if they clearly indicated that a smaller area was being conveyed.'
6 2004 GWD 30-620.

Nicholson Hunter as trustees foresaid, as said part of the said lands and estate is shown hatched black on the said plan annexed and signed as relative hereto.

The difficulty affected the exception. As shown in the plan, the exception[1] included a substantial area of some 400 acres known as the Shank of Freoch. But the land which, in terms of the description, belonged to the Trustees and was to be conveyed on did not include the additional land. There was no declaration as to whether the plan was taxative or demonstrative. Which should prevail: the verbal description or the plan? Unhappily, but correctly, the answer given by Lord Kingarth was that there were 'no hard and fast rules of construction in such cases' although, if anything, a verbal description should be taken as controlling'.[2] Indeed Professor Gordon, in a passage cited by the court, has gone so far as to offer the rule that '[i]n general it would seem that a verbal description of the boundaries will be regarded as controlling the extent of the land granted and as overruling conflicting indications',[3] but much turns on the words 'in general' and the case law discloses a confused and confusing picture. Perhaps the only true rule is that there is no rule. As a result it may often be difficult to establish conclusive priority without the help of prescription help which, as will be seen later, was forthcoming in *Rutco*.

Plans v presumptions

Where land adjoins water certain presumptions operate as to the location of the boundary.[4] In the case of non-tidal rivers, the presumption is of ownership to the mid-point (*ad medium filum*). And that presumption, it has been held, operates even where the land is described as bounded 'by' the river.[5] So the presumption is sufficiently robust to displace the usual rule that where property is bounded 'by' something, the bounding feature is excluded from the land. But if the presumption can thus overcome words can it also overcome plans? That was one of the issues litigated in *Dalton v Turcan Connell (Trustees) Ltd*.[6] The pursuer sought declarator of ownership of various properties in Edinburgh including, at a certain point, the *alveus* of the Water of Leith. The deed plan showed a boundary which excluded the river. It was held that the presumption was defeated by the plan. This does not make new law: a decision of 1862 was to the same effect.[7] But it is a useful reminder of the limits of presumptions.

Not all issues in this area are yet settled. In *Dalton* the land was described as lying to the 'north side of the Water of Leith'. The result might possibly have been different if the land had been described as bounded 'by' the river.

---

1 Which was an area hatched black. A complication was that the Shank of Freoch, although hatched black, was also, and uniquely, over-coloured in blue.
2 Paragraph 14.
3 W M Gordon, *Scottish Land Law* (2nd edn 1999) para 4-08.
4 K G C Reid, *The Law of Property in Scotland* (1996) para 278(3).
5 Eg *Gibson v Bonnington Sugar Refining Co Ltd* (1869) 7 M 394.
6 2005 SCLR 159 (Notes).
7 *North British Railway Co v Magistrates of Hawick* (1862) 1 M 200.

Conflicts in the Land Register

Conflicting elements in descriptions are usually regarded as a feature of Sasine titles. But the same problem could arise in the Land Register. For property in a title sheet is typically described twice, once by postal address or other general description and then again by plan. But they might disagree. Suppose that a title sheet gives the address as 43 Acacia Avenue but shows number 45 on the title plan. Does the person registered as proprietor own number 43 or number 45—or both or neither? In Sasine titles the rule (if there is one) is that the plan must give way to the verbal description, unless declared taxative. In Land Register titles the rule (if there is one) is likely to be the opposite. The Land Register is plan-based. In making up a title sheet the Keeper is directed by the legislation to enter 'a description of the land which shall consist of or include a description of it based on the Ordnance Map'.[1] There is no requirement to include a verbal description. The description by plan is thus the 'main' description.

In a muddle like this matters are more readily put right in a case involving the Land Register than the Register of Sasines, for possession is likely to indicate which of the two descriptions is correct and the Register can be rectified accordingly.[2] But the question of who owned what *before* rectification will remain open and, in some cases, important.

Prescription: foundation writs

What qualities are needed if a deed is to found prescription? The answer is given in s 1 of the Prescription and Limitation (Scotland) Act 1973. The deed must be recorded in the Register of Sasines.[3] It must be sufficient in respect of its terms to constitute the title being sought (and so must not be invalid *ex facie*). And it must contain a 'description habile to include the particular land'. *Rutco Incorporated v Jamieson*[4] is a useful reminder that for a description to be habile to include the land it is not necessary to apply the most natural interpretation of the words used. The question is merely whether inclusion of the land is a *possible* interpretation. If so, the description is habile. The rule was expressed by Lord Kingarth in this way:[5]

> It is clear that a party seeking to establish right to land by proof of possession founded upon a habile title does not need to show that the land was in fact conveyed by that title, or that the proper and only reasonable construction is to that effect. Rather, it seems plain, it is enough to show that that title in question is capable, or susceptible,

---

1 Land Registration (Scotland) Act 1979 s 6(1)(a).
2 Is the owner who thus conclusively gains, say, 43 Acacia Avenue (being the property he possessed) then entitled to indemnity for the definitive loss of number 45? The answer depends on what is taken to be the legal effect of the original registration.
3 Positive prescription can also operate in the Land Register. But it is unusual for it to do so, and the principles are not the same as for the Sasine Register. Land Register prescription is not covered here.
4 2004 GWD 30-620.
5 Paragraphs 12 and 13.

of being construed in a way consistent with the possession which has followed. Only a title 'obviously and indubitably exclusive' (such as, for example, a bounding title) could not form the basis beyond its terms.

This is a low standard—so low indeed that it may put into question the value of insisting on a title at all. (Many other countries do not.) But among its advantages is a sure solution to the problem, discussed above, of competing elements in a description. If a description contains three separate elements, each indicating different boundaries, the title is habile in respect of any of the possible sets of boundaries. Possession for the prescriptive period will do the rest. Thus it was that in *Rutco* itself the title, though subject to contradictions only some of which were mentioned above, was nonetheless a good foundation writ for the acquisition of the Shank of Freoch.

Prescription: walking on water

For prescription a habile title must be followed by possession for 10 years. But not all property is readily susceptible of possession. In *Dalton v Turcan Connell (Trustees) Ltd*[1] the thing to be possessed was the bed (*alveus*) of a section of the Water of Leith. How is a river bed to be possessed? The issue has been considered once before in recent years, in the context of whether a person was a proprietor in possession for the purposes of registration of title. In that case it was held that the removal of a rival's marker posts was not possession. Nor could possession of the bank be treated as possession of the *alveus*.[2] The possessory acts in *Dalton* were, if anything, even less convincing. They consisted merely of the fact that the river was crossed by a bridge which supported pipes. It was not suggested that the pipes were used. The court rejected this as obviously insufficient. It seems unlikely that actual use of the bridge, whether by pipes or people, would have made any difference. It would have evidenced only possession of the bridge and not of the *alveus* beneath.

STAMP DUTY LAND TAX[3]

Introduction

It is safe to say that the introduction of stamp duty land tax has not been among the happier experiences of recent law reform. It provides no comparison with the unbridled joy among practitioners which has accompanied the abolition of the feudal system and the legislation consequent upon that major change. Practitioners are not alone in worrying about the new tax—the Inland Revenue itself seems far from thrilled about aspects of what it has done. More to the point, it is not exactly clear about the new law and seems to delight in keeping such insights as it does

---

1 2005 SCLR 159 (Notes).
2 *Safeway Stores plc v Tesco Stores Ltd* 2004 SC 29.
3 This part is contributed by Alan Barr of the University of Edinburgh.

have to itself. Practitioners are often reduced to having to gamble on what the legislation might mean.

The Finance Act 2004 has not improved the position either in substance or in form. There are large quantities of new provisions, although some are newer than others. For example, part 2 of sch 39 is headed 'Re-enactment, with changes, of amendments made by section 109 Regulations'. This is a reminder that the original legislation, which derives from the ancient history of the Finance Act 2003, was full of gaps and errors. Some attempt was made to cure these by some very detailed Regulations, brought into force (and print) just before SDLT itself on 1 December 2003. But these Regulations had a limited shelf life and had to be replaced within 18 months. So the cure has been re-enacted—but 'with changes'. Unhappily, these changes are not highlighted in the new legislation and are not easy to spot. As this example shows, it is necessary to be exceptionally careful when dealing with anything other than the most standard of transactions in relation to SDLT. The chances of error are greatly increased by the piecemeal and constantly altering rules.

Partnership transactions

The biggest change of substance in Finance Act 2004 relates to partnership transactions. These are dealt with in sch 41, which replaces Finance Act 2003 sch 15 part 3.

It may be recalled that part 1 of sch 15 of the 2003 Act makes general provisions, the most important of which is that the separate juristic personality of a partnership is disregarded, and that a partnership is to be treated as continuing notwithstanding a change in its members.

Part 2 of sch 15 deals with 'ordinary partnership transactions', including the responsibilities of partners and their joint and several liability where, for example, a partnership purchases land from an unconnected third party.

The new part 3 deals with 'transactions to which special provisions apply'. They are certainly special and many may consider them impenetrable. One of the main reasons that they are so impenetrable derives from an attempt to reduce or remove the charge on family partnerships. The special provisions may apply to certain transactions in three circumstances:[1]

(a) the transfer of a chargeable interest to a partnership
(b) the transfer of an interest in a partnership, and
(c) the transfer of a chargeable interest from a partnership

At first sight, this might seem to include virtually anything involving both a partnership and land but that is not so. For instance, the special provisions in relation to the transfer *to* a partnership apply only where the transferor is a partner or someone connected with a partner, or receives an interest in the partnership in return for the chargeable interest.[2] So a true third party sale to the partnership

---

1 Finance Act 2003 sch 15 para 9 (as substituted by Finance Act 2004 sch 41 para 1).
2 FA 2003 sch 15 para 10(1) (as substituted).

is not covered by these rules (although it will of course be covered by the normal rules).

Transfers of land into a partnership

As regards the transfer of land to a partnership, the most difficult issue is likely to be chargeable consideration. To give a flavour of the (unnecessary) complexity it is worth quoting the legislation:[1]

(2) The chargeable consideration for the transaction shall (subject to paragraph 13) be taken to be equal to

$$(RCP \times MV) + (RCP \times AC)$$

where –

RCP is the relevant chargeable proportion,
MV is the market value of the interest transferred, and
AC is the actual consideration for the transaction.

(3) The relevant chargeable proportion in relation to the market value of the interest transferred is

$$(100 - SLP)\%$$

where SLP is the sum of the lower proportions.

(4) The relevant chargeable proportion in relation to the actual consideration for the transaction is

$$SLP\%$$

where SLP is the sum of the lower proportions.

This is, to say the least, uninviting material. 'RCP' (the 'relevant chargeable proportion') has a different meaning in relation to the market value as compared to its meaning in relation to the actual consideration.

The net effect is that there is a need to distinguish two things: the market value and the actual consideration. SDLT may be chargeable on both, or on elements of both. To generalise, it seems that the charge will normally not arise in relation to the market value where the partners are connected other than as partners; but this will not exclude the charge in such partnerships where there is actual consideration. And what constitutes actual consideration remains a subject of some mystery.

Transfers of partnership interest

The second possible category of charge under the special provisions arises where there is a transfer of a partnership interest; consideration is given for that transfer; and the partnership holds an 'interest in land'.[2] This involves a possible charge on the admission of a partner or on changes in profit-sharing ratio, at least where there is a partner reducing his interest or withdrawing who gets money's worth out of the partnership as a result of the change. This charge is only based on

---

1 FA 2003 sch 15 para 10 (as substituted).
2 FA 2003 sch 15 para 14(1) (as substituted).

market value of the relevant land, not on the amount of consideration passing.[1] There are also anti-avoidance provisions aimed at situations where there has been a nil or small charge on the introduction of land to the partnership, followed by changes in partnership interests.[2]

Transfers of land out of a partnership

Since there is an actual transfer of land, a charge can arise. Again it is based on a combination of market value and actual consideration. But it will only apply to the extent that actual consideration is given by the partner taking land out, or to the extent that he is getting more than he is entitled in terms of what has already been charged on the entry of the land to the partnership or previous changes in partnership interests. To this extent the rules are thus relieving provisions.[3]

Vigilance and reflection

It follows from what has been said that in any situation where there is a partnership movement, or a movement of partnership land into or out of a partnership (including on the dissolution of the partnership), it will be necessary to consider whether these special provisions will apply. Often the result of considering them will be that no charge is due, especially in relation to family partnerships—but getting to that result may take a bit of effort. Above all, it must not be assumed that because no money is changing hands, or only money within partnership accounts, there is no SDLT charge. That may very well be wrong. And since it may well be possible to change partnership interests, to bring property into and out of partnership, and to create and dissolve partnerships without the need to register any document, these new provisions are perhaps the best example yet of the fact that SDLT is nothing to do with the stamping of deeds. It is a tax on transactions—and there may be more chargeable partnership transactions around than were ever realised.

Other changes

A number of other changes are made in Finance Act 2004. Many of these are rather mysterious and are probably ill-targeted anti-avoidance provisions, which of course catch the entirely innocent as well as the tax avoider. There are also problems of organisation. In particular the distinction between changes made in the body of the 2004 Act and those made by part 1 of sch 39 (general amendments) is not immediately obvious. For example, s 297 is headed, and deals with, some aspects of leases, including variations. But sch 39 para 2 deals specifically with the very same topic. And para 11 of sch 39 has a number of further minor changes

---

1 FA 2003 sch 15 para 14(6), (7) (as substituted).
2 FA 2003 sch 15 para 17 (as substituted).
3 This (imperfectly) summarises the complex provisions found in FA 2003 sch 15 paras 18–24 (as substituted).

to the rules on leases contained in Finance Act 2003 sch 17A—which changed schedule is then somewhat bizarrely re-enacted in part 2 of the same sch 39.

Variations of lease

A variation of a lease is only to be treated as the acquisition and disposal of a chargeable interest where it takes effect, or is treated, as the grant of a new lease. This would seem to include lease extensions; it certainly includes variations to increase the rent, which are treated as a new lease for the amount of the increase.[1] An anti-avoidance provision extends chargeable land transactions to include lease variations under which the term or the rent is reduced.[2] This is aimed at sale transactions which start as long leases. The lease is then varied to remove demanding lease conditions in return for the bulk of the 'purchase' price. Such a variation will now be chargeable.

Executries

A new exemption is introduced—or confirmed—in relation to appropriations by executors from the estate of a deceased person in favour of beneficiaries, as long as no consideration is given. Previously, this would have fallen under the heading of transfers for nil consideration; now there is a specific exemption.[3] It is also confirmed that any debt assumed on such an appropriation will not count as chargeable consideration.[4] In a related area, it is confirmed that the exemption for deeds of variation[5] is not affected by consideration in the form of *other* variations in the estate.[6]

Charities relief

There are some slight changes, involving both tightening and relaxation, to the charities relief from SDLT.[7]

Building licences and sub-sales

A new s 44A is inserted into the Finance Act 2003[8] to deal with an avoidance device utilising 'building licences'. These involve a developer taking occupation without title, carrying out the development and then directing transfer to a third party purchaser. The intermediate transaction was apparently in danger of escaping SDLT. Further provisions dealing with sub-sales and other transfers of contractual

---

1 FA 2003 sch 17A para 13 (as substituted by FA 2004 sch 39 para 22).
2 FA 2004 s 297.
3 FA 2003 sch 3 para 3A (inserted by FA 2004 s 300).
4 FA 2003 sch 4 para 8A(1) (inserted by FA 2004 s 301(5)).
5 FA 2003 sch 3 para 4.
6 FA 2003 sch 4 para 8A(2) (inserted by FA 2004 s 301(5)).
7 FA 2004 s 302.
8 By FA 2004 sch 39 para 4.

rights largely follow from the new s 44A but are wider in scope.[1] Supplementary provisions relate to the effective date and the notification of such transactions, emphasising the dangerous self-assessed nature of SDLT. The whole area of sub-sales and nominee purchasers requires a great deal of care and attention if double charges are to be avoided.

Contracts before 11 July 2003

11 July 2003 was the date of Royal Assent of that year's Finance Act. The implementation of contracts from before that date is generally unaffected by SDLT. Such implementation would generally fall under the rules on stamp duty and thus in certain circumstances would not involve tax at all (eg where no deed required to be registered). This transitional relief is not now to apply where the pre-11 July 2003 contract has been varied or assigned after 11 July 2003.[2] The net spreads and the mesh gets smaller.

Administrative changes

The assignation of a lease is to be notifiable where at the time of the assignation the grant of the lease itself would have been notifiable, or where there is consideration for the assignation chargeable to SDLT in its own right.[3] The second is confirmation but the first is new, as the assignation of a lease for no consideration (whatever the terms of the lease) would generally not have been notifiable.[4]

Residential purchases for less than £1,000 are made exempt from notification, which may be useful in transactions which tidy up boundaries and the like.[5] Unfortunately, the exemption will not affect rural non-residential transactions, which are perhaps where such small purchases are most likely.

A new sch 11A to the Finance Act 2003[6] introduces a procedure for matters such as repayments of tax and claims for exemption. Hitherto this has been dealt with through the notification and return requirements, and it had been hoped that returns and the amendment process would preclude the need for a special procedure for claims.

EX FACIE ABSOLUTE DISPOSITIONS

Until 1970, it was competent to transfer ownership to a creditor in security of a loan.[7] This was called the *ex facie* absolute disposition. Viewed from the standpoint

---

1 FA 2004 sch 39 para 5.
2 FA 2004 sch 39 para 12.
3 FA 2004 s 298.
4 FA 2003 s 77(2A) (inserted by FA 2004 s 298(2)).
5 FA 2003 s 77(3)(b) (as substituted by FA 2004 s 298(2)). This is apparently aimed at purchasers in England and Wales of reversionary interest under long leases.
6 Inserted by FA 2004 s 299(3), sch 40.
7 Section 9(3) of the Conveyancing and Feudal Reform (Scotland) Act 1970 provided that any such transactions entered into after 1970 would be invalid.

of Roman law, it was an example of *fiducia cum creditore contracta*. If the loan was repaid, the creditor would reconvey. If it was not, the creditor would sell. Most loans secured on heritable property were done in this manner.

Sexton v Coia[1] was a dispute about the ownership of property at 27 and 29 Main Street, Coatbridge, arising out of an *ex facie* absolute disposition. The parties have, it seems, been litigating for more than 30 years: the present action, however, has been before the courts merely since 1997. Even the latest decision apparently will not bring the dispute to an end. As the Lord Ordinary, Lord Emslie, said:[2]

> I now dismiss the action. In one sense, this is a step which I take with some regret, because it is obvious that dismissal of the action will not resolve the parties' long-standing dispute regarding ownership of the subjects.

The dismissal of the action was not because the court held that the defenders had a good title. On that matter no decision was made. Nor, indeed, was it held, strictly speaking, that the pursuers had a bad title. The action was dismissed because the pursuers had not relevantly pled that they had a good title. The pursuers were party litigants, and the Lord Ordinary found their averments 'rambling and discursive ... obscure and difficult to follow'. His difficulties were made greater by lack of access to the relevant deeds: 'None of the apparently significant charters, dispositions, deeds and documents is incorporated *brevitatis causa* in the pleadings, and neither party sought to refer me to the terms of any of them at any stage of the debate.'[3] The case leaves the dispute where it was. Possibly the pursuers did have a good title, but merely failed to present it properly. If so they are free to litigate again, because decree of dismissal does not settle a dispute. Equally possibly, the defenders had a good title. A third possibility is that neither side had a good title. So much of the story is obscure that it is difficult to form a view. But in all the confusion, there is a nugget of pure gold. That, however, comes later.

The tale is one of horrendous complexity. It is a tale of actions, interdicts, declarators, reductions, notices of title, dispositions, more dispositions, yet more dispositions, back-letters, deaths, confirmations, trusts, charters of novodamus and what you will. Once upon a time Charles Coia owned the subjects. In 1927 he disponed them to Eugenio Coia. That was the last moment of clarity. The disposition was an *ex facie* absolute disposition.

The present phase of litigation was between the successors of the respective parties, both laying claim to ownership of the property. The pursuers founded on Eugenio Coia's rights and the defenders founded on Charles Coia's rights. In this action the pursuers sought declarator that they were the owners, and

---

1 There were two stages of a single debate, with amendment happening in between. An interim opinion was issued after the first stage of the debate, summarised at 2004 GWD 17-376. The final opinion is summarised at 2004 GWD 38-781. These two opinions will be referred to as the 'January Opinion' and the 'November Opinion'.
2 Paragraph 18 of the November Opinion.
3 Paragraph 14 of the January Opinion.

for reduction of (i) the confirmation in favour of the second defender (Carmela Coia) as executrix of the late Charles Coia in 1969, (ii) a notice of title in favour of Carmina Coia or Taylor in 1996, (iii) a notice of title in favour of the second defender in 1999, and (iv) an unregistered disposition by the second defender in favour of herself and the first defender dated 3 December 1999. Carmina Coia or Taylor had been a defender in the action when it was raised in 1997 but had since died. The first defender, Marco Coia, was her executor.

Whether the 1927 loan had ever been repaid was a matter of dispute. The question of which party or parties had had possession since 1927 was also unclear. There was some suggestion that for much of that period it had been used by the Coia family in general.

The pursuers' title, as originally pled, was as follows. Eugenio (the creditor) had died in 1938 and his heir, Agostino Coia, had done nothing to complete a title. The pursuers had at some stage acquired the superiority and, having done so, had granted a charter of novodamus to Agostino's trustee, Gusto Coia, and this Gusto had in 1995 and 1996 granted two dispositions of the subjects to the pursuers.[1] Whether these dispositions had been registered in either the Register of Sasines or the Land Register was unclear. The pursuers did assert that land certificates had been issued to them, but the details remained wholly obscure. In the middle of the debate the pursuers amended their pleadings so as to aver that they also held a disposition from a successor of Charles Coia, the debtor. Whether this disposition had ever been registered is unclear. The nature of the defenders' alleged title does not emerge from the Lord Ordinary's opinion.

The Lord Ordinary held that the pursuers had not pled a stateable title. Gusto Coia might have been the trustee of Agostino, Eugenio's heir, but neither he nor Agostino had ever done anything to take up Eugenio's title. The title based on the charter of novodamus did not stand up. The superior held only the superiority and thus could not grant a title to the *dominium utile*. Nobody can give more right than they themselves have.[2] As for the amendment, which sought to found on a disposition to the pursuers from a successor of Charles Coia, the Lord Ordinary dismissed that too, and here one can surface from the confusion and uncertainty of the facts of the particular case into the bracing, if chill, air of legal theory.

An *ex facie* absolute disposition could be done in two ways:

(1) The debtor, who is owner, dispones to the creditor.
(2) The debtor is buying the property. He or she directs the seller to dispone direct to the creditor.

In both cases the creditor acquires an *ex facie* absolute title. The difference is that in a type (1) case the debtor was at one stage the owner, whereas in a type (2) case the debtor was never the owner.

---

1 Why two dispositions is unclear possibly one for No 27 and one for No 29.
2 *Nemo plus juris ad alium transferre potest quam ipse haberet.*

There existed disagreement about how the effect of the *ex facie* absolute disposition should be analysed.[1] In type (2) everyone agreed that the effect was that the creditor acquired the real right of ownership, and that the debtor had merely a personal right to a conveyance upon repayment.[2] The disagreement was about type (1). Some took the view that the effect was the same as type (2). Others took the view that the debtor remained owner, and that all that the creditor acquired was a subordinate real right. In other words, they took the view that the effect was the same as that of a bond and disposition in security, or, in modern terms, a standard security. This disagreement is an old chestnut, and today's youthful conveyancers who have hardly even heard of the *ex facie* absolute disposition do not know all the fun they have missed.

This disagreement was a major issue in *Sexton v Coia*, where the *ex facie* absolute disposition had been type (1). For the starting point of the whole case was this: once the 1927 disposition had been recorded in the Register of Sasines, who was the owner? In feudal terms, who was infeft and seised as of fee? Was it Charles? If so, anyone setting up a title now would need to derive that title from Charles. Or was it Eugenio? If so, anyone setting up a title now would need to derive that title from Eugenio.[3]

The predominant view of the law was that type (1) had the same effect as type (2), which is to say that the creditor acquired the real right of ownership, so that the debtor's reversionary right was a personal right. If that predominant view was correct, Eugenio had acquired ownership, albeit subject to Charles's right to a reconveyance upon repayment. But in 1899 in *Ritchie v Scott*[4] Lord Kinnear said that this standard view was not correct, and that an *ex facie* absolute disposition was, in terms of property law, like a bond and disposition in security, or, in modern terms, like a standard security. In a standard security, ownership is retained by the granter. The grantee does indeed acquire a real right, but it is a subordinate real right of security. Thus there are two real rights in the same property at the same time. If that approach was correct, the 1927 disposition did not transfer ownership to Eugenio.

In tabular form the position is thus:

Type of security	Debtor's right[5]	Creditor's right
Standard security	Real (ownership)	Real (security)
Bond and disposition in security	Real (ownership)	Real (security)
Ex facie absolute disposition (type 2)	Personal	Real (ownership)

1 For references, and exploration of the issues, see G L Gretton, 'Radical Rights and Radical Wrongs' 1986 *Juridical Review* 51 and 192.
2 And also a right to possess the property so long as the loan repayments were kept up.
3 Unless of course someone else could establish a title fortified by prescription.
4 (1899) 1 F 728.
5 The debtor's right can be described as a 'reversionary' right; but this leaves open the question of its precise nature in property law.

Type of security	Debtor's right	Creditor's right
Ex facie absolute disposition (type 1) – traditional view	Personal	Real (ownership)
Ex facie absolute disposition (type 1) – Lord Kinnear's view	Real (ownership)	Real (security)

Lord Kinnear's view gained strength when it was adopted by Professor Halliday. But the weight of authority was against it. Lord Emslie, in a careful examination of the authorities, felt able to reject Lord Kinnear's approach. Orthodoxy was thus affirmed. The effect, in terms of pure property law, of a type (1) *ex facie* absolute disposition is the same as that of type (2). Hence if there was indeed a disposition in favour of the pursuers by a successor of Charles Coia that could not help them, because Charles Coia had lost ownership in 1927 and seemingly neither he nor any successor had reacquired it. On this issue of pure property law the decision is to be welcomed.

TENEMENTS (SCOTLAND) ACT 2004

Introduction

The Tenements (Scotland) Act 2004 (asp 11) received Royal Assent on 22 October 2004 and, with the exception of s 18 (insurance), came into force on 28 November 2004, the day on which the feudal system was abolished.[1] Section 18 is expected to come into force during 2005.

The Act replaces the common law rules regulating tenements and known as 'the law of the tenement'.[2] That law was unsatisfactory in a number of respects. It was sometimes uncertain; it was sometimes unfair—particularly by imposing sole liability for the roof on the owner of the top flat; and it made no provision for management and inadequate provision for maintenance. The Act seeks to solve these problems. Under the Act all tenements are potentially subject to a management scheme set out in sch 1 to the Act and known as the Tenement Management Scheme. The Tenement Management Scheme provides both for management and for maintenance. Decisions are to be arrived at by a simple majority; and maintenance of the strategic parts of the building is a shared responsibility, usually on the basis of equality. At the same time, the Act takes the opportunity of clarifying the rules as to ownership.

The origins of the Act lie with the Scottish Law Commission's Report on the *Law of the Tenement*, which was published in 1998.[3] A full explanation of

---

1 Tenements (Scotland) Act 2004 (Commencement No 1) Order, SSI 2004/487.
2 For the common law of the tenement, see K G C Reid, *The Law of Property in Scotland* (1996) paras 227–252; W M Gordon, *Scottish Land Law* (2nd edn 1999) paras 15-35–15-48.
3 Scot Law Com No 162, 1998 (available on http://www.scotlawcom.gov.uk).

the Act, and of the policy behind it, will be found in the Law Commission's Report. The Act departs in a number of respects from the draft Bill put forward by the Scottish Law Commission. Quite often this is to take account of the Title Conditions (Scotland) Act 2003, which was not on the agenda at the time when the Commission reported in 1998. Further a small number of provisions which appeared in the Commission's Bill are omitted from the current Act as beyond the legislative competence of the Scottish Parliament, but it is understood that they are likely to be included in an order of the Westminster Parliament made under s 104 of the Scotland Act 1998.[1]

A default law

The common law of the tenement applied only to the extent that titles did not provide otherwise. It was thus a default law, providing rules where none otherwise existed. In modern practice titles often made detailed provision for matters such as ownership or maintenance, leaving little or nothing to the common law. When the Tenements Bill was first in Parliament, an initial controversy was whether its provisions should equally be in the nature of a default law, or whether they should be mandatory, over-ruling the titles. At stage 1 a number of those giving evidence spoke strongly in favour of a mandatory code. In the end, however, the Justice 2 Committee supported the principle of 'free variation', ie the principle that the titles could vary the underlying law.[2] That had been the view of the Scottish Executive and, before them, of the Scottish Law Commission.[3] Thus in principle the new law, like the old, is a default law. Indeed the whole reform can be characterised merely as a change in default rules. Out go the old rules and in come the new, but otherwise everything remains the same. In particular, provisions in the titles remain the same.

The default status means that if the titles provide for every matter which the Act provides for, the Act does not apply. But since the Act makes much fuller provision than the common law, it will be unusual for the Act not to apply at least to some extent. In addition, a few provisions of the Act—for example in relation to insurance, or access for repairs—are not default rules and apply whatever the titles may or may not say.

Meaning of 'tenement'

The Act is not confined to traditional Victorian stone tenements. Like the common law, it applies to any block of flats, of whatever size or age, and whether put to residential or to any other use.[4] Thus a 'tenement' includes a modern block of flats, or a conversion of a Victorian villa, or a tower block.

---

1 Clauses 20 and 21 of the Law Commission's Bill, conferring rights to have television aerials, satellite dishes and gas. See below. It is possible that other matters may also be included in a s 104 Order.
2 Justice 2 Committee, *Stage 1 Report on Tenements (Scotland) Bill* (2004) paras 20–22.
3 Scottish Law Commission, Report on *Law of the Tenement* paras 3.8 and 3.9.
4 T(S)A 2004 s 26(1).

Where, as traditionally, tenements are built in terraces, it may occasionally be difficult to tell where one tenement ends and the next begins. The problem is most likely to arise with corner buildings, or where what might be a single tenement is served by two closes. Another difficult case is the Victorian semi-detached house, where one half has been flatted and the other not: is the tenement then (i) the whole house, or (ii) merely the half that has been flatted? If, as in this last example, the structure of the building does not yield a clear answer, the titles will usually make the position plain. If maintenance of the whole building is a common responsibility, then the whole building is a tenement; but if the flatted half is treated separately from the non-flatted half, then only the former is a tenement. The Act expressly allows recourse to the titles for this purpose.[1]

The Act applies to all tenements, both new and old. Thus tenements already in existence on 28 November 2004 were immediately subject to the new law. And all tenements created after that date are, equally, affected.

Ownership

A tenement is a series of houses which, by some mischance, happen to have been built one on top of the other. That at least was the approach of the common law. This meant that little attention was paid to the building as a whole. Instead the focus was on the flats of which it was comprised. The result was uncompromisingly individualistic. Each flat comprised four walls, a floor and a ceiling. Each boundary was an exclusive part of the flat in question. For the top flat one of those boundaries was the roof, and for the bottom flat the solum, both being the sole property of the flat in question. Proceeding in this way, most of the tenement was rapidly accounted for, and there was little scope for common property.

With one minor exception (mentioned later), the Tenements Act simply reproduces the previous law as to ownership. There were two main reasons for what may seem an unduly cautious approach.[2] One was human rights. To alter the rules as to ownership would have been to redistribute existing rights and so risk a contravention of article 1 of the First Protocol of the European Convention on Human Rights.[3] The other reason was merit. Common property—scrupulously avoided by the common law—is often a highly unsatisfactory arrangement. Where resorted to in a tenement it is often as a means of achieving common maintenance. Under the Act, however, the prize of common maintenance comes without the price of common property, for the Tenement Management Scheme imposes maintenance obligations without reference to the question of ownership. As a result the need for common property is much reduced.

The new provisions are contained in ss 2 and 3 of the Act; and, as s 1 makes plain, they are default provisions and so subject to contrary provision in the titles

---

1 T(S)A 2004 s 26(2).
2 Scottish Law Commission, Report on the *Law of the Tenement* paras 3.3–3.5. For restrained criticism, see C G van der Merwe, 'The Tenement (Scotland) Act 2004: a brief evaluation' 2004 SLT (News) 211 at 211–213.
3 By s 29(2)(d) of the Scotland Act 1998 an Act of the Scottish Parliament is outside legislative competence so far as it is incompatible with any of the ECHR rights.

(or to positive prescription). Thus, in considering who owns what, the titles must be consulted and not just the general law.

In three respects the new provisions improve on the previous law. First, they are accessible and clear. Secondly, they resolve uncertainties. For example, there has always been doubt as to ownership of the common passage and stair.[1] Rankine thought that, while it was owned in common, owners dropped out at the point at which the stair ceased to give access to their particular flat, so that for example the final flight of stairs was owned only by the owners of the top flat or flats. Other writers took the view that the entire passage and stair was the common property of everyone. There was no decided case on the point. The Act awards ownership of the whole to everyone, thus copying the provision which is normally found in titles.[2] Thirdly, the new provisions fill gaps in the law, and, by means of a general provision as to pertinents,[3] anticipate future developments.

Registration of title increases the importance of these provisions. Unlike the position for other properties, the boundaries of flats are not shown on the title plan. Instead, reliance continues to be placed on a verbal description, drawn in many cases from an elderly Sasines writ, and the plan gives no more than the footprint of the building together with any ground forming part of the tenement. Other countries have often done better than this, providing detailed sectional plans in their registers. That idea was considered by the Scottish Law Commission but rejected as impracticable, following discussions with the Keeper.[4] In the absence of a sectional plan, the rules as to ownership contained in the Act assume considerable importance.

The Act approaches the question of ownership in two ways. One is to set the limits of each flat and the boundaries between them. The other is to award all remaining parts of the tenement to an individual flat or flats as pertinents. The relevant provisions, contained respectively in ss 2 and 3, may now be considered in turn.

Limits and boundaries

Section 2 applies to 'sectors', an expression which includes not only flats, but also closes, lifts and any other three-dimensional space.[5] ('Close' is the word used in the Act for what is sometimes called the common passage and stair.) The basic rule is the familiar one that 'the boundary between any two contiguous sectors is the median of the structure that separates them'.[6] This means that, for example –

- the boundary between two adjacent flats is the middle (*medium filum*) of the wall which separates them;

---

1 For an account of the dispute, see K G C Reid, *The Law of Property in Scotland* (1996) para 231.
2 T(S)A 2004 s 3(1), (2).
3 T(S)A 2004 s 4(4).
4 Scottish Law Commission, Report on the *Law of the Tenement* para 4.17.
5 T(S)A 2004 s 29(1).
6 T(S)A 2004 s 2(1).

- the boundary between a flat and the close is, likewise, the middle of the wall; and
- the boundary between a lower and an upper flat is the middle of the joists.

The absence of common property should be noted: each owner has exclusive rights to his or her own side of the boundary feature. However, a door or window which serves one flat only—for example the door into a flat from the close—is the sole property of the owner of that flat.[1]

The limits of a flat are thus (i) the median of any shared boundary, and (ii) the whole of any boundary which is not shared (eg an external wall).[2] Consistent with this are the special rules for the highest and the lowest flat, and for the close. The Act expresses the position thus:[3]

- 'A top flat extends to and includes the roof over that flat.'
- 'A bottom flat extends to and includes the solum under that flat.'
- 'A close extends to and includes the roof over, and the solum under, the close.'

As before, ownership of the solum includes ownership of the airspace directly above the tenement—a curious-sounding rule which upholds the importance of the land itself. For land is owned *a coelo usque ad centrum*,[4] a principle which has to be modified for tenements by excepting the intermediate flats. A new exception is added by the Act. Where the roof of a tenement is pitched, ownership of the roof includes ownership of the airspace above the roof, as far as its highest point. The purpose of conferring ownership of this wedge of airspace is to allow dormer windows—and to homologate the many dormers already built which encroach into the airspace of the owner of the solum.

Pertinents

Following the rules just discussed, not much of the tenement is left. As well as the individual flats, the roof and solum are also accounted for. That leaves only the close, any garden ground, chimney stacks, pipes and other miscellaneous parts. Just in the same way as break-off writs would typically include such items in the pertinents clause ('together with …'), so s 3 attaches the items to the flats as pertinents. Sometimes an item is attached solely to one flat. Much more commonly, however, the item is shared by some, or all, of the flats as common property. Except in the case of chimney stacks (discussed below), rights of common property are shared equally.[5]

The distribution effected by s 3 is as follows.

---

1 T(S)A 2004 s 2(2).
2 T(S)A 2004 s 2(1).
3 T(S)A 2004 s 2(3)–(5).
4 From the heavens to the centre of the earth.
5 T(S)A 2004 s 3(5).

Close

As already mentioned, the close is a pertinent of every flat in the building other than a main-door flat if there is no access from the close.[1] Thus the close is the common property of everyone. 'Close' is defined as 'a connected passage, stairs and landings within a tenement building which together constitute a common access to two or more of the flats'.[2] The rule is the same for lifts (other than a lift which serves one flat only).

Garden and other ground

Ground forming part of a tenement is owned, section by section, by the owner of 'the bottom flat most immediately adjacent'.[3] That is the same as the previous law, save that the Act makes an express exception for paths or other common means of access. Usually this rule is found to be unattractive (except, sometimes, for front gardens) and so is displaced in the titles. In particular it is normal for titles to make the back green common property.

Chimney stacks

Little used but prone to crumble and expensive to maintain, chimney stacks are the common property of the owners of the flats served by the stack in question. Following what was probably the common law position,[4] ownership is apportioned by reference to the number of flues which lead into the stack.[5]

Miscellaneous parts

What is left? Section 3(4) gives a non-exhaustive list: paths, outside stairs, fire escapes, rhones, pipes, flues, conduits, cables, and tanks. For such miscellaneous parts, ownership is determined by a service test. If the part serves one (and only one) flat, it attaches solely to that flat. If, however—as much more commonly—it serves two or more flats, it attaches to the flats in question as common property. The way in which this is done deserves attention. Even if one section of the thing serves only one flat and one section another, the thing is viewed as a whole, and each flat has common property in the whole.[6] The rule, in other words, is the same as for closes (mentioned above). An entryphone system, for example, is treated as a single thing and is the property of the owners of all the flats which it serves, despite the fact that individual wires might serve one flat and not another.

---

1 T(S)A 2004 s 3(1), (2).
2 T(S)A 2004 s 29(1).
3 T(S)A 2004 s 3(3).
4 *Whitmore v Stuart and Stuart* (1902) 10 SLT 290. This is a sheriff court decision which followed what was said to be the practice in Edinburgh.
5 T(S)A 2004 s 3(4), (5).
6 Like s 3(1), s 3(4) uses the phrase 'a right of common property in *(and in the whole of)*' the part in question.

Occasionally there might be doubt as to whether a part is one thing or two. Take the case of a path which runs from the street to the entrance to the close, but then continues round the side of the building, through a garden which is the sole property of a flat on the ground floor, finishing at a door leading only to that flat. Is there one path or two? If there is only one, it is the common property of everyone. But if, as seems more likely, the section of path which leads round the side is to be treated separately, then that section would be the sole property of the owner of the ground floor flat.

Section 3(4) is deliberately couched in general terms: it is a residual provision, applying to all *other* parts of a tenement. This acknowledges both the diversity of existing tenements and also, with advancing technology, the inevitable development of new things for which specific provision could not be made in the legislation.

Ownership not lost by non-use

Ownership is not lost by non-use. So if a water tank in the roof space formerly served eight flats but now serves only seven, the eighth flat retains a right of common ownership. This is likely to be important only in relation to maintenance. Like a number of other pertinents, water tanks are not among the strategic parts of a building. This means that they are commonly maintained only if they are common property or if a real burden so provides. If, therefore, a person were to lose ownership, he would lose with it any liability for maintenance (in the absence of a real burden).

Tenement Management Scheme

Under the Act every tenement is to have a management scheme, and frequent reference is made to 'the management scheme which applies as respects the tenement'.[1] In the absence of anything else, the management scheme which applies is the Tenement Management Scheme ('TMS'), which is set out in sch 1 to the Act. The TMS is thus a set of default rules—just in the same way as the rules as to ownership (set out in ss 2 and 3 and discussed above) are default rules. And, as with ownership, the rules are severable. Thus the TMS compromises six substantive rules (rules 2–7) and three ancillary rules (rules 1, 8 and 9) which amplify the substantive rules. It is possible for one substantive rule to apply but not another. A particular tenement, for example, may be subject to rule 3 of the TMS but not to rule 2. Furthermore, with the exception of rule 2 (which applies either entirely or not at all) it is possible—indeed will be normal—for *parts* of a rule to apply but for *other parts* not to apply. Whether a rule or part applies will depend on whether the title makes alternative provision by *tenement burden* (ie by a real burden which affects the tenement).[2] If the title is silent, the relevant

---

1 Defined in T(S)A 2004 s 27.
2 T(S)A 2004 s 29(1).

rule (or part rule) of the TMS applies. But if the title provides, the rule (or part rule) is superseded.[1]

It follows that the TMS does not apply at all if the title makes provision on all the matters which the TMS covers. However, few if any current titles will achieve this, if only because the TMS deals with certain matters—such as paying money for repairs in advance, or emergency repairs—which are not usually provided for in titles. Thus all—or practically all—tenements are subject to the TMS to some degree. In the future, however, it is possible that deeds of conditions will be drafted so as to ensure that the TMS does not apply.

There is one other case where the TMS does not apply. A separate management scheme, known as the Development Management Scheme ('DMS'), is introduced by the Title Conditions (Scotland) Act 2003.[2] The Scheme itself will be prescribed by an order made under s 104 of the Scotland Act 1998, probably during 2005. Once the s 104 order is made, developers will be able to apply the DMS to property—including tenemental property—by registering a deed of application under s 71 of the Title Conditions Act. They will probably not do so unless the development is extensive, for the DMS is likely to be complex and suitable only for large developments. Where the DMS is applied in this way, the TMS is automatically excluded.[3]

The possibilities, for any given tenement, are therefore that:

(a) the DMS applies;
(b) the TMS applies in its entirety;
(c) the TMS applies in part and tenement burdens apply in part; or
(d) tenement burdens (only) apply.

Of these possibilities, (a) must await the enactment of the DMS, (b) will occur only where the title is entirely silent as to management and maintenance, and (d) will occur only where the title covers everything that is covered by the TMS. It follows that, almost always, the position will be governed by (c).

The TMS is an expanded version of the rather rudimentary management provisions in ss 28–31 of the Title Conditions (Scotland) Act 2003 which apply to 'communities' in general.[4] A 'community' is a group of properties regulated by community burdens—for example, a housing estate.[5] Since a tenement is also a 'community',[6] the rules in ss 28–31 of the 2003 Act would, in principle, apply to tenements also; but this would duplicate the TMS. As a result, ss 29 and 31 are wholly disapplied to a community which comprises a single tenement and s 28 is disapplied in part.[7] Another way of looking at it is to say that the TMS is thus supplemented by s 28 (in part) and by s 30 (in whole). Occasionally that will be

---

1 For further details, see T(S)A 2004 s 4.
2 For further details see *Conveyancing 2003* p 128.
3 T(S)A 2004 s 4(2).
4 *Conveyancing 2003* p 112.
5 Title Conditions (Scotland) Act 2003 s 26(2).
6 Unless the title contains no (community) burdens.
7 Title Conditions (Scotland) Act 2003 s 31A.

important, but only in relation to matters not covered by the TMS. The topic is too specialised to merit further discussion here.

Scheme property (rule 1)

Not all parts of the tenement are subject to the TMS. The TMS applies only to 'scheme property', as defined in rule 1. Importantly, the effect of rule 4 of the TMS is that all scheme property is to be commonly maintained (see below).

At the heart of the definition of scheme property are the 'strategic parts' of the tenement (although the term, used by the Scottish Law Commission, does not appear in the Act itself). These are of critical importance. The strategic parts are those parts which, under the TMS, are to be maintained by everyone on an equitable basis *whether they are common property or not*. They are listed in rules 1.2 and 1.3 as follows:

- the solum
- the foundations
- the external walls (but not chimney flues or windows and doors serving one flat only)
- the roof (including supporting structures but excluding chimney stacks, and skylights etc serving one flat only)
- any mutual gable wall to any adjoining building, to the mid-point only
- any wall, beam or column that is load-bearing.

An extension which serves only one flat—for example, an offshoot to the rear of the building which forms the kitchen of a ground floor flat—is excluded from the strategic parts.[1]

The importance of these parts is self-evident. In the words of the Scottish Law Commission:[2]

> [U]nless these parts are adequately maintained the building as a whole would cease to be viable and ownership of individual flats would count for nothing. In our view such parts are properly the concern of everyone, and ought to be maintained by everyone.

It is true that the TMS is only a default code and so can be altered by the titles. But unless the titles provide that a particular part is to be maintained by one owner only—which would be highly unusual—the result is that strategic parts will always be commonly maintained, whether under the titles or, to the extent that the titles are silent, under the TMS. The most important change concerns the roof. At common law the roof belonged to, and had to be maintained by, the owner of the top flat. Under the Act it still belongs to the owner of the top flat but, as scheme property, must be maintained by everyone.

---

1 TMS, r 1.3(a).
2 Report on the *Law of the Tenement* para 5.6.

The strategic parts do not, however, exhaust scheme property. There are two further categories. The first is any part of the tenement which is the common property of two or more owners. Under the Act, as already seen, that would include the close, any lift, chimney stacks (if shared), and certain other pertinents such as an access path or pipes. Although the titles are likely to add to this list, the additions are usually strategic parts (eg walls, roof, and solum) and so are scheme property already.

The second category is any part of the tenement which, by virtue of a tenement burden,[1] is to be maintained by two or more owners. Again, although such burdens are common, they are likely to concern mainly strategic parts.

Scheme decisions (rule 2)

Quite often there are provisions in the titles about how decisions are be made. These range from the elaborate to the minimal. Thus a deed of conditions might provide for a factor, an owners' association, a management committee, regular meetings, and so on. Or there might be merely the bare provision that acts of maintenance can be carried out with the agreement of the majority. If there is provision in the titles—however basic it may be—that provision prevails, provided only that it applies as respects each flat.[2] All decisions are then to be made in that way, including decisions on matters not mentioned in the titles but allowed only under rule 3 of the TMS (for which see below).[3] Conversely, if no provision is made in the titles, decisions are made in accordance with rule 2 of the TMS. In either case the decision is referred to in the TMS as a 'scheme decision' (ie a decision for the purposes of the Scheme).[4]

Rule 2 is easy to read and understand, and only a summary is given here. Decisions are made by the owners of a majority of flats;[5] but if only some of those owners are liable for a particular repair (eg to a chimney stack), only a majority of the paying owners is needed.[6] A special protection exists where the dissenting minority is liable for at least 75% of the cost of the work.[7] One vote is allocated to each flat.[8] If a flat is owned in common, any co-owner can exercise the vote; but if two wish to do so but disagree, the vote does not count unless it represents the agreed view of the holders of more than a one-half *pro indiviso* share.[9]

Voting can occur in one of two ways. One is for the owner seeking a decision to go round and speak to everyone, collecting votes on the way. But he or she cannot then stop once the magic 50% has been reached because there is an obligation to

---

1 Ie a real burden affecting a tenement: see T(S)A 2004 s 29(1).
2 T(S)A 2004,s 4(4).
3 Scottish Law Commission, Report on the *Law of the Tenement* para 5.17.
4 TMS r 1.4.
5 TMS r 2.5.
6 TMS r 2.3.
7 TMS rr 2.10 and 2.11.
8 TMS r 2.2.
9 TMS r 2.4.

consult every owner (or, if a flat is owned in common, one of the owners).[1] The other way is to call a meeting. At least 48 hours' notice must be given, including a note of the purpose of the meeting.[2]

A decision, once made, must be notified to everyone—other than, in the case of a decision taken by meeting, to those attending the meeting.[3] In practice notification will be by the person who proposed that the decision be made (or by a factor/manager acting on his or her behalf). It must take place 'as soon as practicable'. Notice may be given by post, by delivery, or by electronic means.[4] Where the owner's name is not known, it is sufficient to address the notice to 'The Owner' or similar.[5] If the name is known, and the flat is co-owned, each co-owner must be separately notified.[6] The date of notification is the date of sending.[7] As will be seen, that date marks the running of the 28-day freeze period during which decisions cannot usually be implemented.

The rule 2 procedure is designed to represent, more or less, what any sensible owner would do in order to secure the support of the other owners. Thus, even if an owner has never heard of the TMS, it is likely that he or she will follow this kind of procedure before embarking on expensive repairs. But sometimes not all will be done as it should. For that reason, rule 6.1 excuses 'procedural irregularity'. But an owner who was prejudiced by such an irregularity (eg a failure to notify) may be excused the cost of the work.[8]

Subject-matter of decisions (rule 3)

As already mentioned, a scheme decision is a decision of the owners made either (i) in terms of the titles, or (ii) if the titles are silent, under rule 2 of the TMS. Not everything, however, can be the subject of a scheme decision. The owners could not decide to buy additional land or run a lottery syndicate or employ a psychiatrist or publish a lifestyle magazine. Scheme decisions may only be made in respect of certain approved topics. There are two sources of such topics. One is the titles themselves—which commonly provide for decisions in relation to matters such as maintenance or the appointment of a factor. The other is rule 3 of the TMS. In principle, both sources apply to all tenements; or in other words rule 3 supplements whatever is in the titles. If the titles already make provision on a topic covered by rule 3, that part of rule 3 is displaced. Otherwise rule 3 applies.[9]

Rule 3.1 sets out the basic matters in respect of which a scheme decision may be made. The remainder of the rule makes further provision as to maintenance (see below). Rule 3.1 allows owners to make a scheme decision:

---

1 TMS rr 2.7 and 2.8.
2 TMS 2.6.
3 TMS r 2.9.
4 TMS r 9.2.
5 TMS r 9.3.
6 TMS r 2.9 read with T(S)A 2004, s 28(4).
7 TMS r 9.4.
8 TMS, r 6.2.
9 T(S)A 2004, s 4(5).

(a) to carry out maintenance to scheme property;

(b) to arrange for an inspection of scheme property to determine whether or to what extent maintenance is necessary;

(c) to appoint or dismiss a manager. But this power cannot be exercised for as long as the tenement is subject to a manager burden, ie a real burden, typically of five years' duration, which allows the original developer to manage the property or to appoint someone else as manager;[1]

(d) to delegate any of their powers to the manager including, for example, the power to decide on repairs (perhaps with a financial ceiling);[2]

(e) to arrange a policy of common insurance;

(f) to install an entryphone system;[3]

(g) to determine that an owner is not required to pay a share of maintenance or other scheme costs. Any vote by the owner in question is disregarded for the purposes of assembling the necessary majority;[4]

(h) to authorise any maintenance of scheme property already carried out by an owner. This covers the situation where an owner has jumped the gun and carried out repairs without first getting a scheme decision. Authorisation turns an irregular expenditure into a regular one, and allows the owner to recover a share from the other owners; and

(i) to modify or revoke any scheme decision.

Although scheme decisions[5] can be taken by a bare majority of owners, they have the effect of binding everyone. Successors are also bound.[6] So a decision to employ a manager is binding on an incoming owner, even if he or she dislikes the idea of a manager, questions the quality of the service provided, and would like to do without. In practical terms this means that the new owner must pay his or her share of the cost in question, whatever his or her views on the matter. But, as has been seen, a decision once taken is capable of being reversed.[7] So it is open to the new owner to persuade the others as to the errors of their ways.

Challenging scheme decisions in court

Unless work needs to be carried out urgently—a leaking roof, for example—no step can be taken to implement a scheme decision for a period of 28 days after the decision was intimated (or, if the decision was taken at a meeting at which all owners were present, 28 days after the meeting).[8] This is to allow a disaffected owner time to apply to the sheriff court to have the decision annulled. In the event

---

1 Title Conditions (Scotland) Act 2003, s 63. See p 00 above.
2 TMS r 3.1(d) read together with Title Conditions (Scotland) Act 2003 s 28(1)(b) (which, by s 31A of that Act, applies to tenements).
3 This was added by amendment at stage 3, following representations in particular from Sarah Boyack MSP.
4 TMS r 3.5.
5 At least under rule 2.
6 TMS r 8.2; Title Conditions (Scotland) Act 2003 s 30.
7 TMS r 3.1(i).
8 T(S)A 2004 s 5(10), (11).

that a court application is made, the decision is frozen until the application is disposed of (including any appeal). If, however, there are no disaffected owners—if, in other words, the decision was reached unanimously—there is no possibility of a court application, and the freeze period can be disregarded. The rules as to a freeze period apply to scheme decisions reached under the titles as much as to those made in accordance with rules 2 and 3.

By s 5 of the Act an owner who did not vote in favour of a decision can apply to the sheriff court to have the decision annulled. The application must be made within 28 days of the meeting at which the decision was taken or, if the owner did not attend that meeting or there was no meeting, within 28 days of notification of the decision. The sheriff is entitled to annul the decision if it is not in the best interests of all the owners, taken as a group, or if it is unfairly prejudicial to one or more of the owners. Where the decision concerns maintenance or improvements, the sheriff is directed to have regard to a number of factors, such as the age and condition of the building and the reasonableness of the cost.

An order under s 5 annuls decisions which have already been made, but it cannot make a new decision on behalf of the owners. It is a shield and not a sword. Thus an owner who fails to carry a majority in favour of some pet project cannot win the day by applying to the sheriff.

Maintenance: making the decision

Titles frequently allow for decisions on the subject of maintenance. But where the titles are silent,[1] the position is regulated by rule 3.1(a) of the TMS by which owners can make a scheme decision[2] to carry out maintenance to scheme property.

Limitations

Two limitations should be noted at once. First, the right under rule 3.1(a) is to carry out maintenance but not improvements. 'Maintenance' is defined[3] as including

> repairs and replacement, cleaning, painting and other routine works, gardening, the day-to-day running of a tenement and the reinstatement of a part (but not most of) the tenement building, but does not include demolition, alteration or improvement unless reasonably incidental to the maintenance.

The 'unless reasonably incidental' qualification will be noted. Repairs often involve a degree of betterment, as technology advances (or at least changes). That is allowed. So an old thing can be replaced by a new (and, it may be, better) thing. But what is not allowed is to add a thing which did not previously exist. So the owners can make a scheme decision to paint the close, but not to install a sauna in the cupboard under the common stair. That is a clear example, but the distinction

---

1 T(S)A 2004 s 4(5).
2 Ie a decision using the mechanism provided by the titles or, if none is provided, by TMS r 3.
3 TMS r 1.5.

between betterment and improvements will not always be easy to draw. This does not mean that improvements can never happen. The titles may allow a decision for improvements (with or without limits). But otherwise improvements require the agreement of everyone.

There is also a second limitation. A decision under rule 3.1(a) must relate to scheme property—that is to say, to the strategic parts of the tenement (roof, walls, and so on) together with any other parts that are common property or in respect of which maintenance under the titles is a shared responsibility.[1] In fact, however, the definition of scheme property is sufficiently wide for this limitation to be unimportant.

Mixing titles with the TMS

Sometimes it will be necessary to use a combination of the titles and the TMS.

> *Example.* A tenement burden[2] provides that the owner of each flat must maintain the roof, paying an equal share of the cost, and that a decision to maintain can be taken by a majority. It then happens that repairs are needed both to the roof and to a chimney stack (for which no provision is made in the titles).
>
> Since the title provides a mechanism for decisions, the scheme decision is to be made in accordance with the titles, and not with rule 2 of the TMS. Further, the titles allow a decision as to maintenance of the roof, so once again the TMS (rule 3.1(a) this time) is not needed. But there is no provision as to chimney stacks. By s 3(4), (5) of the Act, a chimney stack is the common property of the owners of the flats which it serves, in proportion to the number of flues. Assuming the stack to serve more than one flat, it is the common property of the owners of the flats in question. Hence it is scheme property. Hence a scheme decision to repair it can be made under rule 3.1(a) of the TMS. But the mechanism for making the decision comes, not from the TMS, but from the titles—ie decision by majority.[3]
>
> This long explanation leads to a simple result—as it will in most cases. A majority of owners can decide to repair both the roof and the chimney stack. No doubt owners would often proceed in this way anyway, without knowing why.

Further decisions

Once a decision for maintenance has been made (whether under the titles or the TMS), further scheme decisions are allowed under the TMS.[4] Thus the owners can decide to instruct the work (if this was not part of the original decision). They can decide to appoint a person to manage it—which might be useful if the tenement is not factored (or, sometimes, even if it is). The person could be another owner. The owners can take such other steps as are necessary to ensure that the maintenance

---

1 TMS r 1.2.

2 Ie a real burden which applies to the tenement: see T(S)A 2004 s 25(1).

3 That makes a difference. The decision will be made by a majority of *all* owners, whereas, if the TMS had applied, it would have been made by a majority of those who own the particular chimney stack (r 2.3).

4 TMS r 3.2.

is carried out to a satisfactory standard and completed in good time. Finally, and most importantly, the owners can require that money be paid up front.

Money up front

For a repair of any size it will often be prudent to collect the money first. This avoids unpleasant surprises for tradesmen or for those owners who were unwise enough to sign the contract. At the same time it solves the problem of changes in the ownership of flats (discussed below).

Under the previous law there was no right to demand money in advance, unless (unusually) the titles so provided. The position is now changed by the TMS. By rule 3.2 a scheme decision can be made requiring each owner to pay a sum of money not exceeding that owner's apportioned share of a reasonable estimate of the cost of the repair. A similar rule for non-tenemental properties is contained in the Title Conditions Act.[1]

The procedure is laid down in some detail in rules 3.3 and 3.4. Normally a written notice must be sent to each owner which includes:

- a summary of the nature and extent of the maintenance;
- its estimated cost;
- a note of why the estimate is reasonable;
- the apportioned shares of the other owners;
- an explanation of how the sum requested, and the apportionment, were arrived at;
- the date on which the decision to carry out maintenance was made and the names of those by whom it was made;
- a timetable for the carrying out of the maintenance, including the dates by which it is proposed the maintenance will be commenced and completed;
- the location and number of the maintenance account (which must be with a bank or building society and be interest-bearing) into which the money is to be paid;
- the names and addresses of the persons who are authorised to operate the account; and
- if desired, the refund date (see below).

Any money in the maintenance account is held in trust for the depositors.[2]

The projected timetable should be a realistic one—or at least the refund date should be many months away; for, unless work is begun by the refund date (if there is one) or by 28 days after the date set in the notice for commencement (if there is not), the owners are entitled to the return of their money on demand, and the whole process must start again.

This rather complex procedure does not apply if the amount requested is £100 or less—unless this would raise the amount requested, without formal notice, during

---

1 Title Conditions (Scotland) Act 2003 s 29.
2 TMS r 3.4(h).

the previous 12 months to over £200. For such small amounts it is sufficient to ask for payment to a person nominated for that purpose.[1] Of course, if the amount involved is small, the owners may not trouble to collect it in advance anyway.

Maintenance: apportionment of liability

The question of who pays for what is, naturally, of critical importance. The common law left upon the possibility of a disproportionate liability falling on one person. That possibility is largely removed by the TMS. In particular, the strategic parts (roof, walls etc) are *always* scheme property; and under the TMS the cost of maintaining scheme property is almost guaranteed to be apportioned on an equitable basis.

The position is regulated by a combination of the titles and rule 4 of the TMS. The hierarchy of possibilities is as follows:

(1) Any tenement burden is given effect, provided that it disposes of the entire liability for maintenance of the part in question.[2] This is just the usual rule by which the title always prevails over the TMS. If, however, the total liability under the burdens does not reach 100% the title is disregarded.

(2) If (1) does not apply, liability for any part which is common property is allocated in accordance with the *pro indiviso* shares.[3] In practice, these are almost always equal in size, meaning that each owner is liable for an equal share. A part may be common property either under the titles or as a result of s 3 of the Act.

(3) If neither (1) nor (2) applies, the owner of each flat must pay an equal share of the cost—unless the flats are markedly unequal in size in which case liability is apportioned in accordance with floor area.[4] Flats are markedly unequal if the floor area of the largest flat is more than one and a half times that of the smallest. In the calculation of floor area (i) lofts and basements are disregarded if used only for storage, and (ii) the area occupied by internal walls is included.[5]

There is a special rule for the roof over the close.[6] If the titles are silent as to its maintenance or ownership, it is governed by rule (3)—even although, as common property under s 3(1)(a) of the Act, it would ordinarily be governed by rule (2). The reasoning seems to be that, if the titles are silent as to the roof over the close, they are likely to be silent as to the roof in general. And since the rest of the roof would not, under the Act, be common property and so would be governed by rule (3), it is practically convenient that the rule should be the same for the roof over the close.

---

1 TMS rr 3.2(c), 3.3.
2 T(S)A 2004 s 4(6).
3 TMS r 4.2(a).
4 TMS r 4.2(b).
5 T(S)A 2004 s 25(2).
6 TMS r 4.3.

Some examples

The rules as to liability are easier than they sound. Here are some examples (which, for convenience, assume a tenement of eight flats):

Example 1. Repairs are carried out to the roof, following a scheme decision. The titles impose liability on each flat in proportion to feuduty. Rule (1). Each owner pays a proportionate share. The abolition of the feudal system (and hence of feuduty) does not affect the basis of liability. This is same result as under the former law.

Example 2. Repairs are carried out to the roof, following a scheme decision. The titles make no mention of the roof. Rule (3). Each owner pays an equal share (or, as the case may be, in proportion to floor area). This departs from the former law, which imposed sole liability on the owner of the top flat.

Example 3. The close is repainted, following a scheme decision. The titles make no mention of the close. Rule (2). By s 3(1)(a) of the Act the close is the common property of everyone, in equal shares. Each owner pays an equal share. Probably this is the same result as under the former law.

Example 4. Repairs are carried out to the roof, following a scheme decision. The titles impose liability for a one-eighth share on seven of the flats but the burden is omitted from the title of the eighth. The titles also make the roof common property in equal shares. Rule (2). Each owner pays an equal share. Rule (1) cannot apply because liability under the titles does not add up to 100%. This departs from the former law, which would have limited the liability of the owner of the eighth flat to a one sixty-fourth share (ie an eighth of the missing one-eighth share).

Example 5. Repairs are carried out to the rhones, following a scheme decision. The titles make no mention of the rhones. Rule (2). Since the rhones serve all the flats, they are common property, in equal shares, under s 3(4) of the Act. Each owner pays an equal share. Under the former law the position as to rhones was uncertain.

As can be seen from these examples, the new law often follows the old. Where it does not, it is because the old law was either unfair (as in examples 2 and 4) or unclear (as in example 5).

Other costs

Scheme decisions do not always involve maintenance. For example, it is possible to make a scheme decision to appoint a manager, or to arrange a common policy of insurance.[1] Special provision is made in rule 4 for costs arising from decisions of this kind, but as always the rule applies only where the titles are silent.[2]

Recovering what is due

Where an owner is liable *under the titles* (ie rule (1) above), the money due can be recovered by any other owner who has title and interest to do so. The effect

---

1 TMS r 3.1(c), (e).
2 T(S)A 2004 s 4(6).

of s 53 of the Title Conditions Act is that all owners in tenements have title to enforce any burdens created before the appointed day.[1] In burdens created after that day, the benefited properties must be nominated in the constitutive deed.[2] In practice such burdens are likely to be community burdens, enforceable by the owner of each flat.

Where an owner is liable *under the TMS* (ie rules (2) and (3) above), each owner has likewise a right to recover the money.[3]

In appropriate cases, former owners who are out of pocket also have title to recover.[4]

If a flat is owned in common, each co-owner is jointly and severally liable for the whole, but with a right of relief against the other co-owners proportionate to the size of the *pro indiviso* shares.[5]

Occasionally, an amount due will turn out to be irrecoverable. The result under the former law was unclear (unless the titles made provision). The Act provides that the shortfall is to be met by the other owners in the same proportions as before.[6] The same is true in the event unlikely to be common in practice that a scheme decision is made to exempt a particular owner from a cost for which he or she would otherwise be liable.[7] The forthcoming Housing Bill may give local authorities power, on request, to meet an unpaid share, which would then be recovered by means of a charging order on the flat in question.[8]

Hesitation in recovery may lead to the extinction of the debt by negative prescription. Under the former law, liability under a real burden prescribed only after 20 years, but this is now reduced to five years, both for real burdens and for liability arising under the TMS.[9]

Maintenance: acting alone

Strategic repairs

If a repair is needed for the physical integrity of the building, it may be assumed that it will almost always command the necessary majority of owners. But where this is not so the Act allows individual owners to act alone.

The key provision, s 8, applies to those parts of a building—particularly the external walls and the roof—which provide shelter and support, and imposes on the owner of the relevant part a duty to carry out such maintenance as is needed for that purpose. In practice s 8 can be used in one of two ways:

---

1   This is because flats in the same tenement are likely to be regarded as 'related properties': see s 53(2)(d).
2   Title Conditions (Scotland) Act 2003 s 4(2)(c)(ii), (4).
3   TMS r 8.3.
4   Title Conditions (Scotland) Act 2003 s 8(2)(c); T(S)A 2004 s 14.
5   Title Conditions (Scotland) Act 2003 s 11(5) (liability under the titles); T(S)A 2004 s 28(7) (liability under the TMS).
6   TMS, r 5. This is subject to any contrary provision in the title: see T(S)A 2004, s 4(7).
7   Under TMS r 3.1(g).
8   Scottish Executive, *Maintaining Homes Preserving Homes* (2004) pp 28–29.
9   Title Conditions (Scotland) Act 2003 s 18; Prescription and Limitation (Scotland) Act 1973 sch 1 para 1(ab) (inserted by the T(S)A 2004 s 15).

- The owner of the roof (or other part) can carry out a repair even without a scheme decision to that effect.[1]
- Any other owner can require the owner of the roof (or other part) to carry out the repair.[2]

But although a s 8 repair is by unilateral act, its cost is a shared responsibility. A repair under s 8 is treated as a repair carried out by virtue of a scheme decision, and the rules for liability already described apply.[3] In the case of the roof, for example, each owner will typically be liable for an equitable share. In this respect s 8 departs from the common law doctrine of common interest on which it is otherwise based.

Section 8 does not apply where it would be unreasonable to carry out the repair 'having regard to all the circumstances (and including, in particular, the age of the tenement building, its condition and the likely cost of any maintenance)'.[4] This prevents s 8 being used to promote the pointless repair of derelict buildings.

Other unilateral acts

There are two[5] other occasions on which a unilateral act is permitted.

First, an owner is always at liberty to alter or repair his or her own property, although in the case of property held in common a co-owner living alone is restricted to necessary repairs.[6] In principle, however, the owner must meet the full cost him- or herself.[7] But the cost will be shared with the other owners where either (a) the repair is carried out under s 8 (discussed above), or (b) the repair is subsequently homologated by scheme decision.[8]

Secondly, in any emergency any owner can carry out repairs to scheme property if they are needed to prevent damage to any part of the tenement or in the interests of health and safety.[9] For this purpose it does not matter that it belongs to another owner. The cost is divided among the owners as if the repairs had followed on from a scheme decision.[10]

---

1 Of course an owner can always repair his own property. But the cost of s 8 repairs can be recovered from the other owners: see below.

2 T(S)A 2004 s 8(3).

3 T(S)A 2004 s 10.

4 T(S)A 2004 s 8(2). The previous law was similar: see *Thomson v St Cuthbert's Co-operative Association Ltd* 1958 SC 380.

5 A possible third is where a tenement burden imposes a direct obligation to repair (as opposed to an indirect obligation to pay for the cost of repairs). Arguably this can be used in the same way as the repair obligation imposed by s 8. In other words, the owner bound by the obligation can carry out the repair in question, or at least can be made to do so by any of the other owners.

6 K G C Reid, *The Law of Property in Scotland* (1996) para 25.

7 This is so even where the property is owned in common, contrary to the common law: see T(S)A 2004 s 16.

8 This is permitted by the TMS r 3.1(h) provided that the part repaired is scheme property.

9 TMS r 7. But this is a default rule and so subject to different provision in the titles: see T(S)A 2004 s 4(9).

10 TMS r 7.2.

Maintenance: access

Sometimes a repair cannot be done without using, or taking access through, an individual flat or some other part of the tenement in single ownership. Especially if the owner in question was opposed to the repair, there may be a reluctance to grant access. Section 17, however, confers a general right to access for maintenance and also for certain other purposes, such as to measure floor area.[1]

The procedure under s 17 is straightforward. In principle any owner is entitled to access for maintenance and certain other purposes over any part of the tenement which he or she does not own. The maintenance need not be common maintenance, following a scheme decision, but can also be private maintenance to one's own flat. Reasonable notice, in writing,[2] must be given unless the work requires to be carried out urgently.

Normally a request for access must be granted. It can be refused, either entirely or at the particular time requested, only where it is reasonable to do so, and this in turn will depend on the reasonableness of the original request.[3] The Scottish Law Commission explained the position in this way:[4]

> We are conscious that rights of access are potentially open to abuse. Inspection could be used as a pretext for gaining entry to a neighbour's flat. A neighbour who is officious, or merely curious, might seek access more often than is really necessary. It is not clear that an obsessive repairer should be allowed access over his neighbour's flat whenever he feels the urge to take up tools. Nor is it clear that access should be allowed merely on the ground that it is more convenient to work from a neighbour's flat if the repair could in fact be carried out from one's own property.

For example, it may not be reasonable to reach the ceiling void in one's own flat by breaking open the floor of the flat above.[5] Access, once granted, does not have to be taken by the owner in person but can, for example, be taken by a tradesman.

If the part over which access is taken is the part being repaired, it will (or should) finish up in a better condition than before. But in any event s 17 requires that it be left in no worse a condition. If it is, the owner can have it restored and recover the cost from the person who took access.[6]

Flat sold in mid-repair

A persistent difficulty with tenement repairs is the turnover of flats which, in some areas at least, is alarmingly high. An owner who is shortly to sell is unlikely to agree to repairs which will benefit only his or her successor. And if, nonetheless,

---

1 A complete list is given in s 17(3).
2 T(S)A 2004 s 30.
3 T(S)A 2004 s 17(5).
4 Scottish Law Commission, Report on the *Law of the Tenement* para 10.17.
5 The facts of *Taylor v Irvine* 1996 SCLR 937. In the event the issue did not require to be decided.
6 T(S)A 2004, s 17(8), (9). There is a right of recovery from the owner who requested access, even if the damage was caused by a workman.

the repairs are carried out, the former law was not entirely clear as to whether liability lay with the old owner or with the new.

The position is much improved by the Act. Since only a majority of owners is needed for a scheme decision, a repair can be agreed over the opposition of an owner who is on the brink of selling. To avoid possible difficulties of recovery, payment of the estimated cost can be required at once, in advance of the repair.[1]

Even if the money is not collected in advance—or not until after the sale has gone through—the position is still more favourable than under the former law.[2] Despite the sale, the outgoing owner remains liable for the repair costs on the basis that he or she was owner at the time the decision was taken.[3] Whether the incoming owner is also liable depends upon whether the repairs have already been carried out. Thus:

- Where the repairs have been agreed but not carried out, the buyer is jointly and severally liable with the seller for the share attributable to the flat.[4] This gives the other owners in the tenement a choice of debtor, thus facilitating repairs. But it is unwelcome to the buyer. The assumption, however, is that, having had the property surveyed, the buyer is alerted to the possible need for repairs. Further, even if the buyer is made to pay, he has a right of relief against the seller.[5] So in the end the liability rests with the seller.

- Where the repairs have been carried out but not paid for, the buyer has no liability unless a notice of potential liability for costs was registered against the property at least 14 days before settlement.[6] This is because repairs which have been completed might otherwise be undetectable. The effect of a notice is to make the buyer jointly and severally liable in the manner already described. Although it has been said that such notices are open to abuse,[7] the greater risk seems under-use.

The notice of potential liability was added to the Tenements Bill (as it then was) only at stage 3, following representations from various sources. The owner of any flat in the building can register such a notice against any other flat, and the same notice can be used for all the flats.[8] Once registered, a notice lasts for three years,

---

1 TMS r 3.2(c), discussed above.
2 Although that law itself was not entirely clear. For a discussion, see Scottish Law Commission, Report on the *Law of the Tenement* part 8.
3 T(S)A 2004, ss 11(1), (2) and 12(1). Section 12 is a close copy of s 10 of the Title Conditions (Scotland) Act 2003, which applies to real burdens generally.
4 T(S)A 2004 s 12(2). The seller is liable from the moment the decision was made, and does not lose liability by selling the flat: see ss 11(1), (2) and 12(1).
5 T(S)A 2004 s 12(5).
6 T(S)A 2004 s 12(3).
7 Donald Reid, 'Fair notice?' (2005) 50 *Journal of the Law Society of Scotland* Jan/44. The danger is said to be of speculative notices in respect of repairs which have not yet been agreed. But a notice can impose liability on a buyer only where repairs have actually been carried out. For other repairs it serves merely to warn of possible liability, notably under T(S)A 2004 s 12(2), for repairs which are agreed but not yet carried out.
8 On notices see generally T(S)A 2004 s 13.

but it can be re-registered before the end of that period in which case it lasts for a further three years. There is a mandatory form of notice, set out in schedule 2 to the Tenements (Scotland) Act, as amended.[1] It looks like this:

NOTICE OF POTENTIAL LIABILITY FOR COSTS

This notice gives details of certain maintenance or work carried out, or to be carried out, in relation to the flat specified in the notice. The effect of the notice is that a person may, on becoming the owner of the flat, be liable by virtue of section 12(3) of the Tenements (Scotland) Act 2004 (asp 11) for any outstanding costs relating to the maintenance or work.

Flat to which notice relates:
Number 2/6 Feudal Court, Aberdeen, registered under title number ABN 24371.

Description of the maintenance or work to which the notice relates:
Stripping roof, replacing felt, and re-slating.

Person giving notice:
Duncan Barron, residing at and owner of 2/2 Feudal Court, Aberdeen.[2]

Signature:

Witness:[3]

Date of signing:

If the same notice is used for more than one flat—as will often be the case—a conveyancing description is needed for each flat. The notice can be signed by the person giving it or by an agent on his or her behalf. Service is not required. It is understood that the Keeper does not ask to see the land certificate.

Of course no buyer likes to have to pursue a seller two years after the sale, and it will usually be wise to make a retention from the price. That in turn requires knowledge of the potential liability. There is no difficulty where a notice has been registered, but no notice is needed for repairs which have yet to be carried out. To cover both of these points there is something to be said for a clause in missives, for example:[4]

---

1 By the Tenements (Scotland) Act 2004 (Notice of Potential Liability for Costs) Amendment Order 2004, SSI 2004/490. This adds the words 'to be carried out' to the opening of the notice, thus making clear that a notice can be served at any time after repairs have been agreed even if work has not yet begun.

2 A notice may be registered only by an owner in the same tenement or by the manager. The Keeper requests that the notice should make clear into which category the person giving notice falls. Where notice is given by a manager, the Keeper suggests adding: 'The person giving notice is the manager of the tenement'. See (2005) 50 *Journal of the Law Society of Scotland* Jan/49.

3 Although this is not required by the statutory style, the Keeper asks for a witness (or equivalent): see (2005) 50 *Journal of the Law Society of Scotland* Jan/49. Given the terms of s 6(3)(a) of the Requirements of Writing (Scotland) Act 1995, however, it seems unlikely that this could be insisted on.

4 For a different approach, see Donald Reid, 'Fair notice?' (2005) 50 *Journal of the Law Society of Scotland* Jan/44, 47.

Before the date of entry the seller will provide full details of –

(a) any common repairs which have been agreed by the owners in the building of which the subjects form part or which are otherwise in prospect; and

(b) any common repairs in respect of which a notice of potential liability for costs has been, or is to be, registered.

The buyer may retain from the price such sum as is reasonably required to meet any costs for which he may be contingently liable under section 10(2) of the Title Conditions (Scotland) Act 2003[1] or section 12(2) of the Tenements (Scotland) Act 2004.

A variant would provide for the retention to be placed on deposit receipt in joint names of the two sets of agents.

Insurance

The Act imposes an obligation on owners to insure their flats.[2] The reasons given by the Scottish Law Commission were these:[3]

> Within a tenement each owner is uniquely vulnerable to the physical condition of the property of his neighbours. Since a flat is no more than a single unit in a larger building, an owner may often be affected by damage to parts of the building which are not his. Hence he has an interest not merely in the insurance of his own flat but in the insurance of the other flats in the building. In the most extreme case, where a tenement is badly damaged or destroyed, the fact that even one of the flats is uninsured, or underinsured, may be enough to prevent the building from being restored. In summary, in a tenement an owner is not adequately insured unless his neighbours are insured also.

Insurance must be for reinstatement value and in respect of the prescribed risks. At the time of writing the risks had not yet been prescribed, and the relevant provision of the Act was not yet in force.

Insurance is not required to the extent that it is unavailable, or only available at a cost which is unreasonably high.[4] This recognises the difficulty of obtaining cover for certain properties or for certain owners.

In a tenement insurance can either be taken out for the building as a whole or, piecemeal, for individual flats. The Act makes no choice between these methods and either is allowed. However, under the TMS owners are able to make a scheme decision to move to a common policy of insurance for the whole building, and to determine on an equitable basis the liability of each owner to contribute to the premium.[5] In addition, common insurance is sometimes required by a tenement burden, although, at least in older tenements, the level of cover stipulated may be inadequate. Unless the burden provides otherwise, the cost of premiums is to be shared equally among the owners.[6]

---

1 This refers to the equivalent provision in the Title Conditions Act in respect of non-tenemental repairs.

2 T(S)A 2004 s 18.

4 T(S)A 2004 s 18(4).

5 TMS r 3.1(e).

6 T(S)A 2004 s 4(6); TMS r 4.4(b).

The impact of the obligation to insure will be relatively modest. It is thought that at least 90% of flats are insured already, often no doubt because there is a secured loan and hence an insurance requirement imposed by the lender. Presumably this percentage will now rise, but there will continue to be an irreducible minimum of uninsured flats. One problem, of course, is enforcement. Failure to insure is not a criminal offence under the Act. No public body is charged with monitoring compliance. Instead power lies with the individual owners, who are entitled to see evidence of insurance and, if necessary, to enforce the statutory obligation.[1]

Common interest

No interference with support or shelter

Owners and occupiers must desist from any activity on their part of the tenement which threatens support or shelter. It is enough if there is a material risk, even if it could not be said for certain that disaster will result.[2] The standard case is the D-I-Y enthusiast who demolishes structural walls on a Sunday morning. If a telephone call or visit does not put an end to it, interdict is available under the Act.[3]

This provision, along with the next and the obligation under s 8 to carry out strategic repairs already mentioned, are the statutory replacements for the common law doctrine of common interest, which is formally abolished by the Act in so far as it applies to tenements.[4] There is existing case law on the obligation not to interfere with support and shelter which may be of assistance in interpreting the new provision.[5]

No interference with light

Natural light must also be respected, a statutory version of the (former) servitude *ne luminibus*.[6] In practice this restricts building operations on the back green or other garden. Thus no building is allowed which obstructs the light of a flat.

Demolition and abandonment

Demolition

Occasionally a tenement has to be demolished, because it is unsafe, or derelict, or damaged or destroyed by fire or other peril. The cost of demolition is often substantial, but there was no guidance under the former law as to how it was to be divided. Under the Act the owner of each (former) flat must usually pay

---

1 T(S)A 2004 s 18(5), (6).
2 T(S)A 2004 s 9(1)(a).
3 T(S)A 2004 s 9(2).
4 T(S)A 2004 s 7. It remains in one or two other cases, principally non-tidal waters and boundary walls and fences.
5 For references and a discussion, see K G C Reid, *The Law of Property in Scotland* (1996) para 233.
6 T(S)A 2004 s 9(1)(b).

an equal share of the cost, but if the flats were markedly unequal in size (ie if the floor area of the largest flat was more than one and a half times that of the smallest) the cost is apportioned according to floor area. This is a default rule only and so subject to different provision in the titles—although few titles are so pessimistic as to provide for demolition. Demolition has no effect on ownership, so that the owner of an upper flat continues to own the airspace which the flat formerly occupied.[1]

The former law was hardly more clear as to the disposal of the site, but again the Act makes provision. The practical choice is between rebuilding or selling the site unbuilt. Under the Act, rebuilding is allowed only where the titles so provide (as quite often they do) or, failing the titles, the owners all agree. Otherwise any owner can apply to the sheriff court to have the site sold and the proceeds divided.[2] By 'site' is meant the solum of the building together with any access path.[3] Garden ground is not included, although if it was owned in common there is a similar right of division and sale as a matter of general law.

The procedure is set out in schedule 3. Unlike division and sale of common property, the court has a discretion to refuse the application in respect of the site if sale is not in the best interests of the owners, taken as a group, or is unfairly prejudicial to one or more of the owners.[4] Assuming the application is granted, the court grants an order which must be registered in the Land Register or Register of Sasines (or both).[5] The property is then sold and the net proceeds divided. Any secured loan is paid off from the proceeds attributable to the flat in question.[6] Entitlement mirrors liability for the cost of demolition, so that the proceeds are either divided equally or, if the size of the flats was markedly unequal, by reference to floor area.[7] But this is a default rule which can be altered in the titles.

Abandoned tenements

A tenement which is wholly abandoned is subject to the same rules as the site of a tenement which has been demolished.[8] This means that any owner can apply for its sale and the division of the proceeds. For the rules to apply the tenement must have been entirely unoccupied (other than by squatters) for more than six months, and it must be unlikely that it will be occupied again in the future.

Missing items: aerials and gas pipes

The Scottish Law Commission's original Bill was produced before devolution and was designed for implementation by the Westminster Parliament. Two, relatively

---

1 T(S)A 2004 s 20(1).
2 T(S)A 2004 s 22(1)–(3).
3 T(S)A 2004, s 22(8).
4 T(S)A 2004 sch 3 para 1(4).
5 T(S)A 2004 sch 3 para 3.
6 T(S)A 2004 sch 3 paras 4–6.
7 But only if, despite demolition, that floor area can still be determined: see T(S)A 2004 s 22(5).
8 T(S)A 2004 s 23.

minor, provisions concern reserved matters and so have been omitted from the current Act. It is possible that one or other may be the subject of an order made under s 104 of the Scotland Act 1998 and hence become enacted law.[1]

The first concerns television aerials, satellite dishes and other similar equipment. Unsurprisingly, the common law made no provision for things like this, and it is difficult to explain the basis on which television aerials are allowed to adorn the roofs of tenements. Since the roof, and the airspace above, are either the sole property of one of the owners or, at best, the common property of everyone, most aerials would seem to involve encroachment into property which belongs solely or partly to others. Under the Law Commission's provision there is an absolute right to place aerials and satellite dishes on the roof or chimney stacks, and to lead such wires from them as are necessary.[2]

The other provision concerns gas. To introduce gas to a tenement involves running pipes through or over property which is in either individual or common ownership. This means that those affected must agree, and hence that a gas supply can often be blocked by a single owner. The Law Commission's provision confers on individual owners a right to lead gas pipes.[3]

Sale of new flats: some drafting implications

Where individual flats are being sold for the first time it is necessary to consider in particular issues of (a) management and maintenance, and (b) the distribution of ownership within the tenement including the incidence of common ownership. Neither issue is straightforward, and both depend on the type of property and on its size. Thus an approach which works well for large block of flats may work less well for the sale of a single flat in a small block under the right-to-buy legislation or for the conversion of a Victorian house into two flats.

Management and maintenance

The first concern is likely to be with the rules for management and maintenance. What parts of the building are to be maintained jointly? How is liability to be divided? And how are the owners to make decisions? This is the territory of real burdens and deeds of conditions. Since the Tenements Act came into force there are, roughly speaking, three ways of proceeding:[4]

(1) *Silence*. The titles can make no provision. In that case the position would be governed solely by the Tenement Management Scheme ('TMS').

(2) *Business as usual*. The same provisions could be put in as under the former law. Any gaps would then be made good by the TMS.

---

1 Some of the ground is covered by T(S)A 2004 s 19 which confers a right to install pipes and cables for such services as Scottish Ministers may prescribe. At the time of writing no SSI had been made.
2 Clause 20. See Scottish Law Commission, Report on the *Law of the Tenement* paras 10.1–10.5.
3 Clause 21. See paras 10.6–10.9 of the Scottish Law Commission's Report.
4 T(S)A 2004 s 4.

(3) *Replicating the TMS*. The deed of conditions could repeat, and possibly augment, the rules contained in the TMS. In that case the TMS would be wholly excluded.

(4) *Applying the Development Management Scheme* ('DMS'). If the DMS applies, the TMS is wholly excluded.

Options (1), (3) and (4) have the advantage that all the rules are contained in the one place in the TMS for option (1), in the deed of conditions for option (3), and in the DMS for option (4). Option (2), on the other hand, requires the owners to flit from titles to the TMS and back again.

For tenements which are small and straightforward, option (1) has something to commend it. The rules in the TMS are rather basic, but they cover all the main points. Decisions are taken by a majority and, usually, everyone has to pay for everything in equal shares.

Conveyancers will often be tempted by option (2). There is no doubt that it is workable. It is already the case that, for existing tenements, the provisions in the title must be read alongside the TMS. But plainly it is not the best way to proceed. It would seem odd—perverse even—to draft title provisions without an eye to the default rules set out in the TMS. And once these rules are engaged, it would be natural to use them as a basis for the deed of conditions. That in turn leads in option (3).

Option (3) can be achieved in broadly two ways. One is to use the same kind of deed of conditions as before, but to make sure that it covers at least the ground which is covered by the TMS. The change will thus be to scope rather than to drafting style or general approach. The alternative is to begin with the TMS, reproducing its terms in the deed of conditions and then adding to them as appropriate. The result will be a radical change of style, from the wordy circumlocutions of traditional drafting to a new world of numbered rules, short sentences, and clear layout. Often this will be the best approach. Drafting in short rules is simple to do as well as to read. In practice it will usually be possible to exclude some of the rules in the TMS as inapplicable—for example rules 2.10 and 2.11 (a minority of owners liable for 75% of the cost of repairs), rule 4.2(b)(i) (liability by floor area), and rule 4.3 (roof over the close). And the rules can be modified and added to. An obvious quarry for additional rules is the DMS.

Options (2) and (3) depend on the creation of real burdens—even if, under option (3), the burdens do no more than reproduce the terms of a statutory management scheme. Obviously it is necessary to comply with the new rules set out in the Title Conditions (Scotland) Act 2003. These include requirements: to identify the benefited property or, in the case of community burdens, the community; to use the term 'real burden' or some equivalent term such as 'community burden'; and to register the deed against the benefited property as well as the burdened. In practice, burdens of this kind are likely to be community burdens, ie common to all the owners and mutually enforceable by them.[1]

---

1 Title Conditions (Scotland) Act 2003 s 25.

Option (4) is likely to be attractive only for large developments, including those which mix blocks of flats with villas.[1] But it must await the order under s 104 of the Scotland Act 1998 which, sometime in 2005, will bring the DMS into life.

Amenity conditions

Whichever option is used, it will usually be necessary to add further real burdens to deal with use and general amenity. These are matters for the general law of real burdens and are not touched on by the Tenements Act. As a practical matter, real burdens added under options (3) and (4) are likely to be drafted in the form of additional rules rather than in the more traditional manner.

Common ownership

In drafting deeds of conditions and break-off writs, the modern trend is to make a great deal of the tenement common property. This practice, not always advisable even under the former law, is put into question by the new law.

In considering which parts of a tenement should be made common property, the following points should be borne in mind:

(1) Common property is an essentially undesirable arrangement. Roman lawyers described it as *mater rixarum* (the mother of quarrels). All things being equal, it is better that each should have his or her own property and that as little as possible should be shared. This is particularly true of the boundary features of individual flats. The modern tendency to make common property of external walls is almost always unwise. It means that an individual owner has no greater rights to the walls of his or her flat than any other owner in the building. Strictly, wallpaper cannot be changed, or the walls painted, without the consent of everyone, and the Adam fireplace, installed at great expense, becomes, by accession to the wall, the common property of all owners in the building.

(2) Common property is often used as a means of achieving common maintenance. But common maintenance can be achieved more directly, and economically, by the use of real burdens. That will remain true under the new law. And under that law the strategic parts of the tenement (in particular the roofs and external walls) are already the joint responsibility of all owners, even without either common property or real burdens for maintenance.

(3) Common property is often conferred in respect of the solum as a means of protecting the owners of upper flats in the event of the tenement being destroyed. However, the special rules of the new law for demolished tenements now make this unnecessary.[2]

---

1 For the DMS see further *Conveyancing 2003* p 128. The draft DMS can be found on pp 426–444 of the Scottish Law Commission's Report on *Real Burdens* (Scot Law Com No 181, 2000; available on http://www.scotlawcom.gov.uk).

2 T(S)A 2004 s 22.

(4) Even if the titles are silent, s 3 of the Act will create a certain amount of common property. Thus the close, and any lift, will be common property; and paths, pipes, water tanks, chimney stacks and other parts are common property of the owners of the flats which they serve.

None of this means that common property should cease to be used in break-off writs of new flats. But it should be used more sparingly than hitherto, and against the background of the new law. It is suggested that common property is of value for two purposes in particular:

- *Use.* First and foremost, common property confers a right of use. This means that if a part of a tenement is to be used by everyone, it should be made common property. The most obvious examples are the back green, amenity ground, and paths and other means of access. Depending on the circumstances, the roof and roof space may be another example.

- *Transparency and clarity.* It is will usually be satisfactory that the, relatively minor, parts covered by s 3 of the Act should be common property. (Where it is not satisfactory, s 3, which is a default rule,[1] can be avoided by conveying the part in question to a particular owner.) It is probably helpful to owners if the main parts affected are listed in the break-off writ (and, if desired, in the deed of conditions). In effect this is for information only, for the result would be the same even if the deed were silent. If it is unclear whether a particular part 'serves' flats in the sense of s 3, its inclusion in the list will have the effect of resolving any doubts.

Except where one of the above purposes is being served, the conveyancer should hesitate before creating common property.

Purchase of flats: some implications for practice

We now turn from sale to purchase, and from new flats to all flats. What are the implications of the new law for the purchase of tenement flats? Four in particular can be identified:

(1) Whereas before titles had to be read against the background of the common law of the tenement, they now have to read against the background of the Act and the TMS. One default regime is thus replaced by another. The difference mainly concerns management and maintenance, because the new rules on ownership are much the same as the old.

(2) The potential liability of one's client for maintaining shared parts[2] can usually be determined from the client's title alone. Thus:

- If, in that title, a real burden imposes a share of the cost of maintaining a particular part, that share represents the actual liability unless,

---

1 T(S)A 2004 s 1.
2 Shared as to use and function. Obviously an owner is solely liable for the maintenance of his or her own flat.

exceptionally, the burdens in the titles of the different flats add up to less than 100% of liability.[1]

- If there is no real burden but the part is common property (whether under the title or s 3 of the Act), liability for maintenance is determined by the size of the client's *pro indiviso* share.[2] (In some cases, however, this can only be discovered by examining the titles to the other flats.)
- If there is no real burden and the part is not common property, there is no liability for maintenance except in respect of strategic parts (mainly the roof and external walls).[3] Liability is then either equal or (if one flat in the tenement is more than one and a half times the size of another) by floor area.[4]

One notable consequence is to relieve the purchaser of a top flat from having to examine the titles of the other flats in order to determine liability for roof repairs. The roof is a strategic part. If the titles do not divide the cost, the cost is divided by the TMS, and (unless the title to the flat so provides) there is no question of the owner of the top flat being left with sole liability.

(3) In the purchase of an upper flat, it no longer matters whether the title includes a right in common to the solum. In the event of the tenement being destroyed, any owner (including the owner of an upper flat) is entitled to have the site sold and the net proceeds divided, and no special rights attach to the person who happens to own the solum.[5]

(4) It is necessary to be alert for repairs which have already been agreed upon by the owners for in some circumstances the purchaser will have joint and several liability for the cost with the seller.[6]

---

1 Tenement burdens prevail over the default rules in the TMS. See T(S)A 2004 s 4(6).
2 TMS r 4.2(a).
3 Strategic parts are scheme property under TMS r 1.2(c).
4 TMS r 4.2(b).
5 T(S)A 2004 s 22.
6 T(S)A 2004 s 12.

❈ PART V ❈
TABLES

TABLES

CUMULATIVE TABLE OF APPEALS 2004

This lists all cases digested in *Conveyancing 1999* and subsequent annual volumes in respect of which an appeal was subsequently heard, and gives the result of the appeal.

Adams v Thorntons
2003 GWD 27-771, OH, 2003 Case (46) *affd* 2004 SCLR 1016, IH, 2004 Case (44)

Anderson v Express Investment Co Ltd
2002 GWD 28-977, OH, 2002 Case (5) *affd* 11 Dec 2003, IH, 2003 Case (13)

Armstrong v G Dunlop & Sons' JF
2004 SLT 155, OH, 2002 Case (48) *affd* 2004 SLT 295, IH, 2003 Case (39)

Burnett's Tr v Grainger
2000 SLT (Sh Ct) 116, 2000 Case (21) *rev* 2002 SLT 699, IH, 2002 Case (19) *affd* 2004 SC (HL) 19, 2004 SLT 513, 2004 SCLR 433, HL, 2004 Case (24)

Caledonian Heritable Ltd v Canyon Investments Ltd
2001 GWD 1-62, OH, 2000 Case (69) *rev* 2002 GWD 5-149, IH, 2002 Case (61)

Cheltenham & Gloucester plc v Sun Alliance and London Insurance plc
2001 SLT 347, OH, 2000 Case (63) *rev* 2001 SLT 1151, IH, 2001 Case (73)

Conway v Glasgow City Council
1999 SCLR 248, 1999 Hous LR 20 (Sh Ct) *rev* 1999 SLT (Sh Ct) 102, 1999 SCLR 1058, 1999 Hous LR 67, 1999 Case (44) *rev* 2001 SLT 1472, 2001 SCLR 546 (Updates), IH, 2001 Case (51).

Glasgow City Council v Caststop Ltd
2002 SLT 47, OH, 2001 Case (6) *affd* 2003 SLT 526, 2004 SCLR 283 (Notes), IH, 2003 Case (6)

Grampian Joint Police Board v Pearson
2000 SLT 90, OH, 2000 Case (18) *affd* 2001 SC 772, 2001 SLT 734, IH, 2001 Case (17)

Hamilton v Mundell; Hamilton v J & J Currie Ltd
20 November 2002, Dumfries Sheriff Court, 2002 Case (13) *rev* 7 October 2004, IH, 2004 Case (11)

Inverness Seafield Co Ltd v Mackintosh
1999 GWD 31-1497, OH, 1999 Case (19) *rev* 2001 SC 406, 2001 SLT 118, IH, 2000 Case (13)

Kaur v Singh (No 2)
1999 Hous LR 76, 2000 SCLR 187 (Notes), 2000 SLT 1324, OH, 1999 Case (34) *affd* 2000 SLT 1323, 2000 SCLR 944 (Updates), IH, 2000 Case (26)

Kingston Communications (Hull) plc v Stargas Nominees Ltd
2003 GWD 33-946, OH, 2003 Case (35) *affd* 17 December 2004, IH, 2004 Case (31)

Labinski Ltd v BP Oil Development Co
2002 GWD 1-46, OH, 2001 Case (16) *affd* 2003 GWD 4-93, IH, 2003 Case (17)

McAllister v Queens Cross Housing Association Ltd
2001 Hous LR 143, 2002 SLT (Lands Tr) 13, 2002 Case (26) *affd* 2003 SC 514, 2003 SLT 971, IH, 2003 Case (28)

Minevco Ltd v Barratt Southern Ltd
1999 GWD 5-266, OH, 1999 Case (41) *affd* 2000 SLT 790, IH, 2000 Case (36)

Robertson v Fife Council
2000 SLT 1226, OH, 2000 Case (84) *affd* 2001 SLT 708, IH, 2001 Case (82) *rev* 2002 SLT 951, HL, 2002 Case (69)

Royal Bank of Scotland plc v Wilson
2001 SLT (Sh Ct) 2, 2000 Case (53) *affd* 2003 SLT 910, 2003 SCLR 716, 2004 SC 153, IH, 2003 Case (40)

Scottish Youth Theatre (Property) Ltd v RSAMD Endowment Trust Trustees
2002 SCLR 945, OH, 2002 Case (3) *affd* 2003 GWD 27-758, IH, 2003 Case (8)

Souter v Kennedy
23 July 1999, Perth Sheriff Court, 1999 Case (69) *rev* 20 March 2001, IH, 2001 Case (81)

Spence v W & R Murray (Alford) Ltd
2001 GWD 7-265, Sh Ct, 2001 Case (9) *affd* 2002 SLT 918, IH, 2002 Case (1)

Stevenson v Roy
2002 SLT 445, OH, 2002 Case (67) *affd* 2003 SC 544, 2003 SCLR 616, IH, 2002 Case (54)

Tesco Stores Ltd v Keeper of the Registers of Scotland
2001 SLT (Lands Tr) 23, 2001 Case (30) *affd* sv *Safeway Stores plc v Tesco Stores Ltd* 2004 SC 29, 2004 SLT 701, IH, 2003 Case (25)

Thomas v Allan
2002 GWD 12-368, Sh Ct, 2002 Case (7) *affd* 2004 SC 393, IH, 2003 Case (22)

Wilson v Inverclyde Council
2001 GWD 3-129, OH, 2001 Case (29) *affd* 2003 SC 366, IH, 2003 Case (27)

TABLE OF CASES DIGESTED IN EARLIER VOLUMES
BUT REPORTED IN 2004

A number of cases which were digested in *Conveyancing 2003* or earlier volumes but were at that time unreported have been reported in 2004. A number of other cases have been reported in an additional series of reports. For the convenience of those using earlier volumes all the cases in question are listed below, together with a complete list of citations.

Advocate General for Scotland v Taylor
2003 SLT 1340, 2004 SC 339

Amalgamated Roofing and Building Company v Wilkie
2004 SLT 509, 2004 SCLR 267

Anderson v Express Investment Co Ltd
2004 GWD 16-355

Armstrong v G Dunlop & Son's Judicial Factor
2004 SLT 295

Bluestone Estates Ltd v Fitness First Clubs Ltd
2004 SLT (Sh Ct) 140

City Wall Properties (Scotland) Ltd v Pearl Assurance plc
2004 SC 214

Glasgow City Council v Caststop Ltd
2003 SLT 526, 2004 SCLR 283 (Notes)

Homebase Ltd v Scottish Provident Institution
2004 SLT 296, 2004 SCLR 44

Howgate Shopping Centre Ltd v Catercraft Services Ltd
2004 SLT 231, 2004 SCLR 739

Moncreiff v Jamieson
2004 SCLR 135

Royal Bank of Scotland plc v Wilson
2003 SLT 910, 2003 SCLR 716, 2004 SC 153

Safeway Stores plc v Tesco Stores Ltd
2004 SC 29, 2004 SLT 701

Smith v Stuart
2004 SLT (Sh Ct) 2, 2004 SCLR 241

Thomas v Allan
2004 SC 393